AF708644

MACINTOSH® C PROGRAMMING BY EXAMPLE

MACINTOSH® C PROGRAMMING BY EXAMPLE

KURT W. G. MATTHIES
THOM HOGAN

Microsoft® PRESS

PUBLISHED BY
Microsoft Press
A Division of Microsoft Corporation
One Microsoft Way
Redmond, Washington 98052-6399

Copyright © 1991 by Kurt W.G. Matthies

All rights reserved. No part of the contents of this book may be reproduced or transmitted in any form or by any means without the written permission of the publisher.

Library of Congress Cataloging-in-Publication Data
Matthies, Kurt W.G., 1954–
Macintosh C programming by example : a step by step guide to developing programs with Think C / Kurt W.G. Matthies, Thom Hogan.
p. cm.
Includes index.
ISBN 1-55615-357-0 : $34.95 ($44.95 Can.)
1. Macintosh (Computer)--Programming. 2. C (Computer program language) I. Hogan, Thom, 1952– II. Title.
QA76.8.M3M37648 1991
005.265--dc20 91-37506
CIP

Printed and bound in the United States of America.

1 2 3 4 5 6 7 8 9 MLML 6 5 4 3 2 1

Distributed to the book trade in Canada by Macmillan of Canada, a division of Canada Publishing Corporation.

Distributed to the book trade outside the United States and Canada by Penguin Books Ltd.

Penguin Books Ltd., Harmondsworth, Middlesex, England
Penguin Books Australia Ltd., Ringwood, Victoria, Australia
Penguin Books N.Z. Ltd., 182-190 Wairau Road, Auckland 10, New Zealand

British Cataloging-in-Publication Data available.

Apple®, Mac®, and Macintosh® are registered trademarks of Apple Computer, Inc. Macreations™, Tycho™, and Tycho Table Maker™ are trademarks of Macreations Publishing Corp. Symantec® and THINK C® are registered trademarks of Symantec Corporation.

Acquisitions Editor: Marjorie Schlaikjer
Project Editor: Erin O'Connor
Technical Editor: Jeff Carey

CONTENTS

PREFACE

Why anyone would want to do what I do for a living—sit day and night in front of a stolid, one-eyed deity and wrestle with abstract bits of mind-fluff—continues to be a source of wonder—to me and to my long-suffering family. Is it for the long hours, the backaches, the spreading middle, the chronic tic of eye strain? For all this and more.

Sarcastic reflections aside, if you have the right temperament, programming the Macintosh can be one of the most rewarding preoccupations in this wide world. Granted, it can turn ugly as fast as the weather changes here in Colorado's Front Range. To paraphrase Robert Pirsig in *Zen and the Art of Motorcycle Maintenance,* writing a Macintosh application requires "great peace of mind." One thing is for sure: A Macintosh application's ease-of-use is directly proportional to the effort the programmer puts into writing it. Creating a Macintosh applicaton is tricky under the best conditions, and learning to write a maintainable application that's relatively free of errors takes years of experience. We've written this book to reduce the time it takes you to become an effective Macintosh programmer.

You already know how to program? So did we. I came to Macintosh programming in 1986 with a strong background in the UNIX environment, and Thom had spent years in CP/M and MS-DOS programming. In spite of our combined experience, we weren't prepared for the Macintosh's totally different software development requirements. And, unfortunately for us, back then there weren't many Macintosh application examples around to teach us Mac ways.

I've always found that I learn programming techniques best by example. If I can find a code example that does the kind of thing I want to do, I use that code as a foundation and work a "variation on a theme" to solve my particular programming problem. This book provides the foundation common to almost all Macintosh application programming.

The book came out of a relationship between Thom and me that's spanned several years and several ventures. Early in 1990, we started up a series of columns for *MacUser* magazine. The *Power Programming* series ran from February 1990, through June 1991. Each column focused on skills in a particular area of Macintosh programming: windows, menus, dialog boxes, text files, graphics, file-handling, and so on. What was unique in our approach was that we always demonstrated the specialized skill in the context of whole applications.

Writing programs for the Macintosh requires much more than knowing how to use the various Macintosh Toolbox software managers—the utility routines embedded in the Macintosh read-only memory chips that display windows, report the mouse location, and read menu selections. Effective Macintosh application programming also requires that you engineer your program code so that your application uses memory and the Toolbox routines efficiently.

The approach we used in the *MacUser* columns got a lot of positive feedback from readers. Experienced programmers said, "I wish I'd had this when I was learning to write for the Mac." Beginners expressed their gratitude and enthusiastically demanded more.

Last year, Microsoft Press gave us the opportunity to publish the particulars of our approach in book form, a boon that has allowed us to rethink the columns without the magazine's 2500-word limit hanging over our heads. We've rethought, expanded, and rewritten the *Power Programming* columns. Now you'll find three full applications—Generic Application, Loser, and Browser—each of which describes a Macintosh programming paradigm. We develop the applications over the course of the book's chapters, and you'll find fully finished copies on the disk that accompanies the book. And we've added a chapter on the C language that makes a point of going into aspects of the language that require special attention in the Macintosh programming context.

We thank everyone at Microsoft Press for helping this book come into being especially Marjorie Schlaikjer, the acquisitions editor whose superhuman stamina saw the writing of this book through to completion; our technical editor Jeff Carey, who kept us honest; and our manuscript editor Erin O'Connor, who provided an antidote to 20 years of bad writing habits. Principal proofreader Deborah Long made many valuable suggestions, and text processors Debbie Kem and Barb Runyan prepared the manuscript for typesetter Carolyn Magruder's ministrations. Kim Eggleston, Lisa Sandburg, and Peggy Herman collaborated on the design, art, and layout.

While we're at it, we want to thank Paul Somerson, Jim Bradbury, and Rhoda Simmons at *MacUser.* Their work with us on the *Power Programming* series was invaluable.

I'd like to make special acknowledgment of the best software designer I ever met, Dennis K. Ward, whose thinking permeates the code examples in this book. Dennis and I have worked so closely together on Macintosh projects that it's no longer clear where his ideas about Macintosh applications end and mine begin. I also want to thank my good friend David J. Hall, who introduced me to the Macintosh way back when. And eternal love and kisses to Debby, Jason, Adam, and Jamie, who let me hang around the house all day in my pajamas.

I sincerely hope this book helps you become a better Macintosh programmer. With the new, low-priced Macintoshes, System 7.0's interapplication communications facilities, and the latest agreement between Apple and IBM, the Macintosh seems here to stay. The need for Macintosh software is greater than ever, and the opportunities available to Macintosh programmers have never been better. Even if programming is a pain in the neck, it sure beats working for a living.

Kurt W.G. Matthies
Boulder, Colorado
September 13, 1991

1

PROGRAMMING THE MACINTOSH WITH THINK C

Why would anyone want to become a Macintosh programmer? The answer is more complex than you might think. Several circumstances make a familiarity with programming the Macintosh helpful if not downright necessary.

- Mac users are becoming more sophisticated and are demanding more from their machines. Many state-of-the-art application programs allow user programming through either macros or a built-in control language such as Basic.
- Apple has privately indicated that a scripting language might eventually become part of the Macintosh operating system.
- HyperCard and SuperCard give Mac users a taste of programming but lead them on. To accomplish meaningful work, HyperTalk and SuperTalk scripts usually have to resort to external commands (XCMDs) written in a traditional programming language such as C or Pascal.
- The way programs are built dictates the way programs are used. A user familiar with Mac programming restrictions won't be surprised by the behavior of a Mac application.
- Corporate Mac use inevitably leads to custom applications and the need to tie the Macintosh into existing database and entry applications running on other machines.

But more to the point, we've seen over time that virtually all Mac users eventually express an interest in learning how the Mac does what it does. Apple's documentation doesn't always explain underlying concepts, and the curious Mac user consequently senses a wall between him or her and the inner confines of the Toolbox built into the Mac ROM. We've written this book to help you break through that wall.

No Degree Necessary

You won't need a degree in computer science to become a Mac programmer, but you will need some preparation. We know that the main hurdle in writing a first Mac application is the volume of code it takes to put up a single window. That's where we can help. Our charter for this book is to help the casual programmer explore the wealth of system software that comes with the Mac.

How This Book Will Proceed

Before we get down to writing applications, we'll take care of a few important preliminaries. We'll introduce you to the THINK C compiler in Chapter 2, and in Chapter 3, we'll take a look at C language fundamentals.

Then in Chapter 4, we'll develop a simple application. We'll step back in Chapter 5 to see how the Mac manages memory, and then in Chapters 6 through 8 we'll develop a generic application that will form the basis of all your future programming projects. In later chapters, we'll use this generic application to create applications that explore the file system, that demonstrate the graphics capabilities of the Mac, and that show how the Mac handles text. We'll look at a host of other examples of using the Mac's Toolbox. Every project will be a complete working application.

If You're New to C

For the projects in this book we'll use the C programming language. If you're new to C, look at the short C primer in Chapter 3. It's only a primer. It is not an introduction to programming. We assume that you already know about fundamental programming concepts such as variables, subroutines, and assignments. We don't expect you to know C itself.

Know Thy Mac Interface

You do need to be familiar with the conventions of the Mac interface. We'll assume that you know what a menu, a dialog box, a button, and a window are, and we'll focus on how to put them together in an application program.

If you study a Macintosh application carefully, you'll notice how the menus lead to dialog boxes, how button and command names refer to actions that the user takes, and how well-organized dialog boxes lead the user from the most significant choices to the less important ones. Compare two similar applications—two word processors, say—and notice which elements of the user interface are the same in both programs and which differ. Which interface do you like better? Why? If you can answer these questions, you're well on your way to understanding how to design a user interface for your programs.

One advantage of programming the Mac over programming other machines is that much of the Mac's user interface is well defined and directly supported by the operating system. You don't have to invent a window, a menu, a scroll bar, or any of the other features of the Macintosh interface.

The small price you pay for having a standard interface is conformity. All Mac applications have an Apple, a File, and an Edit menu, and these menus have standard sets of basic commands and standard command-key equivalents for their menu commands. That's because Mac programmers have agreed to cooperate with Apple and make their applications conform to the Macintosh user interface guidelines. This set of "suggestions" about what a Macintosh application should look like helps users know where things are when they first sit down to use a program.

Your application designs should follow the guidelines—unless, of course, you have discovered a much better way of doing things; that's progress, after all. If your modifications to the standard interface don't work, if they don't feel right, your users will let you know about it. One of the first applications for the Macintosh was a document outliner very Mac-like in all respects but one: The way the user scrolled text differed from Apple's specification. Users complained directly to the company, in letters to the editor in Macintosh magazines, in online comments on services like CompuServe, and in many other ways. The program was redesigned, and later versions worked according to the guidelines.

The sample applications in this book follow Apple's guidelines, and if you've used your Mac for some time, you probably have a pretty good idea of how a Macintosh application should look and feel. If you need information about a particular interface issue, you'll find the complete user interface guidelines in two books: *The Programmer's Introduction to the Macintosh* and *The Macintosh Human Interface Guidelines,* both published by Addison-Wesley. As a casual programmer, you're not likely to need these books, but they do deserve a browse. A professional programmer should have both.

Know Thy Toolbox

You also need to know something about how Apple divided the Macintosh's resident software into Toolboxes and Managers—roughly, Toolbox routines for the interface goodies and Manager routines for operating system chores like file handling. The six-volume *Inside Macintosh,* also from Addison-Wesley, is the definitive source for Macintosh programming information. Known tersely as *IM* by those of us who frequent the Apple Macintosh Developer Technical Support electronic mail facility, *Inside Macintosh* is the basic reference for system routine call syntax and for data structures. You don't need to rush out and buy all six volumes—the whole set represents a sizable investment. Start by buying Volume I. As you progress, you'll know when it's time to get the other books.

Volumes I and II contain the original Macintosh programming information. Volume I focuses on the user interface, and Volume II on the behind-the-scenes operating system activity. You'll use Volume I a lot and Volume II hardly at all. Volume III describes the Macintosh hardware and fills the reader in on changes to the Toolbox and Manager routines between the initial Mac (128K) and the Lisa XL. Volume IV covers changes that resulted from the introduction of the Plus and 512E models. Volume V describes changes that resulted from the addition of color and other hardware innovations with the Mac II. Volume VI describes changes that accompanied the additional Mac models introduced in late 1990 and System 7.0, the new Mac operating system introduced in 1991.

You might think of the volumes after I and II as "delta documents," documents that describe only changes or additions but that do not recap the original information. This makes *IM* somewhat hard to use. For casual programming, we recommend that you try a third party reference. A professional programmer will need all the *IM* volumes at some point in his or her career because their detailed information will eventually come in handy for troubleshooting.

A good third party resource is *Encyclopedia Mac ROM,* by Mathews and Friedland, from Brady Books. A software utility Kurt finds useful is the *Inside Mac Desk Accessory,* a shareware utility written by Bernard Gallet. This DA, available directly from its author, is first-rate—better than anything available from commercial publishers. It contains a database of the Toolbox calls and the data structures found in *IM.* It really helps to have the information online and quickly accessible. A commercial product of this type is available from Addison-Wesley, but we find the shareware utility much more useful.

Know Thy Programming Language

Picking a programming language is an emotionally charged decision. Everyone has his or her own ideas about which one is best. For the Mac, five general choices were available to us: HyperTalk, Basic, Pascal, C, and assembly language.

We ruled out HyperTalk for many reasons. Although it comes free with every Mac, it simply doesn't have the power to control all aspects of the Macintosh by itself. XCMDs are available, but they must be programmed in one of the other languages. Moreover, the disjointed nature of HyperTalk scripts, scattered as they are within HyperCard stacks, makes it difficult to present finished solutions. HyperTalk also brings along a large overhead because it is interpreted by HyperCard, which eats up a lion's share of the available memory in a 1-megabyte Mac. Finally, HyperCard is mostly object oriented, which we feel makes it less suited for procedural operations such as scientific calculations or for carefully controlled sequences of events.

Basic has many appealing features. You can run it interactively, so you don't have to wait until compile time to see whether a statement is going to execute the way you think it will. Basic is easy to understand. It's inexpensive and readily available. Unfortunately, Basic belongs to the old sequential world of computing, in which instructions are always executed in a particular order. (In the original Basic, that order was dictated by line numbers.) The event-driven Mac interface isn't well suited to this sequential control. Moreover, the Macintosh ROM expects to deal with special groupings of data called data structures, and Basic has no way of dealing with data structures directly, which means that Mac programs would have to be more complicated than they might otherwise have to be.

Pascal has a reputation as a fine teaching language. Better still for our purposes, it was the language of choice internally at Apple as the Macintosh was developed. The data structures that the Toolbox and the operating system expect to deal with are forms Pascal directly understands. Two problems made us avoid Pascal: Coding pointers and handles—two basic types of Macintosh data—is somewhat cumbersome in Pascal; and accessing low-level data such as individual bits is possible only through Toolbox macros.

Assembly language, of course, lets you access the bits and bytes in memory, but we ruled it out because creating data and control structures tends to become quite complex. Assembly language has no data structures or structured loops, leaving you to invent them yourself. And good assembly language code is difficult to read quickly.

That left us with C, the language we have used for most of our programming projects in the last five years. We feel strongly that C does a better job of showing the control and manipulation of data structures for Mac programming than any other language does. The only real drawback to using C is that the Macintosh's native language is Pascal, and C data types and calling conventions differ from their Pascal counterparts. Another drawback is that C lets you do some very stupid things. C is a *laissez-faire* language: It usually lets you do what you want to do as far as assignments and pointer arithmetic are concerned, but, because it's so lenient about checking for compatible data types across assignment operations, it will let you do nonsensical things in your code without much warning or complaint from the compiler.

C assumes that you know what you're doing. This is the Pascal aficionado's major complaint against C, but it's a feature that we enjoy. Be forewarned, though, that novice C programmers are virtually guaranteed to fall into one of C's traps at some point early in their careers. Guard against C's traps by double-checking every change you make to a program and by constantly double-checking your data types.

As a prospective Mac C programmer, you need to be familiar with the syntax and semantics of the C programming language. Sure, we'll supply you with working code, but you'll need to understand the language if you want to write your own code and get the most benefit from this book. You'll need to learn the fundamentals of C—variable declarations, assignments, function definitions, function calls. Don't worry if you don't have any experience with the language—we'll meet you halfway. Chapter 3 is a brief C primer you can use as a reference. We do suggest that you pick up a copy of Kernighan and Ritchie's *The C Programming Language,* published by Prentice Hall, if you're serious about learning C. This classic, known by the blue *C* on its cover, was the first book on the language. Recently revised, *K&R* is still our favorite, despite competition from dozens of other introductory books on C.

Although the Kernighan and Ritchie book is excellent for learning how to use C, it doesn't teach you a thing about programming the Mac. As you read along in this book, we'll alert you to common pitfalls that await the new C programmer of the Mac, and we'll beef up our efforts when we get to more advanced topics like data structures, pointers, and dynamic memory allocation—and their relationship to the Mac. Of course, we think the best way to learn a language is by example. In each chapter, study the examples and read the code. We can't emphasize that enough. The code will teach you more about how to put a Macintosh application together than any description can.

If you are a C programmer experienced in other development environments, forget everything you've learned about console-based systems. You'll find that all the basic *stdio* library routines for console input and output—routines such as *getch*, *scanf*, and the ubiquitous *printf*—are provided with the THINK C environment, but you'll be hard-pressed to find any real use for them in a Mac application. The good news is that you already know a lot about C that you can put to immediate use on the Mac.

Know Thy Development Environment

But why Symantec's THINK C? Why not Apple's own Macintosh Programmer's Workshop C (MPW C)? That's an easy question to answer. MPW C is definitely a big-league compiler, but with roots in UNIX, it isn't exactly the interactive, event-driven product Mac users are used to. MPW C comes with all kinds of special tools, but they're all invoked with cryptic command-line instructions or macros. The THINK C environment follows the Mac Interface Guidelines; it's easy to learn; it's as full-featured as MPW C; it produces code that is as small, reliable, and fast as MPW C code; and it costs less.

We're not the only ones who think so, either. Some of the largest development houses in the industry, companies like Aldus (PageMaker, Freehand, and Persuasion), Claris (MacWrite and others), and Quark (XPress), have selected THINK C as their primary development environment. Indeed, we would guess that if you were to poll all applications developers, you'd find that more commercial programs had been developed with THINK C than with any alternative.

Although THINK C is one of the easiest development environments to use, the next chapter is geared toward those who have little or no experience with THINK C. We might even have a thing or two to teach THINK C veterans.

The Programming Process

All of this brings us to the actual act of writing a program for the Mac. We'll start with an oversimplification. A program usually starts with your idea for a computer-based tool, which you then break into smaller, logically oriented pieces. Until you've figured out what it is you're trying to accomplish, you shouldn't start to code. The first steps often take the form of notes, diagrams, samples of screens, or printouts. The more you refine your ideas before you sit down to code, the more likely you are to produce a useful program.

A case in point: We spent two man-years sketching out our ideas and designing before we started the programming that eventually became Tycho Table Maker, our commercial table-editing program. We spent much of that time looking at examples of tables and extrapolating the basic concepts our program had to treat. And we looked at how to put information into Tycho. (It doesn't make any sense to retype something that already exists, does it?)

Our ruminations resulted in several paper designs for specific pieces of Tycho. In particular, we spent a great deal of time designing the underlying database the program uses. But we wouldn't have even realized that a table editor needs an underlying database if we hadn't done the preplanning. Had we simply jumped in and started to program, we probably would have spent a great deal of time inventing a database by trial and error—which, as you might suspect, is not the most efficient way to design software.

When you fully understand the product you want to create, it's time to start programming. You take your ideas and your paper design, and you begin to type source code into an editor. Source code is a sequence of computer-specific instructions for performing the process that carries out your program idea. All a computer does is process a sequence of instructions in a tightly controlled fashion. The real key to successful programming, therefore, is to identify the right process to encode, to think of all potential exceptions to the process that your program might encounter, and to keep the sequence of execution correct.

A good computer language helps in these tasks. C is a structured language—which lets us create data structures and control structures that imitate the real-life elements we try to model in programs. C also provides the low-level access to data objects, such as pointers or the bits of a data word, that we need for writing efficient programs.

THINK C has an adequate editor for typing in and organizing your source code. It also has a compiler and a linker and a debugger for examining your program in detail as it executes. Until this point in the programming process, you have used only the editor as you typed in your first-pass source code. Next in our programming sequence, you use the compiler to parse the source code instructions you typed into machine code, usually called object code, that the computer can understand directly. On the Mac, that object code must be linked into a file that the operating system can understand and execute. Figure 1-1 on the next page illustrates the process.

Finally, you've got a runnable application. Of course, if you didn't do a good job of designing it or if you put in illogical or nonsensical instructions, it might not run too well. Then you use the Debugger to explore your code. Rarely does the first pass at a program come even close to working. (You'll have an advantage with the examples in this book, though, because we'll provide source code listings that we know will work.) In real life, you often find yourself back at step 2 (entering and modifying source code) or even at step 1 (isolating and designing key modules of the program on paper). And so it goes. You edit, compile, link, and run your program, find the errors, and go back through the sequence again.

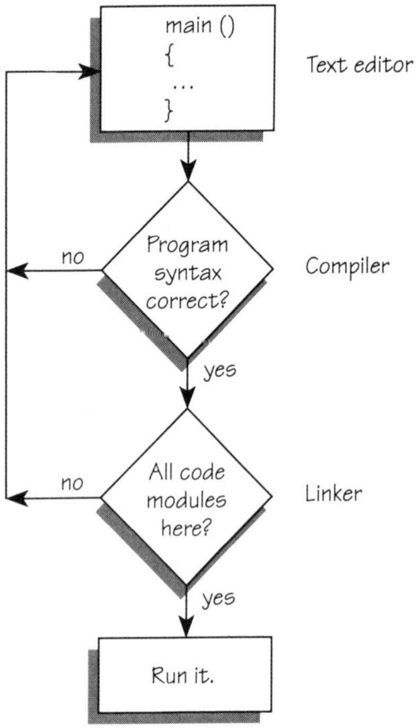

Figure 1-1.
The programming cycle.

What to Do Next

To get yourself ready:

- If you're a newcomer to programming, get some exposure to programming concepts and terms. We'll explain advanced concepts, but you need to know what a bit, a byte, an assignment, a loop, and a conditional expression are.
- Get familiar with the C language. Chapter 3 is a helpful introduction, but we also recommend that you read *The C Programming Language,* Second Edition, by Brian Kernighan and Dennis Ritchie.
- Know why you want to program the Mac. Are you merely curious about what it takes? Do you have specific needs that aren't met by existing programs? Are you looking for shortcuts? Do you want to be the next Andy Hertzfeld? If you understand why you want to know about programming, you'll get more from this book.

So start up your editor. You're about to tackle your first Macintosh program.

2

USING THINK C

THINK C is one of the best-integrated programming environments to come along in years. You edit, compile, link, and run your program without leaving the environment. And, under MultiFinder with at least 2 megabytes of memory, you can use the THINK C Debugger to trace the execution of your program, stepping statement by statement through your source code.

The editor in THINK C behaves as any Macintosh text editor or word processor you might be accustomed to does. As in most programming editors, text doesn't wrap at the end of a line as it does in a word processor and the editor supports automatic indentation of subsequent lines, which is handy for writing structured code. You can cut and paste text, find and replace text strings, and take advantage of other features that are useful for programmers, such as the ability to find curly brace pairs.

THINK C's built-in compiler converts your source code into machine readable instructions and stores this object code in the project file. You might be accustomed to development environments in which you have to keep track of the object files, the .o or .obj files that the compiler creates as a result of compilation. You won't have to do that in THINK C.

Likewise, linking the code, the final step in creating a runnable application out of source code, is automatic in THINK C. Linkage proceeds as a result of running the application. Because the objects are maintained and kept hidden by THINK C, there's no need for a script to control linkage.

The Development Folder

If you haven't installed THINK C on your hard disk yet, now's your chance. You'll find that THINK C works better if you follow the file system organization scheme we describe in this chapter.

Keep all your development projects and the compiler in subfolders within one main folder, the Development folder. (We usually put this folder at the top of the file system hierarchy, although you can put it anywhere.) Inside the Development folder is a folder named THINK C, in which the compiler, the debugger, and associated files will reside. Each programming project folder will reside at this level.

The most important files on the THINK C distribution disks are the THINK C integrated programming environment file and the THINK C symbolic debugger file. Put these two application files, named THINK C and THINK C Debugger, in the THINK C folder. You'll also need ResEdit, the Apple resource editor, if you're to follow some of the examples in this book, so copy ResEdit from the THINK C distribution disks into the THINK C folder.

Along with the compiler environment and the debugger come programming libraries, header files, the precompiled headers file, library sources, and the class library. Minimally, you'll need to put the programming libraries and the header files in the THINK C folder Put the file MacHeaders, the Mac #includes folder, the Mac Libraries folder, and the C Libraries folder in the THINK C folder.

Although we don't use the class library for any of our programming projects in this book, you might want to play with some of the THINK C object-oriented programming (OOP) examples, so you might as well install those files now. Add the oops Libraries folder and the THINK C Class Library folder to your THINK C folder.

If you have a lot of disk space, copy the programming examples from the THINK C distribution disks. The best way to learn programming is to study actual programs that work. The more code you have access to, the more approaches you'll have to your particular programming problems. Some of the example projects are good for starting small applications as well as Control Panel utilities (CDEV) and desk accessories (DA). Instead of putting these code example folders in the THINK C folder, put them in the Development folder, at the same level as the THINK C folder in the file system organization.

Another likely candidate for copying onto your hard disk is the C Library sources folder. This folder contains all source code for the THINK C programming libraries. (We'll talk about these in detail in a moment.) Again, put this folder in the Development folder, at the same level as the THINK C folder. The other file folders at this level can be independent projects, other programming libraries, or other developer's tools.

Finally, put all the project folders from the source code disk for this book into your Development folder. Figure 2-1 illustrates a typical layout of the Development folder.

With all these files in the Development folder, you might wonder how THINK C finds a particular file. It makes use of two hierarchies: the THINK C tree and the project tree. The THINK C tree encompasses every folder and file in the THINK C folder; the project tree encompasses every file in a project folder. This is why we advised you to put project folders at the same level as the THINK C folder. If you put the project files in the THINK C folder, THINK C would search all your project files every time it looked for a file, and it would run into trouble if you had multiple source files of the same name.

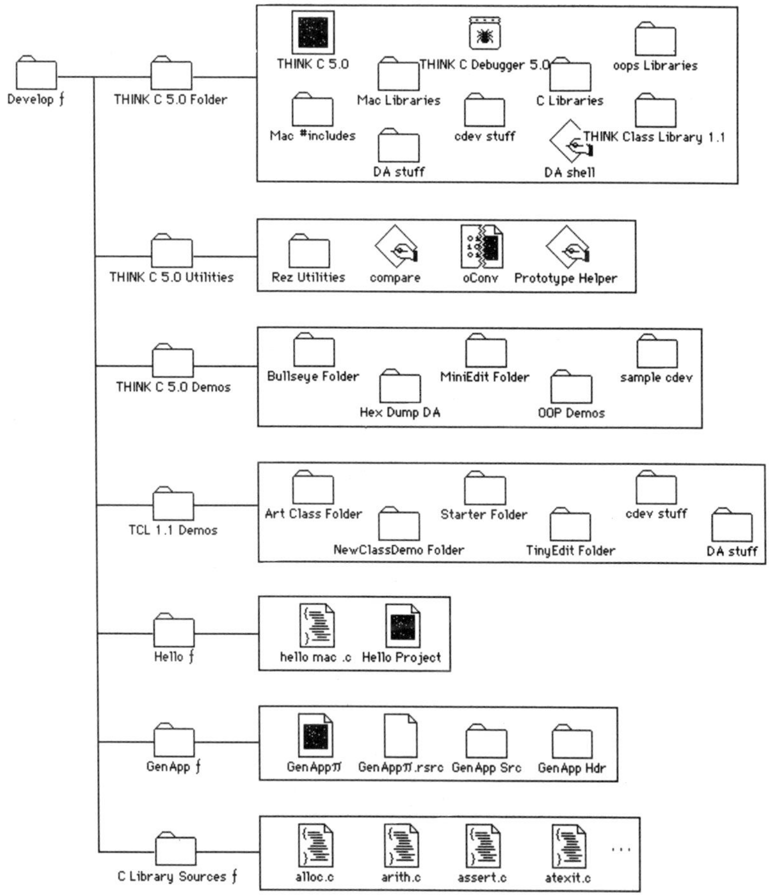

Figure 2-1.
Layout and organization of a generic development folder. The THINK C folder, Utilities folder, Demos folders, C Library Sources folder, and project folders are all at the same level.

Programming Libraries

The header files that come with THINK C and the programming libraries take up the bulk of the THINK C distribution disks. You can't write a Macintosh application without the Macintosh header files and the Macintosh libraries. The Macintosh headers contain definitions of the Macintosh data structures, and the libraries contain the hooks into the Macintosh's programming Toolbox, which includes the routines to display a window, read a menu selection, and get a mouse click.

A programming library is an organized collection of program pieces. These pieces, called functions, can be used by any program that connects, or links, the library with the program. The THINK C environment has a built-in linker for this purpose.

Library functions provide a software toolbox for your program. Included in the many libraries that are shipped with THINK C are routines to process strings, format numeric values, search a list, sort a table, and perform file I/O (input and output), along with a wealth of other routines.

The functions in a library are in compiled, or machine readable, form. The human readable source code for a library is not usually available or, in the case of a commercial library, is available only for a price. This is not the case with THINK C, whose library sources are included on the distribution disks. We salute Symantec for including these sources with the library functions.

Library code is (usually) thoroughly debugged. When you modify proven source code, you run the risk of introducing new bugs into the code. You can't modify library code directly in binary format, so the use of compiled libraries can contribute to software reliability. This impenetrability of library code means, though, that each library function needs complete, descriptive documentation of its name, action, inputs, and outputs. The inputs to a function are called "parameters," or, informally, "arguments." The output of a function is known as its "return value."

The *Standard Libraries Reference*

The THINK C library functions are documented in the *Standard Libraries Reference* manual that comes with THINK C. Symantec has borrowed the style for the entries in this book from the old *UNIX Programmer's Manual,* the original source of C function library documentation. The entries appear one function per page, with four main sections for each entry. At the top of the page, the function name appears, followed by a one-line description of the function's action. The syntax, or usage, section follows. Here's an example, the syntax for the function *toupper()*:

```
#include <stdio.h>
int toupper (char c);
```

The first line tells us that we need to include *stdio.h* in order to use this function. The *.h* indicates that *stdio* is a header file. (We'll go into header files later in this chapter.) The second line tells us that *toupper()* accepts a character argument and returns an integer. This gives us enough information to use *toupper()* in an application:

```
#include <stdio.h>      /* placed at top of source file */
...
myFunction()
{
int upperC;             /* declared inside function */
char c;
...
upperC = toupper (c);  /* converts the character */
...
```

The most important section of a library reference entry is the description, which tells you what the function does. The description for *toupper()* says that it returns the uppercase equivalent character of a lowercase letter c...," so you know that *toupper()* converts lowercase letters to uppercase.

If the function returns a value, the return value section of the entry describes the range of data values or the error value you can expect when the function returns. The function *toupper()* returns the uppercase equivalent of a lowercase letter. (The manual doesn't tell you what *toupper()* returns if the original character wasn't in the lowercase letter range—you have to find that out for yourself.)

The reference manual is organized by library. The names of the several libraries that come with THINK C differ depending on the version of the compiler you are using (version 3.0; version 4.0; or version 5.0, the new System 7.0 compatible compiler). Here are some of the important THINK C libraries:

MacTraps This is the most important library that comes with THINK C because it contains all references for the Macintosh Toolbox routines. Any program that uses a Toolbox function needs to link with the MacTraps library. In other words, virtually any program you write needs to link with MacTraps.

ANSI The ANSI (American National Standards Institute) committee concerned with C has been active for years in an attempt to standardize the language. The functions in THINK C's ANSI library support the new standard. The library contains all of the I/O functions, including *printf()*, file stream utilities, and character I/O primitives. It also contains floating point support. If your application includes floating point (non-integer) calculations, you need to use the ANSI library.

ANSI-small This library is similar to the ANSI library, but it doesn't include the floating point routines. Use this library if your application does not use floating point calculations and you want to save some space.

math If you plan to use the C math functions, such as the square root, trigonometric, or logarithmic functions, you need to use the math library.

unix The unix library is provided to help you convert UNIX applications to Macintosh applications. Some of the unix library functions don't do anything—*setpid()*, for instance, is provided simply for compatibility. We've never needed to use this library when programming the Macintosh, and unless you're coming from the UNIX world, you won't either.

Header Files

THINK C comes with scores of header files, whose names characteristically end with the .h extension. The contents of these files are organized along the lines of *Inside Macintosh,* by Toolbox manager. The names of the files differ depending on which version of THINK C you're using. If you're using anything other than THINK C 5.0, for example, Event Manager constants and structures are defined in the file EventMgr.h, QuickDraw stuff in QuickDraw.h, and Window Manager structures in WindowMgr.h. In THINK C 5.0, the file names conform with those used in MPW C: Events.h, QuickDraw.h, and Windows.h.

C programmers use header files to define constants, macros, data types and structures, variables, and function prototypes. In programming, one header file is usually included by multiple source files, so the header file serves to fix a constant or data structure definition for all files in a project. Defining something, like a constant's value, in one place is organizational good sense: If you need to change the value, you need to do it only once. As your programs become larger and more complex—perhaps encompassing dozens of source code files—the proper maintenance of header files becomes very important.

Header files are sometimes called "include" files because their contents are included in the compilation stream with the contents of other files. In a C source file, you include the contents of one file in the compilation stream of another by using the *#include* directive. Consider the following source file, in which we've used *#include* to include two header files:

```
#include "AppConstants.h"
#include "FileUtil.h"

main ()
{
...
}
```

In Figure 2-2, you see a diagram of the result. The compiler reads the contents of AppConstants.h and FileUtil.h before it looks at the source file code.

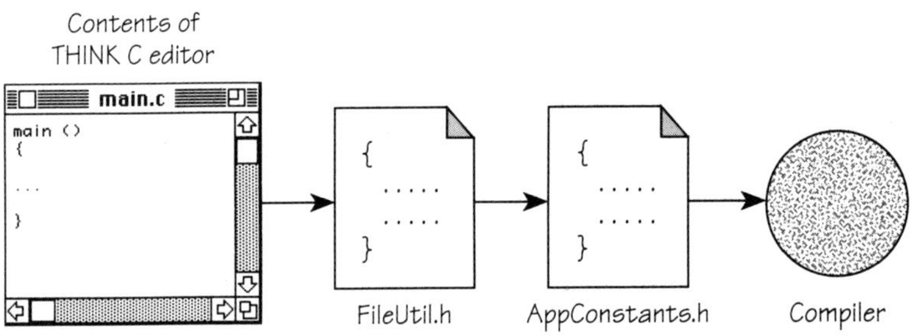

Figure 2-2.
The compilation stream using the #include *directive. The compiler sees AppConstants.h, then FileUtil.h, and then the* main() *code.*

A note about the syntax of *#include* statements: When the compiler sees double quotes around the header file's name, as in

```
#include "constants.h"
```

it searches the current project folder tree, looking for the file constants.h. Conversely, when the compiler finds angled brackets, as in

```
#include <QuickDraw.h>
```

it looks for the header file in the THINK C folder tree. The angled brackets signify that the file is a compiler-supplied header file that resides in the THINK C hierarchy. If you've set up your Development folder as we've recommended, you must use the angled bracket form for THINK C header files.

MacHeaders

Inside Macintosh is the standard guide to which header files you'll need to include in a particular source file. If you are using the Window Manager and accessing a *WindowRecord* data structure, you'll need somewhere in your source file the statement

```
#include <Windows.h>
```

if you're using THINK C 5.0 or

```
#include <WindowMgr.h>
```

if you're using an earlier version of THINK C. Your program needs to know about the Window Manager data structures. (If you don't know what a data structure definition is now, don't worry—we discuss this in the next chapter.)

The problem with this organizational convention is that you need *Inside Macintosh* to get started. The number of files that you'll need to include for most applications runs high. Beginners find that the compiler's syntax-checking error messages can get to be pretty annoying before they come up with a combination of header files that includes all the structure definitions.

One solution to this problem is to use our Generic application, discussed in Chapters 6, 7, and 8, which already includes the necessary header files.

Beginning with THINK C version 3.0, Symantec came up with an elegant solution to this problem: precompiled headers. MacHeaders, the precompiled header file supplied with THINK C, contains definitions for most of the commonly used managers. The file loads more quickly during compilation because it is in binary form, unlike conventional text header files. And you never need to load a manager include file because the compiler includes the MacHeaders file automatically if you set the MacHeaders compiler option. (You'll find compiler options in the THINK C editor's Edit-Options dialog box.)

Custom MacHeaders File

If you really know what you're doing with header files, you can build your own MacHeaders from the text file Mac #includes.c, using the Precompile command on THINK C's Source menu. Just modify Mac #includes.c so that it will include the files you're interested in, and precompile it. If THINK C is to recognize the new file, you have to name it MacHeaders, so you might want to rename the original MacHeaders to avoid duplication.

The Project Folder

A project folder holds all a project's files. Each of your programming projects should be in its own folder. A typical project folder contains four types of files:

- The project file
- C language source files, called ".c files," usually kept in a subfolder
- C language header files, usually kept in a subfolder
- The project resource file

The Project File

The project file is the master file for the project. Each programming project centers around the project file, which contains everything THINK C needs to construct the application from your source files. All project management is done from this file. When you open the project file in THINK C's integrated environment, a list of the source files appears in the project window, as shown in our example in Figure 2-3. To open an individual source file, double-click on its name in this window. You can use the arrow keys to move the selection bar up and down in the window. If you type the first few letters of a file's name while this window is active, the selection cursor jumps to that file's name. If there are multiple files with similar names (for example, FileBuf.c, FileMgr.c, and FileUtil.c), the Tab key will move you to the next file name that contains the matching first few letters.

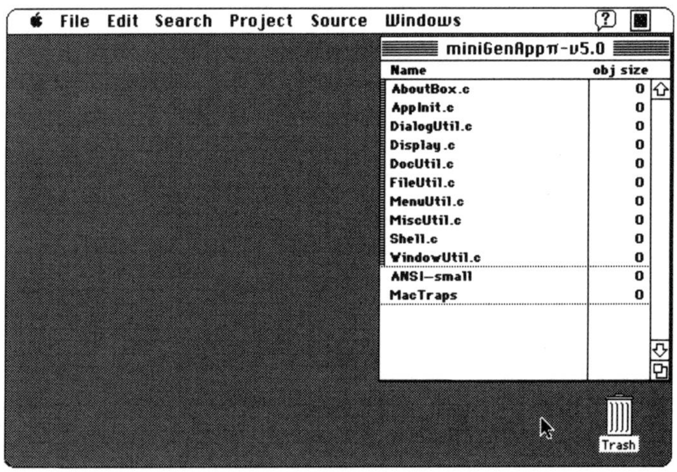

Figure 2-3. *The project file window for miniGenAppπ from Chapter 6. The file names are listed in this window with the file sizes.*

The Full Titles option (from the Windows menu) is useful when you have more than one version of the source code on disk. It displays the file's path in the window title.

For building programs, THINK C offers a built-in, UNIX-like make facility. (When we say UNIX-like, we mean in essence, but certainly, we hasten to add, not in appearance.) This facility keeps track of compilation dates and dependency information for your source files and stores the data in the project file. In UNIX and MS-DOS terms, this means there's no makefile. When you make a change to a file, the date and time are noted internally. When you try to run your program, THINK C reminds you that the project needs to be brought up to date. You can also configure the environment to automatically make the program before you run it, again with the Edit-Options dialog box.

There are no .o files with THINK C. The project file holds the object code (machine language instructions) that is compiled from the source files. The project file also contains debugging data and linking data, such as symbol and line numbers, and code resource segmentation data. As a result, the project file can grow to be very large. Using the Precompiled Headers option can help reduce the size of your project file, but you won't have to worry about the projects in this book taking up too much space.

C Source Files

The C language source files constitute your program code and end with the .c suffix. Generally, you'll have more than one source file to a project. To minimize the number of files in the project folder so that it doesn't become cluttered, put all your source files in a subfolder of the project folder. We organize all of our more extensive projects this way. For example, if the project file name is miniGenApp, we name the source subfolder miniGenApp Src.

C Header Files

Header files end with the .h suffix. They contain constants and the definitions of data types and structures, variables, and function prototypes. Again, you'll usually

Source File Suffixes

The .c or .h suffix in these file names is a holdover from command-line system days. Because the Macintosh system software designers chose a free-form file naming convention, we don't have to suffer with an abbreviated name such as ACCNTS09.DBF, as our MS-DOS counterparts do. The free-form convention means that file names can be more descriptive. We can change ACCNTS09.DBF to Sept. Accounts. (Periods can appear anywhere in the name.) On the Mac, there's really no need for a file name "extension" to classify the file. The Finder notes the file's origin internally, so we don't need the .DBF extension to tell us that this is a dBASE file; the icon tells us that.

Source file names in THINK C are a different story. C source file names must end with .c. That's how THINK C recognizes them as C language source files. Likewise, by convention, header file names always end with .h. It's a throwback, admittedly, but for now, that's the way it is.

have more than one of these files in a project. We like to collect them in their own subfolder, under the project folder.

The Project Resource File

The final item you might put in the project folder is the project resource file. This file contains the program's resources—menu descriptions, dialog box item lists, PICTs, control definition functions, or other resources the application needs at runtime. We build all our resource files with Apple's ResEdit, one of the so-called resource editors. Symantec ships ResEdit with THINK C.

If you come from a different programming environment, the resource file concept is probably new to you. The principle behind resource files is that it's advisable to split program code from the user interface items, that any messages that a program displays to the user belong in the resource file, not in the source code. The idea is that if an application's interface items, such as strings, dialog box contents, menu titles, and other items of text within a program, are accessible from an outside source, the program can be easily converted to another language system.

This principle works pretty well, and we follow it in our examples. Anything a user sees in a program we place in the program's resource file. Each of our example programs has a resource file (except our first example, Hello Mac!, which doesn't really count as a full-fledged application).

In a stand-alone application, the program's resources are built into the program file, in its resource fork (a topic we'll cover in Chapters 10 and 11). But in the THINK C environment, the application has to have access to the resource file. There are two ways to set this up.

If you name the resource file correctly, THINK C automatically opens the resource file when you run your program. You should name the resource file after the project file name and give it an .rsrc extension. If the project name were GenericAppπ, for example, the resource file should be named GenericAppπ.rsrc. The resource file has to be in the same folder as the project file.

The alternative is to use the *OpenResFile* call in your program. For example, the call

```
OpenResFile ("GenericAppπ.rsrc");
```

will open the resource file for your program's use. You must make this call before your program accesses any resources. A program will eventually bomb if it doesn't have access to the resource file. There is no warning or safeguard against this in THINK C, and there shouldn't be. C programmers are masters of their own destinies.

Working with THINK C

Application development centers on the project file, and the THINK C environment won't operate unless a project file is open. So, the best way to begin a THINK C session is by double-clicking on the project file name. If you open THINK C without a project file, the environment will ask for one by presenting the Open Project dialog box. You must either select a project file to open or create a new project file.

You're going to become very familiar with the features and commands in the THINK C environment as you spend hours and hours getting your programs up and running. You might spend most of your time in the editor. The multiwindow editor supports just about everything you'll need to edit your program's code. It is fast, it is highly functional, and it works as most Macintosh editor applications do.

After the project file is open, you open the source code files by double-clicking on their names in the project file window or by choosing Open from the File menu. THINK C's Windows menu is handy for managing these files—it lists each open file. You bring an open window to the top by selecting it. The first nine open files get Command-key equivalents, Command-1 through Command-9, which you can use to bring a window to the top. Command-0 selects the project window.

You save a file by using the File menu's Save command. Save As works a little differently than you might expect. Save As not only creates a new file with a new name, but it also changes the file name stored in the project file. If you want to save a file with another file name without changing the name in the project file, use Save A Copy As.

You edit text in a THINK C editor window as you would in a Macintosh word processor. Text does not wrap in the editor; you must use the Return key to start a new line. The editor automatically indents (autoindents) each line of text, which means that the next line begins under the first character of the previous line.

You use the mouse to select text ranges. A double-click selects a word; a triple-click selects a line. There's no overstrike mode as there is in WordStar-like editors. The editor is always in insert mode. You overstrike text by selecting it and then typing the replacement text. Typed text always replaces any selected text on the Mac.

You can use the arrow keys to move the text cursor around the screen. Alone, the arrow keys move the cursor character by character horizontally and line by line vertically. The Option-arrow key combinations move the cursor as far as it can go in a particular direction: Option-up moves the cursor to the top of the file; Option-down to the bottom of the file; Option-left to the beginning of the current line; Option-right to the end of the current line. The Shift-arrow key combinations extend the

Changing the Default Font

The THINK C editor uses a 9-point Monaco font as its default font. Some people don't like this font for one reason or another. The default font number, size, and tab size reside in the second, third, and fourth words of the THINK C CNFG #0 resource. You can change these values with a little ResEdit-style surgery on your THINK C application. Remember to enter these values in their hexadecimal equivalents.

selection range. These are nice features if you like to work without taking your hands from the keyboard. Pressing the Enter key scrolls the window contents so that the text cursor is in the middle of the window, which is handy for finding your place after scrolling around.

The editor's Edit menu supports full cut, copy, and paste operations, which are all supported by their conventional keyboard shortcuts (Command-X, Command-C, and Command-V). You can shift blocks of text left or right by using the Shift Left and Shift Right commands on the Edit menu or by using the keyboard shortcuts Command-[and Command-]. This feature is illustrated in Figure 2-4. The Balance command (Command-B) on the Edit menu is useful for finding syntax errors caused by your forgetting to close a block with a curly brace.

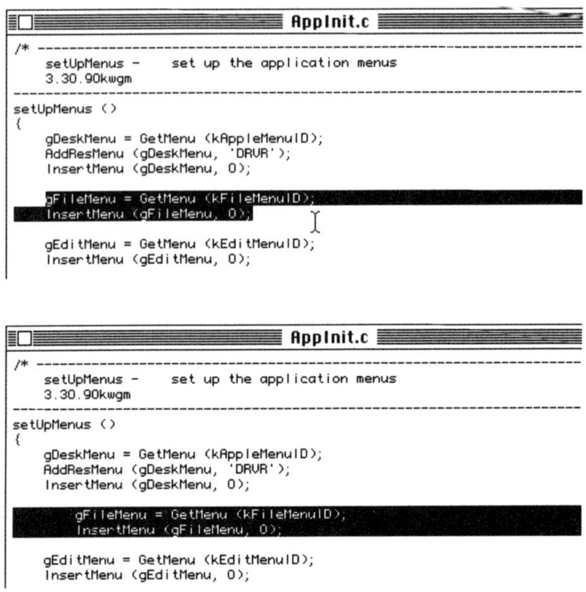

Figure 2-4. *Shifting text right. To use the Shift Right command, select the lines you want to shift, as shown on the top screen, and then press Command-]. The text shifts right, as shown on the bottom screen.*

If you hold down the Option key or the Command key and hold down the mouse button while the cursor is in an editor window title bar, THINK C displays a pop-up menu that lists the names of the header files included by the project file. If you then select one of the header file names, THINK C opens that file in the editor. This feature uses some internal project file information, so the source file must be part of a project and must have already been compiled for this feature to work.

Searching for Text Strings

The Search menu supports full text search and replace capability. You can search for text strings in single or multiple files. The search mechanism finds strings that match the search string and can replace them with the replace string.

You enter the search and replace information into the Find dialog box shown in Figure 2-5, which appears when you choose Find from the Search menu (or use the keyboard equivalent, Command-F).

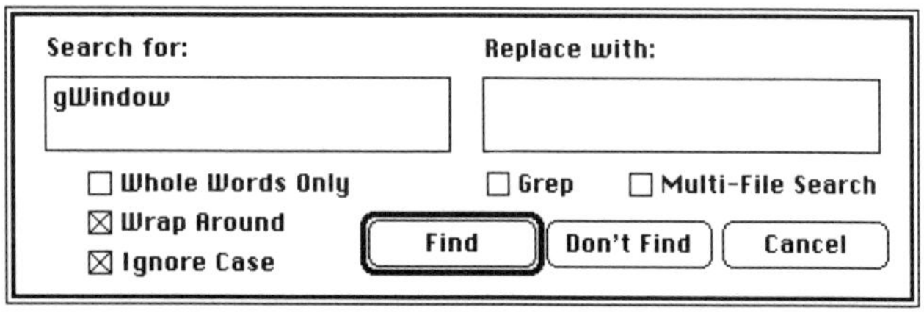

Figure 2-5. *The Find dialog box. Note the check box options in the lower left corner.*

After you specify a search string, you can find each occurrence of the string by using Find Again (or Command-A). You can replace the occurrence of the search string with the replace string by using Replace (Command-P) or Replace and Find Again (Command-W), which replaces the current selection and moves the cursor to the next occurrence of the string.

Say, for example, that you want to change the name of the global variable *gKill* to the more descriptive *gDeleteRefs*. A global variable can occur in any file, so you'll have to search the entire project. Here is how you go about this in a project:

1. Find the first occurrence of *gKill*.
2. Select the word by double-clicking on it.
3. Choose Enter Selection from the Search menu (or press Command-E). This sets the string for the search to the selected text, *gKill*.
4. Type *gDeleteRefs*. Because *gKill* was selected, the typing replaces this string.
5. Double-click on *gDeleteRefs* to select the word.
6. Choose Copy from the Edit menu (or press Command-C) to copy this word to the Clipboard.
7. Choose Find from the Search menu (or press Command-F). Select the Replace With edit box, and press Command-V to paste the Clipboard contents into the dialog box. This sets the replace string to *gDeleteRefs*.

   The Find dialog box reflects the search and replace options shown in Figure 2-6. If you were replacing the search text in this source file only, you'd be ready to go. But because you're looking for all the instances of a global variable, you need to set up the search so that THINK C will scan all source files.

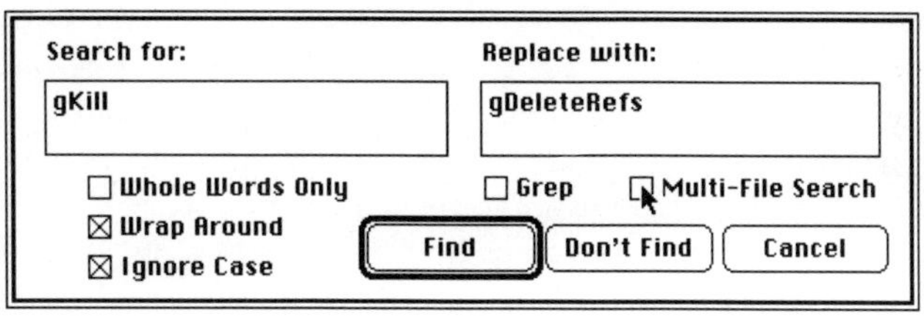

Figure 2-6. *The Find dialog box.* gKill *is the search string and* gDeleteRefs *is the replace string.*

8. Click on the Multi-File Search check box. You're presented with a dialog box that looks something like the one shown in Figure 2-7. Click the Check All button, and click OK.

Figure 2-7.
The Multi-File Search dialog box.

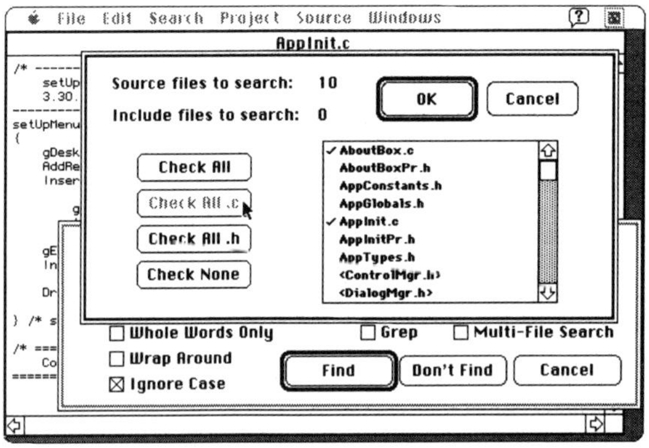

You are ready to start the search. You can replace occurrences of *gKill* one at a time with Replace and Find Again (Command-W) or replace all occurrences in a file at once with Replace All (no keyboard equivalent). When you're ready for the next file, choose Find In Next File from the Search menu (Command-T).

To find function and global variable definitions, hold down the Option key or the Command key and double-click on the function name or the variable name. THINK C will open the source file in which the function or variable is defined and find the first instance of the string. If you include all your global variables in a header file, THINK C will open the source file containing the definition of *main()*.

Using the grep Option

The search routine has a built-in grep facility that lets you use a regular expression instead of a literal string as your match string. Unlike a literal string, which specifies

grep

THINK C's grep feature is derived from a UNIX utility program of the same name. The name grep is an acronym that stands for (g)lobal (r)egular (e)xpression and (p)rint. When it comes to esoterica, UNIX excels. The names of its five string-processing utilities—awk, grep, sed, lex, and yacc—are classic examples of the jargon that permeates the computer sciences. The name awk is made up of the first letters of its authors' names: (A)ho, (W)einberg, and (K)ernighan. The name sed is for a (s)tream (ed)itor. The lex utility builds (lex)ical analyzers, and the name yacc is an acronym for (y)et (a)nother (c)ompiler (c)ompiler, which isn't an entirely accurate name because it's only a parser generator. That's some computer programming folklore. We just thought you'd like to know.

only one string to match, a regular expression specifies a set of strings to match. A regular expression contains both alphanumeric characters and operator characters, called "metacharacters," that control comparisons, repetitions, and other features of the expression-matching facility. Some examples will illustrate what we mean.

Any single character matches itself. For example,

```
a
```

matches *a*. You can freely concatenate expressions, just as you concatenate letters to make words. Any string as a regular expression therefore matches itself. Thus, the regular expression

```
hello
```

matches any occurrence of the string *hello* in the source text. The dot (period character) matches any single character. Therefore, the regular expression

```
.
```

matches *a*, *1*, *K*, . (the period itself), or any other single character. By itself, the dot is useless—it matches everything. But used with other characters, it becomes very handy. The expression

```
c.t
```

matches *cat*, *cot*, *cut*, *cmt*, *c_t*, and any similar string. If you want to find the dot and only the dot, however, you need to tell grep to treat the dot as a dot, not as a metacharacter. You do this by "escaping" the metacharacter with the backslash. For example, if you wanted to find all periods, you'd enter

```
\.
```

The expression that matches the backslash itself is

```
\\
```

DLE

The origin of the term "escape," which means to remove any special context of a character, comes from data communications, in which programs send special control characters in a data stream to control communications. For example, in certain protocols, the end-of-text character (ETX) signals the end of a data block and the beginning of a checksum value. If binary data is being transmitted, however, it is likely that the ETX character (which has a value of *3*) is part of the data. The transmitting software therefore prefixes any control character with the data-link escape character (DLE). The receiving program understands that any character following the escape is data, not control, and therefore places the ETX in its data buffer.

If you wanted to find a word with an embedded blank, you'd escape the blank, as in

```
hello\ world
```

The ^ operator specifies the beginning of a line. Therefore, the expression

```
^c.t
```

matches the word *cat* if it occurs at the beginning of a line, but not the second syllable of the word *concatenate*. The operator *$* matches the end of a line. The regular expression

```
^...$
```

matches all lines that contain a single three-character word.

The * operator specifies zero or more occurrences of an expression. The expression

```
ca*t
```

matches *cat*, *caaaaaaaaat*, or *ct*.

You specify a "character class" between square braces. A character class is a set of characters for grep to match against. The expression

```
[bchm]
```

matches a single character from the set *b*, *c*, *h*, or *m*. Again, this match might not be useful by itself, but its value becomes evident when you concatenate character class expressions, such as

```
[bchm]at
```

This expression matches the words *bat*, *cat*, *hat*, and *mat*.

You use the - operator in a character class to specify a range of characters. For example,

```
[a-z]
```

matches any lowercase character, and

```
[A-Za-z]*
```

matches all text words. If you know C language syntax, you can use regular expressions to find text words. (If you don't know C syntax, you'll learn about it in the next chapter.) For example, the expression

```
^[A-Z_a-z][0-9A-Z_a-z]*[ ]*()[ ]*$
```

works pretty well for finding your function declarations, and

```
^[A-Z_a-z][0-9A-Z_a-z][ ]*=[ ]*^[A-Z_a-z][0-9A-Z_a-z][ ]*;$
```

finds most assignment statements.

Within the bounds of a character class, the ^ operator matches all characters except the one that follows. For example,

```
[^a]
```

matches all characters except *a*, and

```
[^A-Za-z]
```

matches any character that is not a letter. Note that, inside a character class, the circumflex does not match the beginning of a line. An expression such as

```
^[^A-Za-z]
```

therefore matches any nonletter, but only at the beginning of a line. We apologize for this apparent contradiction in meaning, but regular expressions are inherently context dependent. Using grep takes a special mindset. Although grep might offer a little more power than you think you'll ever need, it's nice to know it's there. THINK C's grep supports other operators, and we refer you to the well-written THINK C user's manual for more detail.

Running with THINK C

After you've created your application's source code, you'll probably want to run it. THINK C's Project and Source menus control compilation, code generation, and program execution.

The Set Project Type command from the Project menu brings up a dialog box similar to the one shown in Figure 2-8.

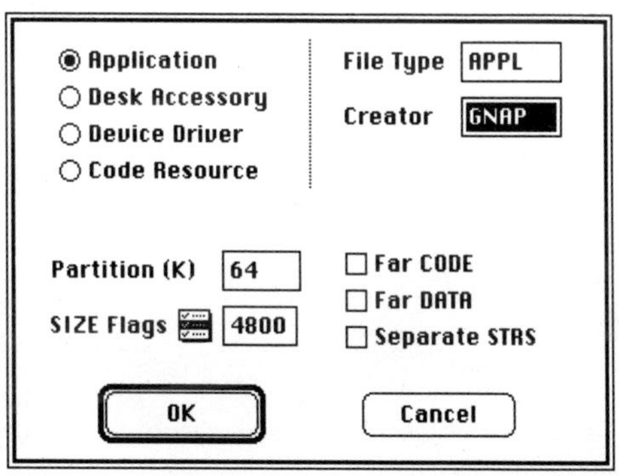

Figure 2-8. *The Set Project Type dialog box.*

Notice the radio buttons in the upper left corner of the dialog box in Figure 2-8. The Macintosh system software has different code configuration requirements for applications, desk accessories, and CDEVs. THINK C can create any kind of executable code on the Macintosh and therefore can create four types of projects: applications, desk accessories, device drivers, and code segments. All the examples in this book use the Application option.

Each application has a file signature that consists of the file type and the creator. An application is always of type APPL. The creator defines how Finder

- Maps an icon to an application
- Associates an application's documents with the application

The partition size defines how much memory MultiFinder will allocate to the application when it starts up. This is all the memory your application will get for both code and data, so it has to be enough. But it should not be so much that it hogs all the space on the user's machine—your user might want to run a concurrent application.

You arrive at a reasonable value for the partition size by some initial guessing and trial and error. If you find that your application is running out of memory, you can bump up the value. It's a good idea to run an application in the smallest partition possible and in the partition that maximizes the number of applications your user can open. Our sample applications all use small partitions, but larger applications require more memory.

To learn the size of your modules, use the Get Info command from the Source menu. Its dialog box displays the code size, data size, STR size, and jump table size for each module and segment and for the entire project. Code size is the size, in bytes, of the object code. The Macintosh system software requires that object code be grouped in segments (taken care of by the compiler's "back end" code generator), and each segment is limited to 32K. The code size value gives you an idea of how large your segments are getting. See the sidebar on segmenting your code for more information on how to keep your code segments under the 32K limit.

There are other limits on Macintosh applications: 32K on data size and 32K on jump table size. If your data size is growing too large, which should occur only in some large projects, or if you've allocated memory for some large arrays on the stack, check the Separate STRS option in the Set Project Type dialog box to move your program's string constants into a resource and free up some space. The jump table limit won't be reached, again, except in large programs. If you're careful about keeping your code modular and using static functions, you shouldn't have any problem with the jump table size. But a vigilant programmer pays attention to organization. Just because you don't need the space in small applications doesn't mean that you can be careless with space. We discuss techniques for managing jump table size in Chapters 3 and 5.

Segmenting Your Code

If one of your code segments grows larger than 32K, you'll observe some strange behavior. When a segment grows too large, you have to move one or more modules to another segment. The segments are separated visually in the project window with a dotted line. It's easy to resegment your project by dragging a module name in the project window to another segment.

You add new source modules to the project file with either of two Add commands from the Source menu. You can't compile a source file until it belongs to a project file because THINK C writes the resulting object code into the project file. The Add command without the ellipsis adds the file associated with the current editor window to the project file. The Add command with the ellipsis opens a standard file dialog box and lets you select files to add to the project file. This dialog box stays open, letting you add multiple files with a single command, until you select the Cancel button. You remove a module from the project file by selecting the module name in the project window and choosing Remove from the Source menu.

For most applications, you will need to add the MacTraps library to the project file. You do that by selecting Add (with the ellipsis) from the Source menu, navigating to the THINK C folder, selecting MacTraps, and clicking the Add button. THINK C will load the MacTraps library contents into the project file either automatically, when you run the program, or when you select the library name in the project window and choose Load Library from THINK C's Source menu.

Compile and Make

To run a program, THINK C first compiles the source code into machine-readable object code. The combination of a source file and its associated object code is called a "module." Whenever you change a file's source code, you need to regenerate the file's object code by compiling it. A source file needs compilation when

- You first create it
- You modify it
- You modify another file that it includes

Compilation occurs on a file-by-file basis. In THINK C, the source file name must end with the .c extension, and the compiler will not compile a file that doesn't belong to a project. You manually invoke compilation of a particular source file by choosing Compile from the Source menu (Command-K) to compile either the file displayed in the currently open source file window of the editor or the file selected in the project window if no source file window is open.

If you're accustomed to other C compilers—say UNIX's cc, the Microsoft Optimizing compiler for MS-DOS, or the MPW C compiler—you're in for a pleasant surprise.

Checking Syntax

You can check a source file's syntax without invoking the compiler's code generator by choosing the Check Syntax command from the Source menu (Command-Y). Because the code generator is not run, you can use this method to check the syntax of a nonproject file or a file that doesn't end in .c. And because it doesn't generate code, this feature proves to be slightly faster than using Compile from the Source menu (Command-K).

The THINK C compiler is very fast. (Early versions of THINK C were called Lightspeed C.) Because THINK C's compiler is so fast, some developers use the compiler to check their code's syntax. The compiler stops when it finds a syntax error, opens a window into the file containing the error, puts the text cursor on the offending line, and opens a message window that describes the error.

In a working environment, most programmers let THINK C's built-in make facility take care of remembering which source files need recompilation. There are no makefiles to create and maintain in THINK C, which uses the project file information and derives the dependency information directly from the source files.

Choosing Run from the Project menu (Command-R) executes the program from within the THINK C environment. The make facility is automatically invoked when you run the program, so you never need to worry about whether your program is in phase with the source code. You can set an environment option to run the program either by beginning the recompilation process automatically or by putting up a dialog box that gives you the choice of compiling or of running the program without changing the object code. You can also invoke the compilation process by choosing Bring Up To Date from the Project menu (Command-U). If the project is already up to date, the environment simply runs the program.

THINK C's make facility is almost always right about which files need compilation. When it's wrong, that's either because you've moved files into the project folder from backup disks and the modification times therefore don't apply to the current project or because you've manually manipulated the flags signaling that a file needs to be recompiled.

Choosing the Make command from the Source menu brings up the dialog box shown in Figure 2-9. You easily turn recompilation on or off by clicking next to the module name. There are also buttons to force compilation of all modules or none. When the make facility becomes confused, it is best to click the Use Disk button and turn off the Quick Scan option by clicking its check box. Then THINK C will reset the make flags according to the results of its search through each header and source file for dependency information and each file's time of modification.

Figure 2-9.
The make dialog box. Click on module name to compile that module. Selection is indicated by check mark. Click on name a second time to clear mark.

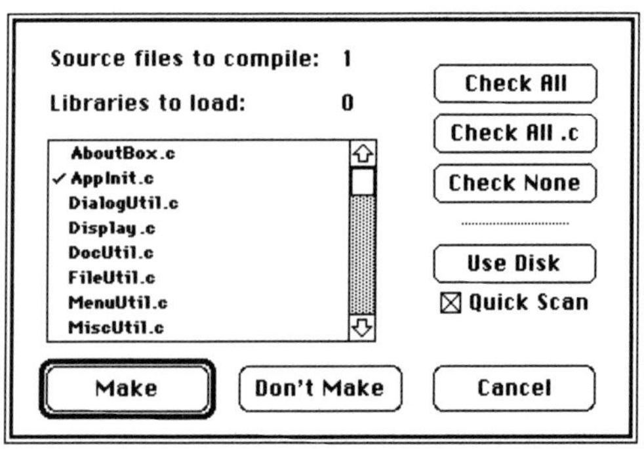

The Debugger

The symbolic debugger completes the THINK C development package. The debugger is a separate application that runs concurrently with the THINK C environment. You must therefore have enough memory to run both the environment and the debugger, and, in System 6, you must be running MultiFinder. (The System 7.0 Finder incorporates the concurrency features of MultiFinder.) You need only 2 megabytes for small projects like the examples in this book. But if you're serious about developing average-size applications, you'll need more memory—about 4 megabytes minimum.

You'll find a second monitor useful when you start to work with the debugger. You can use your primary screen for your program display and configure the THINK C Debugger to run on the second monitor. In our opinion, this is the only way to debug glitches in user-interface software. When we developed our Tycho Table Maker application, we ran into problems with our user interface modules when the debugger windows interacted with the Tycho windows they overlapped. As soon as we moved the debugger to a second screen, the problems disappeared.

To run your program with the THINK C Debugger, choose Debug from the Project menu. If you created your project without the debugging option, you'll need to recompile all your source code so that the symbol information gets generated. Don't worry—THINK C knows this and does it for you automatically the first time you try to run the program with the symbolic debugger.

When you have the THINK C Debugger up and running with your program, you have three applications running: the THINK C environment, the THINK C Debugger, and your program. This can get quite confusing, especially if you use keyboard shortcuts and consequently don't look at the menu bar to see which application is actually in the foreground.

The THINK C Debugger has two main windows: the source window and the data window shown in Figure 2-10 on the next page. If you have a two-monitor system, the source and data windows appear on the second screen. On a single-monitor system, these windows appear on the lower third of the screen.

make and makefiles

The make facility in THINK C is based on a UNIX program that drove compilation. In its day, make was a technological wonder, using a combination of file dependency data and times of file modification data to determine which files in a programming project needed recompilation. The project administrator or a programmer defined the dependency information in a text file called the "makefile." The makefile also contained information about how to generate the object code, how to link the object code, and what programming libraries to include to create the stand-alone program.

Figure 2-10.
The debugger windows.

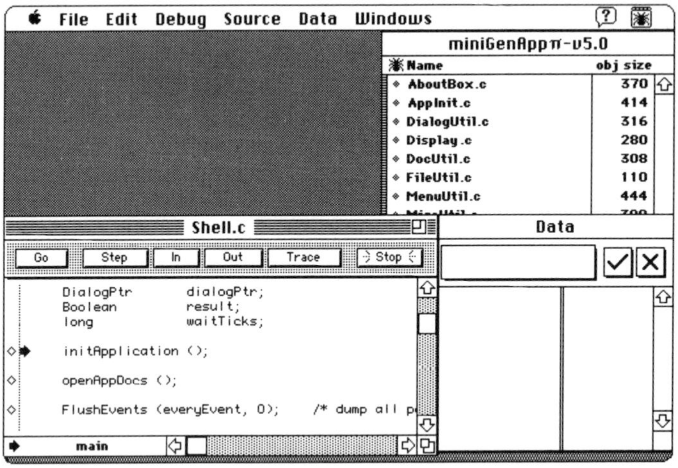

The Source Window

The source window's name is that of the currently active source module (Shell.c in Figure 2-10). When the debugger starts up, the module in the window will be the one that contains the function *main()*. Execution will be at a halt at the first statement in your *main()* function. This statement might be an assignment statement. At the bottom left of the window you'll see the current function's name—when you first start the debugger, *main*. As you continue to run your program within the debugger source window, the name changes to that of the current function. If you hold down the mouse button when the pointer is in this region, a pop-up menu appears that contains the names in the chain of calls that got you to that function. This chain is sometimes called the "call stack." (If the program burrows deeply into function after function, it might take longer than you expect to create this menu. Hang in there—it will show up.) This menu is a live menu: When you select one of the function names, the debugger source window displays that function's source code.

The six buttons at the top of the source window correspond to the first six menu commands in the Debug menu. If you click one of the buttons or choose the corresponding command from the Debug menu, the button appears to be pressed, as shown in Figure 2-11. You can figure out where you are in the debugging process at any time by looking at these buttons.

Figure 2-11.
The Go button is highlighted when you click it.

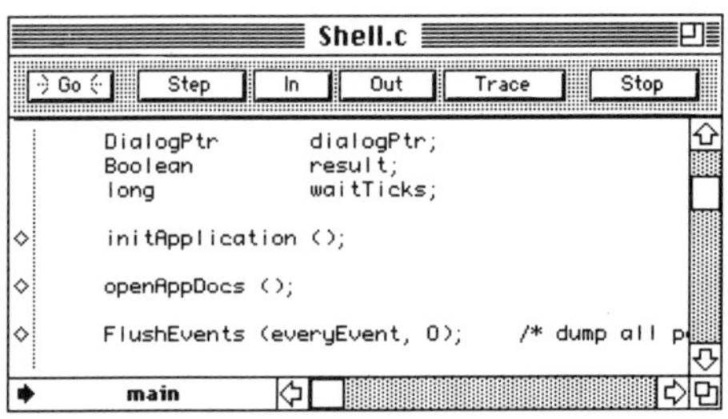

The Go button begins execution of your program and continues execution until a breakpoint or an error occurs.

The Step button executes a single statement and returns control to the debugger. In C, a statement can contain multiple function calls, so if the line contains any function calls, the functions are run as a single statement.

The Trace button works the way the Step button does in that it executes a single statement. But if the current statement is a function call, Trace traces control flow into the function and control stops at the first statement of the function.

The In button also steps into a function, but it executes any number of statements up to the first statement of the next function in the statement stream.

The Out button steps out of the current function. Like In, it executes any number of statements, but it stops at the statement after the current function returns.

The Stop button stops your program regardless of the part that is executing. You can use the Command-period equivalent for Stop.

> **NOTE:** *Be careful when using Out around the main event loop. If you're in the outermost level of your* main() *function and you select Out, the debugger will never return! You'll have to quit and restart your debugging session.*

The arrow on the left side of the source window (visible in Figure 2-10) points to the current statement. The little diamonds to the left of this arrow, called statement markers, correspond to statements in your source file. Each statement marker is a potential "breakpoint" at which the debugger will stop your program, letting you examine variables and other elements.

To set a breakpoint at a particular statement, click on its statement marker. The diamond will turn black to indicate that the breakpoint is set. When you press the Go button and execution reaches the statement, the debugger will stop the program and place the current statement arrow at that line. To clear a breakpoint, click on its darkened statement marker or select the line in the source window and choose Clear Breakpoint from the debugger's Source menu. You can remove all of a program's breakpoints at the same time by choosing Clear All Breakpoints from the debugger's Source menu.

Setting a breakpoint in another module

The source window displays the source module associated with the current statement, and you can set breakpoints only in this module. The THINK C environment and debugger were designed to work together, however, and you can set a breakpoint in another module:

1. Switch out to THINK C by clicking in the project file window or selecting the project window from the debugger's Window menu.

2. Open the file that contains the module in which you want to set the breakpoint.
3. Choose Debug from THINK C's Source menu (Command-G).

The source code for the new module will appear in the debugger's source window, so that you can set the new breakpoint by clicking on the appropriate statement's diamond.

Editing a source file while debugging

The linkage between the THINK C environment and the debugger works both ways: You can invoke the THINK C editor on the source file displayed in the debugger window by choosing Edit from the debugger's Source menu (Command-E). This is a handy feature when you discover a problem and want to make a quick fix in the source code without quitting your program (the program you're debugging, not THINK C or the THINK C Debugger).

Setting a temporary breakpoint

You set a temporary breakpoint in your program by holding down the Command key or the Option key while you click on a statement marker. After you release the mouse button, the debugger will run your program up to that breakpoint and then clear the breakpoint. Two other commands from the Debug menu, Go Until Here and Skip Until Here, create something like temporary breakpoints. Both work with selections in the source window. After you select a statement (by double-clicking on the corresponding line in the source window), choosing Go Until Here (Command-H) will cause your program to execute up to the selected statement.

The Skip Until Here command "jumps" the current statement arrow to a statement selection without executing the code between the arrow's old location and its new location. This feature can be useful for skipping over code that you know has bugs, when you want to test the various cases of a determinant expression, or even when you want to jump backward to re-execute some statements. But be smart about how

Stuck in Auto-Mode

The debugger has what the documentation calls its "auto-mode." A more descriptive name might be "sticky mode." If you hold down the Option key or the Command key when you click on one of the buttons at the top of the debugger's source window (Go, Step, In, Out, Trace, or Stop), the debugger will loop on each command as if the button were stuck. For example, if you're in auto-Step mode, the debugger will execute the next instruction, stop, update the source and data windows, and then step again, as if you had clicked the Step button again. The auto-mode is useful when you would like to watch a variable's value change as the program executes. You cancel auto-mode by pressing Command-Shift-Period.

you use Skip Until Here. Don't skip over allocations and then try to use that memory, for example. And don't skip from one stack frame to another; you'll mess up the program stack.

Coming to a screaming halt

Sometimes programmers inadvertently create infinite loops in their code. If your program is running but isn't responding to commands or if a breakpoint you set hasn't been reached in a reasonable amount of time, you can halt program execution by pressing Command-Shift-Period—what Symantec calls "the panic button." This key combination stops your program, invokes the debugger, and places the current statement arrow wherever the program was when you pressed the keys. The key combination works when the program itself is running in the foreground, but it won't work if your program intercepts the panic button (Command-Shift-Period).

Setting a conditional breakpoint

The THINK C Debugger also supports conditional breakpoints, called "watchpoints" in some debuggers. A conditional breakpoint halts execution only when a condition fails. To set up a conditional breakpoint:

1. Click on the statement marker in the source window.
2. Double-click on the statement line to select the statement.
3. Click on an expression in the data window.
4. Choose Attach Condition from the debugger's Source menu.

The statement marker turns gray to signify a conditional breakpoint.

You clear a conditional breakpoint just as you would a regular breakpoint—by clicking on the corresponding statement marker or by selecting the statement and choosing Clear Breakpoint from the Source menu.

If you want to check the condition associated with a conditional breakpoint, select the statement and choose Show Condition from the Source menu.

The Data Window

The condition governing a conditional breakpoint depends on an expression in the debugger's data window. In the data window, you can examine the contents of your program's variables. The data window has three parts. The upper part is an edit box in which you can enter variable names or C language expressions. Below the edit box are two columns: The left column contains the names of data objects; the right column contains the values of the objects. (Objects in this discussion have nothing to do with object-oriented programming. They're basically variables, but they could be constants or enumeration types.)

To display a variable, either enter its name in the edit box at the top of the data window or double-click on the variable name in the source window to select it and then choose Copy To Data from the debugger's Edit menu (Command-D).

The data window supports many of the fundamental C data types. The types it supports are listed in the debugger's Data menu. When a data object's value is displayed in the right column of the data window, you can format the value by selecting it and then choosing the appropriate format type from the Data menu. To change an object's value, select the value in the right column to place the value in the edit box, enter the new value in the edit text box, and press Return or Enter. The value must be consistent with the object's type and with the rules of the C language. You can't reassign a constant value, for example.

If the data value is a pointer or a handle, double-clicking on it in the right column will create a new dereferenced value in the data window. This feature is handy for tracking through memory to look at objects on the heap. If the data object is a pointer to a structure, a subsequent double-click on the data object's value will open a window on the structure values. The data window automatically uses data structure information from the project file and the header files, so formatting and field information in the data window match the source code in its (the source code's) window.

Each data object in the data window has a specific context in which its value is valid. The rules that govern the validity of data object values in contexts follow the scope rules of the C language. (See Chapter 3 for more information on the scope of data objects in C.) For example, a local variable's value is valid only within the context of the function in which the variable is defined. You can therefore have three local variables named *i* in the data window, each with a different context. And, because you'll probably forget the context of a value, especially if you have three *i*'s in your data window, you can see the context of a data window's data object by selecting the data object's name in the left column of the data window and choosing Show Context from the Data menu. The source window will show the function in the source file in which the object is defined.

Using the THINK C environment with the THINK C Debugger is like using any tool—it takes practice. Some of the features will become second nature to you. Others you'll never get used to. All in all, we're sure that you'll find THINK C as comfortable a development environment as we do. As the product has evolved, Symantec has delivered more features, compatibility with new systems, and compatibility with other development environments, including their popular THINK Pascal and Apple's MPW Pascal. If you use THINK C as your primary development environment, you can rest assured that your investment will be protected. This product is here to stay.

In this chapter, we've made a few assumptions about your knowledge of C. In the next chapter, we'll survey the C programming language as it applies to the Macintosh. If you're already pretty good with C, you might want to catch up with us in Chapter 4. Otherwise, turn the page.

3

A C PRIMER

Developed at Bell Laboratories in the early 1970s by UNIX pioneer Dennis Ritchie, C is today the most popular professional programming language in the world. Described by its author as a "low-level language," C has operators for bit manipulation and pointer arithmetic yet supports most of the functionality of a high-level language with data structures and typing and a wide variety of operators and program control semantics. C is based on ALGOL (short for ALGOrithmic Language), a language of the 1950s and 1960s that has its roots in the work of the computer science pioneers E. Dijkstra, C.A.E. Hoare, and P. Naur. You can trace the ancestry of all the structured languages—Pascal and PL/I as well as C—back to ALGOL. Their common ancestry explains why Pascal and C have similar language constructs, and why we can gratefully program the Mac in C now, instead of Pascal.

C is a primitive language. It has none of the built-in features for input and output, string manipulation, and higher mathematics that you find in many languages. C's features come in function libraries, which makes C an ideal language to implement in a variety of programming environments. The function libraries can contain most of the environmental dependencies. Thanks to this arrangement, C programs tend to be "portable," that is, easily moved from one machine environment to another.

The strategy has been a success: More code is written in C than in any other language. Engineers have ported the C language to dozens of computing environments. Today, you'll find a C compiler for every major computer on the market.

Of course, being all things to all environments has involved trade-offs. As every environment got its C compiler, it became harder to port a C program from one environment to another, primarily because of variations in the function libraries. To standardize the language, the American National Standards Institute (ANSI) convened the X3J11 Committee on C. As a result of their work, we now have an ANSI standard for the C function libraries. THINK C's ANSI library supports the standard, and version 5.0 supports the standard's language extensions.

C Language Fundamentals

Now that you know something about the history and evolution of the C language, we'd like to turn your attention to the language itself. Any section of a C program is likely to contain these language elements:

- Variables. Created by you, the programmer. Used for data storage and expression operands.
- Function calls. Created by you or provided with the compiler in function libraries. Used to direct a program to execute collateral pieces of code, called functions, and then return and pick up program execution in the instruction stream immediately following the function call.
- Operators. Built into the language. Used for assignment, arithmetic, comparison, and so on.
- Control statements. Built into the language. Used to control the order in which functions and other statements are executed.

If we were to compare C to a natural language such as English, the variables, function calls, and operators would be the parts of speech.

Case and Spaces

C, like English, is a case-sensitive language—you can use either uppercase or lowercase letters for variable and function names, but an uppercase letter will be treated distinctly from a lowercase one. In the following example, the *newWindow* variable and the *NewWindow* function are different objects:

```
WindowPtr   newWindow;

newWindow = NewWindow (0L, &winRect, "\p", 0, 0, -1L, 1, 0L);
```

How do you know which is which? The clues are in the code. The position of the element *newWindow* on the left side of an assignment operator signifies that the elements on the right side of the equals sign will be assigned to *newWindow*. An element that is assigned to is a variable, so we know that *newWindow* is a variable.

On the right side of the equals sign, *NewWindow* is followed by an argument list enclosed in parentheses—a tip-off that *NewWindow* is a function. (It is, in fact, a Macintosh-defined routine.)

Of course, you could eliminate any potential confusion of the variable with the function by calling the variable *newWindow* something else—say, *myWindow*. But that's not necessary because C is case sensitive. You can create names that read the same but that are treated differently by the C compiler.

The C compiler is sensitive to case but oblivious to white space (spaces, tabs, extra lines, and other nonprinting characters). You can use white space in your programs to make them more readable, but the compiler doesn't care. Nor does a C compiler care about line and column numbers in a C source file the way compilers of other programming languages, notably Basic and FORTRAN, do. You can write an assignment as

```
i = 1;
```

or as

```
i=1;
```

or as

```
i
=
1;
```

The three statements look the same to a C compiler.

Comments

There's no such thing as self-documenting code! Comments in a program help you remember why you did what you did. In C, one way to treat comments is to put them between /* and */, as in

```
/* this is a comment */
```

A comment can span multiple lines, but you can't "nest" comments. After you open a comment with /*, the comment is closed at the first */. Watch what happens in this example:

```
/* comment out the following code:
    if (ISDIRTY(theDoc))
        SelectWindow (theDoc);    /* bring to front and highlight */
*/
    if (doCloseDoc (theDoc) == kSaveChangeCancel)
    {
        result = false;           /* user canceled */
        break;
    }
```

You'll get a syntax error at the first */, right after the word *highlight*, because of the nested comment after *SelectWindow*. It's a good idea to use comments to describe single lines of source code only. One easy way to avoid nested comment problems is to comment on a whole section of source code using the *#if 0* directive, as in this example:

```
#if 0
    if (ISDIRTY(theDoc))
        SelectWindow (theDoc);    /* bring to front and highlight */
#endif
    if (doCloseDoc (theDoc) == kSaveChangeCancel)
    {
        result = false;           /* user canceled */
        break;
    }
```

The *#if 0* directive tells the compiler to ignore everything between the *#if 0* and the *#endif* in the compilation stream. Of course, you still need to be careful not to nest *#if 0* directives, but along the left edge of the code they're easier to spot than a comment usually is.

ANSI C offers another way to indicate comments, and the THINK C 5.0 compiler supports the new commenting style. The double slash, //, "comments out" an entire line, as in

```
// this is a comment
```

The comment ends with the source line. Double slash comments don't span multiple lines:

```
// this is a comment

this is not!
```

We'll use all three kinds of comment notation in this book. Now, we'll take up the C language elements.

Statements and Expressions

If variables, function calls, and operators are the words of the language, statements are the complete sentences. (The compiler, by the way, will flag an incomplete statement as a syntax error.) A statement is closed with a semicolon. Here are some examples of statements:

```
i = 6;

theDoc->type |= docParams->attributes & kDocTypeMask;

SFGetFile (aPt, promptStr, 0L, 0, 0L, 0L, &reply);
```

Although C has no line numbers, programmers continue to use "line of code" as a unit of measurement that helps them quantify the source size of a program, as in "This program has 100,000 lines of code." Old habits die hard. The number of statements would yield more information about the size of a program, but you'll never hear a C programmer say, "This program has 75,000 statements."

A statement can span multiple lines, as in

```
if (theHandle)                  // if theHandle is nonzero,
    DisposHandle (theHandle);   // dispose of it
```

The example is one statement. To satisfy ourselves that it is, we could rewrite the code:

```
if (theHandle) DisposHandle (theHandle);
```

We prefer the first form because the indentation of the second line illustrates its dependency on the first.

By the way, an empty statement is perfectly legal:

```
;
```

Using an empty, or null, statement is a logical thing to do in some contexts, as in the branch of a conditional:

```
if (!theDoc)        // if theDoc is equal to 0,
    ;               // do nothing
else
    return (theDoc->type);    // otherwise, return its type field
```

In this example, if *theDoc* is equal to *0*, no action is required; otherwise, the fragment returns the value of the document's type field. (We'll explain why in detail as we go on.)

With a little rethinking of the problem, you can usually structure a portion of code so that you don't need the null statement:

```
if (theDoc)
    return (theDoc->type);
```

This statement says, "If the value of *theDoc* is nonzero, return the document's type field." The two example statements are equivalent, but the second requires less code and is therefore more efficient. In programming, efficiency counts.

In both statements, *theDoc* is an "expression," a fragment of code that yields a value. In our example, the value is simply the value of the variable, *theDoc*. Expressions are used all the time in C and are usually the results of assignments or function calls. The following three expressions

```
i = 6
i == 6
getchar (filePtr)
```

all yield values. The first is simply the value of *i*—in this case, *6*. The second compares *i* to the constant *6*. If the value of *i* is actually *6*, the value of this expression is *1*, which stands for *true*. If the value of *i* isn't *6*, the value of the expression is *0*, or *false*. The final expression is a function call, *getchar()*, that returns the next character from some input stream of characters. The value of that expression is the value returned from the function, a character value.

Variables

Variables store data—numbers, characters, strings, pointers, handles, or data structures—the value of which can vary. The data is stored somewhere in RAM. Think of a variable as having two parts: a name and a value.

The name is your access to the variable—for storing a value in the variable or retrieving the value stored in the variable. You can use any of the uppercase or lowercase alphabetic characters in a variable name, as well as the numeric characters and the underscore (_). A variable name cannot begin with a number.

In this book we use a mixed uppercase and lowercase convention in naming our variables. We begin with a lowercase letter and then begin each syllable or word in the name with an uppercase letter. This is a common practice among C programmers in general, and particularly among Macintosh C programmers.

You can create long variable names, as in

```
theDocumentPrintRecordHandle
```

The length of a variable name is up to you. You can use any number of characters in a variable name, although it's usually a good idea to limit the length of a variable name to 32 characters.

The kind of data you store in a variable depends on its use. You might have character data in your variable if the variable will store a person's name. You might need to store fractional numerical data with great precision in your variable. The format of the data determines the variable's type.

A character is small—8 bits. You can store one character per byte in RAM. A fractional numeric value, called a floating point or real number, is 10 times as large as a character—80 bits. It takes 10 bytes to store a floating point number.

The variable's type tells the compiler how many bytes to allocate for a particular variable. The variable's type also lets the compiler know how to operate on the data. Multiplying two real numbers requires different steps than multiplying two whole numbers (called "integers"). The type of the variable operands on either side of the multiplication operator determines what instructions the compiler generates to perform the operation.

The six built-in variable types in C are shown in the following table by their declarators (type names), their sizes, and the kinds of data they can store. Notice that two of the six C variable types aren't used in C programs for the Mac.

Type Name (Declarator)	**THINK C Size**	**Used For**
char	8 bits	character data
int	16 bits, signed	whole numbers (not used on the Mac)
short	16 bits	whole numbers (< 32768)
long	32 bits	whole numbers (> 32767)
float	32 bits	real numbers (not used on the Mac)
short double	64 bits	real numbers
double	80 bits	real numbers

Defining a Variable

You must define a variable in your program before you can use it. When you define the variable, the compiler creates space for it in RAM and maps its name to that memory location. Because you specify a type for the variable when you define it, the compiler knows how much space to create for the variable. The syntax for a single variable definition is

```
typename    varname;
```

You can define a series of variables of the same type in a single statement, as in

```
typename    var1, var2, var3;
```

Character variables—*char*

As our table indicates, the smallest data type, a 1-byte variable, is the *char*. A common name for a *char* variable is *c*, as in this variable definition:

```
char c;
```

Integer variables—*short* and *long*

An integer variable is a simple numeric variable. A common name for an *int* variable is *i*, as in this variable definition:

```
int    i;
```

Symantec chose to use a 2-byte *int* for THINK C versions 1.0 through 4.0 (to coincide with the size of their Pascal integer type), and Apple chose to use a 4-byte *int* for MPW C (to match the register size of the 68000 processor).

> **CAUTION:** *Don't use the* int *type on the Mac.*

In THINK C 5.0, you can configure the compiler to use either a 2-byte or a 4-byte *int*. Even so, when you define an integer in THINK C, it's a good idea not to use *int*; use the *short* or *long* type name instead. The *short* type takes up 16 bits. The *long* type takes up 32 bits. If you use *short* or *long* instead of *int*, you'll know what you're getting, no matter where your code ends up being compiled. Explicitly type your integer variable as either *short* or *long*. Common names for *short* and *long* integer variables appear in these variable definitions:

```
short    i, j;    /* 2 bytes */
long     l;       /* 4 bytes */
```

How do you know whether to use *short* or *long* for your data type? Consider the size of any number the variable might be required to hold. If the number will always be less than 32,768, define your variable as a *short* type. If the number will be greater than 32,767 but less than 2,147,483,648, define your variable as a *long* type. If the number will be larger than 2,147,483,647, define your variable as a *double* type.

Real variables—*float, short double,* and *double*

In THINK C, real variables come in three types. The smallest THINK C real variable takes up 4 bytes and is declared with the keyword *float*. The next largest takes up 8 bytes and is declared with *short double*. The largest takes up 10 bytes and is declared with the keyword *double*.

Which do you use? Unless you're really under a space constraint, we recommend that you use 10-byte *double* variables. These largest real variables follow the IEEE-488 standard for real numbers and are supported by SANE, the Macintosh's built-in floating point routine library, so processing values of this type is faster than processing values of either of the shorter real variables.

> **NOTE:** *Floating point arithmetic is inherently slow. Avoid it unless it's absolutely necessary. (And it rarely is!)*

The fixed point alternative Using fixed point real variables is an efficient alternative to using floating point real variables. While not supported with a built-in declarator as the "native" C types are, fixed point variables are supported by the Macintosh Toolbox. Fixed point values give your application precision approaching that of floating point values, and simple operations on them, like addition and subtraction, are as fast as operations on long integer values.

That's because fixed point addition and subtraction are essentially the same operations as long integer addition and subtraction. A fixed point variable is 32 bits wide, the same size as a *long*. You declare a fixed variable using the *Fixed* type:

```
Fixed       fsin, fcos;
```

The format of the number allows it to contain a fractional part as well as an integer part. Figure 3-1 illustrates how *Fixed* numbers work.

Figure 3-1.
A Fixed *value. The value shown,* 0x00018000L, *represents* 1.5.

The upper 16 bits contain the integer part of the value, so a *Fixed* variable is like a *short* integer variable in that a variable of *Fixed* type can range from –32768 through +32767. The lower 16 bits hold the fractional part of the value. Because a *Fixed* value is simply a long integer, addition of *Fixed* values is a simple matter of *long* addition. Figure 3-2 illustrates the addition operation with *Fixed* numbers. The Toolbox contains routines for performing more complex operations on *Fixed* numbers—multiplication, division, and conversion of fixed point values to floating point values. *Fixed* multiplication and division are of course more complex than integer multiplication and division and are therefore a bit slower. But they are much faster operations than their floating point counterparts.

A *Fixed* type is a user-defined type—one not native to C that is created by a user. In the case of the *Fixed* type, the user was Apple, and the THINK C compiler supports

Apple's *Fixed* type. The user can also define derived data types in C. We'll get into greater detail about user-defined types in a moment.

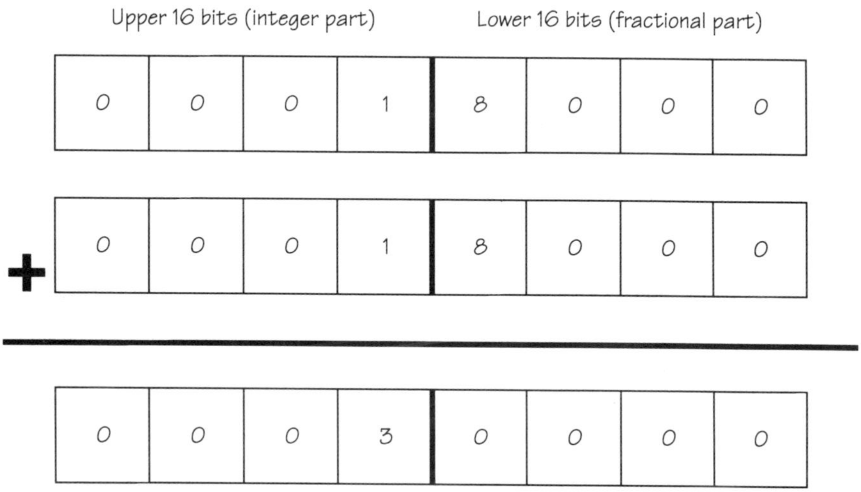

Figure 3-2.
The addition of two Fixed *numbers (*1.5 + 1.5 = 3.0*).*

Unsigned variables

Normally, integer variables are "signed," meaning that they can store either positive or negative numbers. A signed *short* integer can hold values in the range –32768 through +32767. If you're not interested in negative values, you can use the *unsigned* keyword to force the compiler to interpret the contents of the variable in the range 0 through 65535. (See the sidebar on two's complement storage to see how the computer stores signed and unsigned numbers.)

Here are some examples of *unsigned* variable definitions:

```
unsigned char     c;

unsigned short    i;

unsigned long     l;
```

Two's Complement Storage

To understand the *unsigned* keyword's significance, you need to understand that a computer stores positive and negative numbers differently. The computer stores positive numbers as pure binary numbers. For example, 1 is stored as 0001, 2 is stored as 0002, 3 as 0003, etc. But the computer stores negative numbers in two's complement form: –1 is stored as FFFF, –2 as FFFE, –3 as FFFD, and so on.

User-defined types

The types of the variables you use in a program aren't limited to the types native to C. Using the *typedef* keyword, you can declare your own, user-defined, types. Here's an example declaration for a type named *ushort*:

```
typedef unsigned short    ushort;
```

After this declaration, you define your own variable as

```
ushort    i;
```

The Mac System software has many of its own user-defined types. Here are the declarations for a few of them.

```
typedef unsigned short OSErr;

typedef unsigned char Byte;

typedef char * Ptr;

typedef char ** Handle;

typedef short (*ProcPtr)();

typedef long Fixed, Fract;

typedef long Size;

typedef enum { false, true, FALSE = 0, TRUE } Boolean;

typedef unsigned char Str255[256];
```

You should get used to using these Apple-defined types as you program.

Constants

Now that you know how to create variables, you'll probably want to assign values to them and use constant values for those assignments. Here are some native and user-defined variable types and examples of appropriate constant values for them.

Variable Type	*Sample Constant*	*Comment*
decimal short integer	1	Integers are base-10 numbers.
decimal long integer	16L	Notice the "L" after the number.
octal integer	\7	The backslash signifies base 8.
hexadecimal integer	0xFFFF	The leading "0x" signifies base 16.
real	1.44	The decimal point signifies a real number.
character	'x'	Notice the single quotation marks.
string	"Now is the time for all good men"	Notice the double quotation marks.

Symbolic constants

A symbolic constant is a constant value shown by a name, not by the value. Using symbolic constants, assigning names to your constant values, gives meaning to your code. Rather than simply having a naked *15* in your code, as in this expression,

```
right - left - 15;
```

you can help describe what's going on in your code by changing the *15* in the expression to a symbolic constant that has a meaning, as in

```
right - left - kScrollBarWidth;
```

You define symbolic constants with the *#define* preprocessor directive:

```
#define    true             1
#define    false            0
#define    kScrollBarWidth  15
#define    pi               3.141592654
#define    kErrMsg          "Warning: Call tech support"
#define    kBytesPerInt     2
```

Naming symbolic constants

If you've looked at any of the old-time, traditional C books, you've probably noticed that in most of them, the authors put their symbolic constant names in all capital letters. Indeed, when Kurt wrote UNIX-based programs, he too used all capital letters in his symbolic constant names, as did just about everyone else. It used to be that the preprocessor, the part of the compiler that processes *#define* directives, was not case sensitive and therefore couldn't distinguish among words like *ERRMSG*, *errMsg*, and *errmsg*. C programmers therefore chose to adopt the convention of defining constant names using all capitals, in order to foster a means by which a constant could readily be identified in a block of code. The prominence of constant names helped programmers avoid duplicating constant names.

The modern preprocessor is case sensitive, so the name *ERRMSG* is different from the name *errMsg*, and both are different from the name *errmsg*. We think that mixing uppercase and lowercase characters in any constant name helps to break the word up into syllables (and that words that consist entirely of capital letters are ugly!) and therefore like to name our constants as we name our variables, with mixed uppercase and lowercase letters. To distinguish most symbolic constants from variables, though, we begin the name of a constant with a lowercase *k*, for "konstant."

Sometimes you need to define symbolic constants for nonprintable characters such as tab, backspace, linefeed, carriage return, and formfeed and for serial control characters such as XON and XOFF. You represent these characters with octal or hexadecimal constants. You construct octal constants from the character set *0..7*(because they are base-8 numbers) and begin them with a backslash. Here are some examples of octal constants:

```
#define    kBell       \7
#define    kFormFeed   \14       /* octal constants */
```

If you prefer to work in base-16 numbers, you construct hexadecimal constants from the character set *0..9* and *a..f* or *A..F*, beginning with the prefix *0x* (zero-x). Here are some examples of hexadecimal constants:

```
#define    kBackSpace    0x08
#define    kTab          0x09
#define    kLineFeed     0x0A
#define    kReturn       0x0D        /* hexadecimal constants */
```

C defines special "escape sequences" for some of these characters. Although escape sequences are remnants of terminal-based implementations of C, they're supported in THINK C:

```
#define    kBackSpace    '\b'
#define    kTab          '\t'
#define    kLineFeed     '\n'
#define    kReturn       '\r'        /* special C char constants */
```

Assignment

You assign a value to a variable with the equals sign (=). Here are some integer type definitions followed by examples of integer assignment:

```
short x, y;
long  z;

x=0;          /* C ignores white space */
y = 4;        /* both are valid assignments */
z = 12;
```

Here is a floating point type definition followed by some floating point assignments:

```
double sinx, cosy;

sinx = 0.707106781;
cosy = 0.866025403;
```

Here is a character assignment:

```
c = 'K';
```

Here is a user-defined type definition followed by some assignments:

```
Point pt;

pt.h = 40;
pt.v = 10;
```

You can also assign a value to a variable when you define the variable, as in

```
short i = 0, j = 10;
```

Multiple assignments in one statement are also allowed, as long as the assignment doesn't occur during definition. Assignment is performed from right to left.

```
short i, j, k;

i = j = k = 0;
```

This kind of assignment is more efficient than assigning each variable a value separately, as in

```
i = 0;
j = 0;
k = 0;
```

But note that in multiple assignments, values are assigned from right to left. Thus, first $k = 0$, then $j = k$ (which is 0), and then $i = j$. The more complex your assignments, the more likely that multiple assignments might get you into trouble.

Automatic Type Conversion

At assignment, the compiler automatically converts the types of values. The definition

```
double x = 1;
```

defines a variable *x* of type *double* and assigns it a value of exactly *1.0*, even though the constant *1* is an integer.

If you're not careful, you can be surprised by the outcome of a type conversion at assignment, as in this example:

```
short       x;
double      y, z;

y = x = 2.5;
z = x + y; /* what is the answer? */
```

Surprisingly, *z* is *4.0*. That's because the assignment $x = 2.5$ doesn't work the way you might expect it to. The variable *x* is a *short*, so it can store integers only. The compiler therefore automatically reduces *2.5* to *2.0*. The variable *y* gets its value from *x*, so it will be assigned *2.0* as well. And $2 + 2 = 4$.

In the similar example,

```
short       y;
double      x, z;

y = x = 2.5;
z = x + y; /* what is the answer? */
```

z is *4.5*. The difference between the two examples lies in their variable definitions. Although the source code is identical in both fragments, the value of *z* depends on the variable type. In the second example, *2.5* is assigned to the *x* variable now of type *double* and thus retains its full fractional value. But *y*, of the *short* type, is an integer and is therefore assigned the value *2.0*. The value of *z* is therefore *2.5 + 2.0*.

Operators

You haven't learned all you need to know about variables yet—we'll get back to them soon. But data storage is only one aspect of the C language. You need to know something about the operators you use to affect the data. C supports a wealth of built-in operators to manipulate the data held in a variable.

Binary Operators

A binary operator requires two operands. If *a* and *b* are operands—variables, constants, or expressions—expressions using the binary operators take the form

```
a op b
```

where *op* is one of these operators:

<table>
<tr><td>*</td><td>Multiply</td></tr>
<tr><td>/</td><td>Divide</td></tr>
<tr><td>%</td><td>Modulus</td></tr>
<tr><td>=</td><td>Assign</td></tr>
<tr><td>–</td><td>Subtract</td></tr>
<tr><td>+</td><td>Add</td></tr>
<tr><td>>></td><td>Bit shift right</td></tr>
<tr><td><<</td><td>Bit shift left</td></tr>
<tr><td>></td><td>Greater than</td></tr>
<tr><td><</td><td>Less than</td></tr>
<tr><td><=</td><td>Less than or equal to</td></tr>
<tr><td>>=</td><td>Greater than or equal to</td></tr>
<tr><td>==</td><td>Equal to</td></tr>
<tr><td>!=</td><td>Not equal to</td></tr>
<tr><td>&</td><td>Bitwise AND</td></tr>
<tr><td>^</td><td>Bitwise XOR (exclusive OR)</td></tr>
<tr><td>|</td><td>Bitwise OR</td></tr>
<tr><td>&&</td><td>Logical AND</td></tr>
<tr><td>||</td><td>Logical OR</td></tr>
</table>

The operands can be variables, constants, or the results of other expressions. Here are some example expressions:

```
i == 12              /* is the value of i equal to 12? */

c & 0x00FF           /* yields the lower 8 bits of c */

x << 1               /* shift x left by 1 bit */

(count > 0) && theDoc     /* two conditions:
                             count is greater than 0 and
                             theDoc is nonzero */
```

Assignment operators

In addition to the simple equals sign (=), C has a wealth of assignment operators. Any expression of the form

a = a op b

can be rewritten using an assignment operator. For example, the expression

a = a + b;

is rewritten, using the += assignment operator, as

a += b;

These are binary assignment operators because they take the binary form

a op b

The variable on the left side of the operator gets the assignment. Here is a table that shows the binary assignment operators, their uses, and their effects.

Operator	**Usage**	**Result in a After Operation**
=	a = b	b
+=	a += b	a plus b
-=	a -= b	a minus b
*=	a *= b	a times b
/=	a /= b	a divided by b
%=	a %= b	a modulus b
>>=	a >>= b	a shifted right by b bits
<<=	a <<= b	a shifted left by b bits
&=	a &= b	a ANDed with b
^=	a ^= b	a exclusive ORed with b
|=	a |= b	a ORed with b

Unary Operators

A unary operator, as you might expect, affects only one operand, and the operand appears to the right of the operator in the instruction stream. Here's the syntax for a unary operator:

op a

where *op* is the operation and *a* is the operand. Here are the unary operators:

*	Pointer dereference
&	Address
–	Negate value
!	Logical NOT
~	Bitwise NOT
++	Increment
––	Decrement
sizeof	Size in bytes

Pointer dereference and address operators return the result of an address calculation. We'll cover more of pointers and addresses later in this chapter.

Increment and decrement operators

C provides two unary operators for incrementing and decrementing integer variables:

++ and ––

A shorthand means of applying an assignment, the increment and decrement operators were designed to take advantage of special register instructions. The ++ or –– operator means that a variable is assigned itself plus or minus 1:

i++ is the same as i = i + 1

i–– is the same as i = i – 1

You can use the increment and decrement operators as either postfix or prefix operators, but the results can be different. Consider these two examples:

```
x = 5;
y = x++;     /* y equals 5, and x = 6 */
```

and

```
x = 5;
y = ++x;     /* y and x equal 6 */
```

In the first example, *x*++ is a postfix-increment operation, so the assignment occurs first, and then the value of *x* increases. Thus, after the statement executes, *y* is *5* and *x* has become *6*. In the second example, ++*x* is a prefix-increment operation, so the value of *x* gets "bumped" before the assignment takes place. After the statement executes, both *x* and *y* equal *6*.

You would typically use an increment or a decrement operator to manipulate a loop variable, as in a *for* loop:

```
for (i = 0 ; i < someMax ; i++)
```

We'll talk more about *for* loops in a moment.

The Ternary Operator

C's ternary operator has three parts:

?, :, and some operator like -- or ++

You use the ternary operator when you could otherwise use an *if-then-else* statement, as in

```
if (!c)
    return;
else
    c--;
```

According to this statement, if *c* is *0*, execution returns to the caller; otherwise, *c* is decremented. We can rewrite this statement, using the ternary operator:

```
!c ? return : c--;
```

No wonder C has a reputation for being terse! The syntax for using this operator is

```
expression ? true part: untrue part
```

C's evaluation of an expression involving a ternary operator is If the expression is true, do the true part; otherwise, do the untrue part.

Operator Precedence

Operator precedence determines the order in which expressions will be evaluated. A simple expression like

x * y + z

can have two different results, depending on whether the multiplication is performed before or after the addition.

C's built-in sequence of operator precedence, highest precedence to lowest precedence, is shown in this list:

() [] -> .

! ~ ++ -- - (cast) * & sizeof

* / %

+ -

<< >>

< <+ > >+

== !=

&

^

|

&&

||

?:

= += -= /= *= etc.

,

To force evaluation in some other sequence, you can use parentheses. Normally, the expression

```
x * y + z
```

would add *z* to the product of *x* and *y* because the * operator has a higher precedence than the + operator. If you wanted to multiply *x* by the sum of *y* and *z*, you would write

```
x * (y + z)
```

Expressions that appear within parentheses are evaluated first.

Casting

Now that you're familiar with the operators in C, let's continue our discussion of data and storage. Sometimes (usually when assigning pointers) you need to explicitly change the type of a variable. You perform temporary type conversion with a "cast." Casting forces a type conversion for the duration of one statement—the one in which the type cast variable is used. You put the new type name in parentheses, before the variable whose type you want to cast. In the next example, we'll cast *x* to a *short* so that the fractional number will be truncated to a whole number:

```
double    x = 3.141592654,
          y;

y = (short) x;
```

The value of *x* is temporarily cast to *short*. The resulting value of *y* is *3.0*.

You can also use casting to round to the nearest integer, as in this example:

```
double    x, y;

x = 4.67;
y = (short) (x + 0.5);

x = 4.45;
y = (short) (x + 0.5);
```

In the example, when *x* is greater than *4.5*, *x + 0.5* is greater than *5*, and with truncation caused by the cast to *short*, *y* equals *5.0*. When *x* is less than *4.5*, *x + 0.5* is less than *5*, and the truncation results in a return of the integer part, *4*: *y* equals *4.0*.

Storage Classes and Scope

In some languages, Basic, for instance, you can use a variable anywhere in a program. In C, the places in which you can use a variable—the "scope" of the variable—are governed by the variable's storage class. A variable's storage class determines where in RAM the compiler will put the variable. The two storage classes are "automatic" and "static."

Automatic Variables

An automatic variable resides on the stack. If you don't know what a stack is, don't worry about it—you don't have to know anything about the stack to create an automatic variable. You define an automatic variable inside a function definition. The compiler automatically creates the variable (on the stack) when the function begins to execute and destroys the variable when the function returns. (We'll get to more about functions in a moment.) Here's an example of an automatic variable definition:

```
someFunction()
{
    short    i, j;
```

You can reference an automatic variable only inside the function in which it's defined. An automatic variable is also called a "local variable" because it is "local to the function"—available only within the function in which it's defined.

Programmers use local variables for values a program needs for only a short time. It's a good idea to make a loop counter automatic, for example—once the program is finished with the loop, it doesn't need the counter variable.

Static Variables

A program usually needs to keep some variables around much longer—maybe for the life of the program. That's where the static variable storage class comes into play.

Unlike an automatic variable, which resides on the stack, a static variable resides somewhere else in RAM. Where a static variable resides depends on both the particular operating system and the particular implementation of the compiler. In THINK C on the Mac, statics reside in a place in RAM called "the application globals."

You define a static variable outside a function definition. What's important about a static variable is that it sticks around for the life of the program. You can store a value in a static and have it survive over many function calls. Because of this persistence, statics are also called "global variables"—they can be accessed globally by all routines in a program. In this example, *gHasColorQD* is defined as a static variable outside any function, and *i* and *j* are automatics defined within a function:

```
Boolean    gHasColorQD;

someFunction()
{
    short    i, j;
```

The *register* and *static* modifiers

You can use the two keywords *register* and *static* to modify automatic and static storage classes. The *register* directive, when used in an automatic variable definition, will direct the compiler to use a CPU register for the variable instead of the stack if the registers are not otherwise occupied. In THINK C, four data and three address registers are available to your application. With judicious use of the *register* modifier for automatic storage classes, you can really speed up your application. (You don't want to assign the *register* modifier to 50 variables—you'll run out of registers!) The scope of a *register* automatic class variable is limited to the function in which it's defined, and you can't define a pointer to a *register* variable.

You can use the *static* keyword with either an automatic or a static variable. If the variable is an automatic, the *static* keyword limits the variable's scope to the function in which the variable is defined—you can't access the value of the *static* automatic variable outside the function. But the compiler will create the variable in the global variable space of RAM, not on the stack. The *static* automatic variable's value therefore persists across function calls.

When you declare a static variable explicitly with the *static* keyword (as opposed to merely defining the variable outside any function), the variable's scope is limited to the source file in which it is defined. Most programmers modularize their code into separate source files—we're no exception. A judicious use of the *static* static variable can sometimes solve a difficult programming problem.

The *extern* modifier

When you want to use a variable in a source file other than the one in which it's defined, you declare it with the *extern* keyword, as in

```
extern short count;
```

Of course, if you don't have a proper definition of the variable

```
short count;
```

in the proper place in another of the project's source files, you'll get a link error.

Arrays

Data often presents itself in array form. You declare an array with its number of elements in square brackets, as in these examples:

```
char filename [33];

double x [3], y [3];

unsigned short range [100];
```

You can specify any number of dimensions for an array, as in this two-dimensional definition:

```
char symbolTbl [12][48];
```

or this four-dimensional definition:

```
short bigArray [4][4][4][4];
```

but an array is limited to a total of 32K. On the Mac, it's better to allocate memory for an array on the heap, not the stack, and we'll show you how to do this in Chapter 7.

Array subscripting always starts at index 0, which means that the last valid index is the size of the array less 1. For example, if the array is declared as

```
char a [10];
```

it has 10 elements, and the names of these elements are *a[0]*, *a[1]*, through *a[9]*. *a[10]* would not be a valid element for this 10-element array.

C does no bounds checking for you on the index, so if you index off the end of the array, you'll be reading from or writing to something other than the array. Reading from something other than the array is usually nonfatal—you'll just end up with digital junk in your variable. But writing beyond the array bounds is always a fatal programming error. You've been warned.

An array is stored as contiguous bytes—the array elements are stored next to each other. You can speed up array access by taking advantage of this fact, by using a pointer. We'll talk more about pointers in a moment.

Other Data Structures

Any data structure collects one or more simple types into a composite group. You structure data definitions to fit data needs. For example, to model a calendar date, you would need to store information about the month, the day, and the year.

You create a data structure with the *struct* type keyword. Here's the definition for a structure for the calendar date:

```
struct    date
{
    short    month,
             day,
             year;
};
```

The structure's "tag," a name for the structure, is *date*. The structure's "members" are *month*, *day*, and *year*. Now we'll create a variable called *today* that uses the date structure:

```
struct date today;
```

You access the members of a structure with the dot operator (a period). For example,

```
today.month = 12;
today.day = 23;
today.year = 1980;
```

initializes the structure with the date December 23, 1980.

Structures can be embedded in structures. Here's a structure for a personnel record:

```
struct    person
{
    char            name [128],
                    ssnum [12];
    struct date     birthDate,
                    hireDate;
};
struct person    aPerson;
```

Notice the embedded structure *date* in the definition for *person*. We've defined *aPerson* to be a *person* structure variable. You also access the members of an embedded structure with the dot operator, which has left-to-right precedence:

```
aPerson.birthDate.day = 13;
aPerson.birthDate.month = 9;
```

Structure Types

In Macintosh applications, the convention is to type data structures and then use those types to define variables. Here's an example, our personnel record recast as a *typedef*:

```
typedef struct     person
{
    char            name [128],
                    ssnum [12];
    struct date     birthDate,
                    hireDate;
} Person;
```

Notice the change in syntax. We can now declare a variable of type *Person*:

```
Person    employee;

...
employee.hireDate = todaysDate;
...
```

Pointers

A pointer is used to hold the address of something in memory. You declare a pointer with the star operator (*). The declaration

```
char *p;
```

declares a character pointer, *p*. The type declaration is important. The following example demonstrates why. Let's declare a pointer to index through an array.

```
short values [12];          /* the array */
register short *pvalues;    /* the pointer */

pvalues = values;
```

The statement

```
pvalues = values;
```

assigns the address of the first element of the array to the pointer. Now, assuming that we want to copy the several elements of the array into separate variables, we would use the pointer to step through the array, as in

```
value1 = *pvalue;
value2 = *(pvalue + 1);
value3 = *(pvalue + 2);
...
value12 = *(pvalue + 11);
```

This code yields the same result that using the index would:

```
value1 = values [0];
value2 = values [1];
value3 = values [2];
...
value12 = values [11];
```

except that with pointer use, the code is more efficient. Note the use of parentheses. The star operator (*) has a higher precedence than the plus operator, so to do pointer arithmetic (as this is called), we need to perform the address calculation, by adding 1 to the address, before the star operator uses that address to access the value.

Pointers to Pointers—Handles

Because of the way the Macintosh manages memory, we need to take this pointer concept one step further, to the idea of a "handle." A handle is a pointer to a pointer; that is, a handle is a variable that holds the address of a pointer. It's defined this way:

```
char **
```

Why would you use a handle? We'll see why shortly.

Pointers to Structures

Just as you can have a pointer to a simple data type, you can create a variable that points to a structure. One of the most basic Macintosh types is the rectangle, named *Rect.* A *Rect* structure is defined this way:

```
typedef struct Rect
{
    short top, left, bottom, right;
} Rect;
```

In the next example, we define a *Rect* and a *Rect* pointer. We then use the pointer to zero the structure:

```
Rect    r,
        *p;

p = &r;

p->top = p->left = p->bottom = p->right = 0;
```

We've used the ampersand operator (&) to return the address of the rectangle *r*, which we then assign to the pointer *p*. Then we use the -> operator (created with the – and > characters) to access the members of the structure. If the pointer is a register variable, this section of code is highly efficient.

You could also access the members of the rectangle this way, using the dot operator:

```
(*p).top = (*p).left = (*p).bottom = (*p).right = 0;
```

Again, notice the use of parentheses around the **p*. The dot operator has a higher precedence than the star operator, and in this example, we want the compiler to calculate the address of the data structure first, before it adds the offset of the structure's member to this address. When you're dealing with pointers and structures, you have to stop and think about what you want to happen first.

Figure 3-3 illustrates the relationship between a pointer and the data it points to.

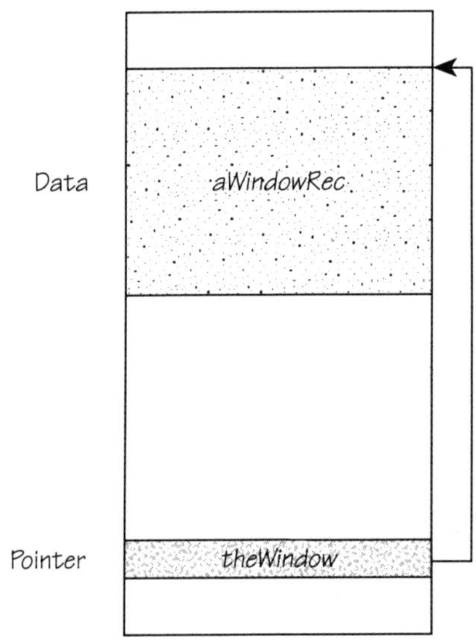

Figure 3-3.
A pointer.

Handles to Structures

More often than not in Macintosh programming, you'll have a handle to a structure and will need to access one of the members of the structure. Given a handle *h* to a *Rect* structure *(Rect **h;)*, you would access the members this way:

```
(*h)->top = 0;
```

or

```
(**h).top = 0;
```

The constructs are equivalent. We prefer the first, although the second offers a singular advantage: If you ever need to find all the handle references in your program, you can search globally for **, which is usually unique to handle accesses.

Figure 3-4 illustrates the relationship of a handle (*ControlHandle*) to its associated structure (*ControlRecord*) in RAM.

Program Flow Control

The C language supports a wealth of program flow control constructs. The simplest is the test and branch, performed by means of the *if* statement. Here's the syntax for an *if* statement:

```
if (expression)
    statement
```

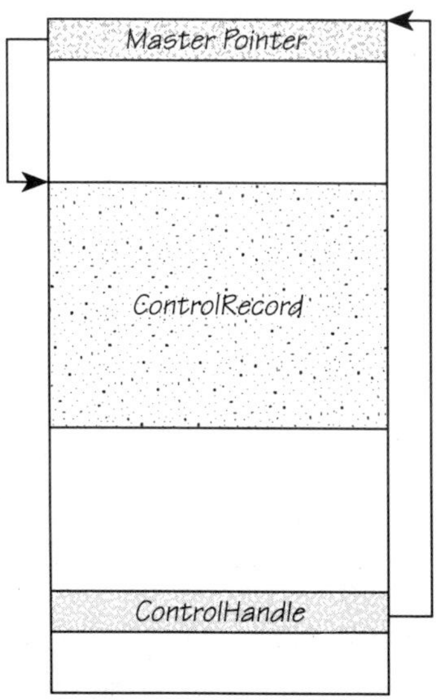

Figure 3-4.
A handle.

In this example, *statement* will execute if *expression* results in a nonzero value. In the next example, *DebugStr* will be called if the variable *gDevel* is nonzero:

```
if (gDevel)
    DebugStr (string);
```

The *if-else* statement provides an alternative branch to be taken when the expression under scrutiny is *0*:

```
if (expression)
    statement 1
else
    statement 2
```

If *expression* is true, *statement 1* is executed; otherwise, *statement 2* is executed. In the next example, if the *gDevel* flag is on, the debugger is entered with the call to *DebugStr*. (We'll get to that call in a later chapter.) Otherwise, the program takes the second branch and puts up a dialog box on the screen with the call to *errorDialog()*:

```
if (gDevel)
    DebugStr (string);
else
    errorDialog (string);
```

Two or more statements are called a "compound statement." You create a compound statement inside curly braces, { and }. In the next example, the *else* part of the *if-else* statement consists of a compound statement:

```
if (gDevel)
    DebugStr (string);
else

{
    SysBeep (1);
    GetPort (&savePort);

    if (!(theDialog = GetNewDialog (kDebugStrAlert, 0L, -1L)))
        return (1);

    ParamText (0L, string, 0L, 0L);

    ModalDialog (DLOGfilterProc1, &itemNumber);
    DisposDialog (theDialog);

    SetPort (savePort);
}
```

A compound statement actually defines a code block, for which a stack "frame" is generated. (You'll find an extensive discussion of stack frames in Chapter 7.) This means that you can define variables within the block, as in

```
if (!gDevel)
{
    GrafPtr     savePort;     /* local to block */

    GetPort (&savePort);
    if (!(theDialog = GetNewDialog (kDebugStrAlert, 0L, -1L)))
        return (1);

    ParamText (0L, string, 0L, 0L);

    ModalDialog (DLOGfilterProc1, &itemNumber);
    DisposDialog (theDialog);

    SetPort (savePort);
}
```

The local *savePort* isn't used outside the *if* statement. If you try to reference *savePort* outside the statement, the compiler will generate an error.

Multiway Branching

A one-out-of-many choice, called a "multiway branch," is a common programming construct. The *if-else if-else* statement is the most flexible implementation of a multiway branch:

```
if (expression 1)
    statement
else if (expression 2)
    statement
else
    statement
```

You use the *if-else if-else* construct when the test expression changes for each branch, as in the next example:

```
if (!listHdl)     /* not found */
    return (0L);
else if (prevListHdl == listHdl)     /* head of list */
    (*objectHdl)->ref = (*listHdl)->next;
else
    (*prevListHdl)->next = (*listHdl)->next;     /* link last to next */
```

In other instances of the multiway branch, an expression is compared to a variety of constants. In the next example, *objectType* is compared to a number of constants:

```
if (objectType == kSquare)
    doSquare (theObject);
else if (objectType == kCircle)
    doCircle (theObject);
else if (objectType == kRoundRect)
    doRoundRect (theObject);
else
    doError (kUnknownTypeErr);
```

Placement of Curly Braces

Three widely acknowledged styles regarding the placement of curly braces for compound statements are in use today. The standard style is adopted from the practice of Thomas Plum, a well-known authority on C programming and the author of many books on the language. The braces appear on lines of their own, beneath the tab stop of the controlling keyword:

```
if (expr)
{
    statements
}
```

The Whitesmith style, from an organization influential in the development of C language standards, puts the braces on lines of their own but indented one tab stop from the controlling keyword's tab stop:

```
if (expr)
    {
    statements
    }
```

The Kernighan and Ritchie style puts the opening curly brace at the end of the line containing the controlling keyword and the closing curly brace on a line of its own beneath the tab stop of the controlling keyword:

```
if (expr) {
    statements
}
```

We choose to use the standard Plum style. You can use whichever style you like, as long as you stick to it.

A more efficient way to achieve a multiway branch is to use a *switch* statement based on a value that can take on a set of constant values. Here's the syntax for a *switch* statement:

```
switch (value)
{
    case constant1:
        statement
        break;

    case constant2:
        statement 2
        break;

    default:
        statement n
        break;
}
```

Here's the previous multiway branch example, recoded as a *switch* statement:

```
switch (objectType)
{
    case kSquare:
        doSquare (theObject);
        break;

    case kCircle:
        doCircle (theObject);
        break;

    case kRoundRect:
        doRoundRect (theObject);
        break;

    default:
        doError (kUnknownTypeErr);
        break;
}
```

Notice how the cases are enumerated. If no case matches the expression, the optional default case is executed. The *break* statement at the end of each case causes control to jump to the bottom of the *switch* statement. If the break were left out, control would continue through the remaining cases.

Loops

Use a loop when you want to repeatedly execute a statement. The loop loops as long as a controlling expression is true. You specify a loop in one of three ways: in a *while* statement, in a *do-while* statement, or in a *for* statement.

while loops

Use a *while* loop when you want to test the expression before the loop is entered. Here's the syntax for the *while* construct:

```
while (expression)
    statement
```

The statement executes as long as *expression* is true. Here's a typical example of a *while* construct:

```
while ((*listHdl)->next)
    listHdl = (*listHdl)->next;
```

In this example, execution loops through a null-terminated linked list of objects stored in the heap. Execution exits the loop when the handle to the next element of the list is null (has a *0* value).

do-while loops

The *do-while* loop is similar to the *while* loop, except that the test of *expression* is made at the bottom of the loop—you are assured that the body of the loop will execute at least once. Here's the syntax for a *do-while* loop:

```
do
    statement
while (expression);
```

for loops

Use a *for* loop when you know how many iterations are necessary. Here's the syntax for a *for* loop:

```
for ( initial expression ; test ; increment )
```

Notice that there are three expressions inside the parentheses of a *for* loop. The first expression initializes the loop counter variable. The second is the test expression. The loop loops as long as this expression is *true*. The third increments the loop variable. The next example illustrates the initialization of an array:

```
short i, c [MAX];

for (i = 0 ; i < MAX ; i++)
    c [i] = 0;
```

This is a simple initialization loop in which *i* takes on all integer values from *0* through *MAX–1*. You can set up your loop variable to take on only even values, or only multiples of 5, or whatever you want it to take on, by selecting an appropriate expression for the incrementing expression of the *for* statement, as in

```
for (i = 5 ; i < SOMEVALUE ; i += 5)
    doSomething (i);
```

Breaks and Continues

You've already seen *break* in the *switch* statement. A break causes execution to jump to the bottom of a switch or a loop. Here's an example:

```
while (1)
{
    c [i] = 0;
    if (i++ > MAX)
        break;
}
```

Whenever *i* is greater than *MAX*, the loop execution exits. Of course, smart C programmers will recognize that this loop could be rewritten as

```
while (i < MAX)
    c [i++] = 0;
```

The *continue* statement causes execution to jump to the top of a loop. Here's an example:

```
while (count--)
{
    if (fileType != kOurType)
        continue; /* jump to top of while loop */

    fileParams = getNextFileName();
    if (doOpenFile (&fileParams))
        loadDoc (&fileParams);

    numOpenDocs++;

    if (msg == doPrint)
        printFile (&fileParams);
}
```

This example, and the preceding one, could be rewritten without the use of either a *break* or a *continue*. Proponents of structured programming would argue that *break* and *continue* aren't actually essential (as far as loops are concerned—*break* is necessary in a switch statement). We occupy the middle ground on this question: If you need *break* and *continue*, use them. We don't frown upon their use, although we do realize that most C code can be structured so that they are not necessary. Use them sparingly.

Functions

We do recommend the use of functions to divide a program into small, logically distinct parts that are reusable: You can call functions from various points in a program, reducing your code size. If you publish the functions in a library, other programmers can use them too, and you'll have reduced their need to "reinvent the wheel."

When your program calls a function, control is passed to the function, and execution continues until the function ends or a *return* statement is encountered. Figure 3-5 illustrates the control process.

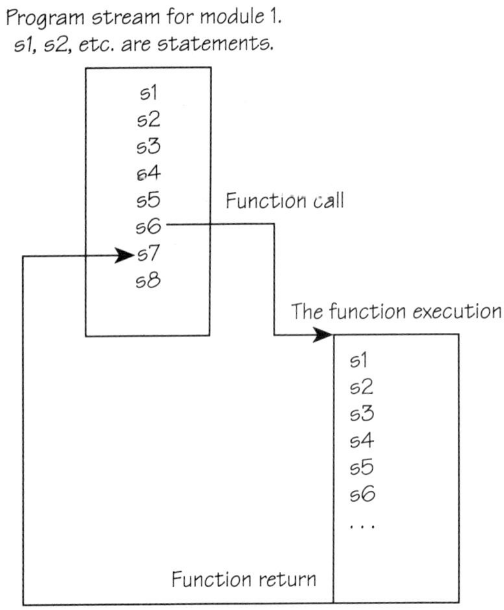

Figure 3-5.
A function call, execution, and return to the next program statement.

You call a function with its name and a parenthesized argument list, as in

```
disposeDocContents (theDoc);
```

Here, the function is called with one argument: *theDoc*. You call a function without an argument with its name and empty parentheses:

```
PenNormal ();
```

A function can return a value on the stack. You receive the value as the result of an expression that contains the function, as in

```
theWindow = FrontWindow ();
```

Here, the return value of the function *FrontWindow()* gets assigned to *theWindow* when the function returns.

All of the Macintosh Toolbox routines are accessible to your THINK C program through a function call if you add the MacTraps library to your project. (We'll discuss this in the next chapter.) The *FrontWindow* function in the previous example is a Macintosh Toolbox Window Manager routine.

You can define your own functions. Here's the syntax for a function definition:

```
return-type
name (argument list)
{
    declarations

    statements
}
```

You have several options for defining functions. You can define a function to return a value by using the *return* statement. In the next example, the function returns a *DocPtr* value.

```
static DocPtr        /* return type */
allocDoc ()          /* function name */
{
    DocPtr    newDoc;        /* variable definition */

    newDoc = 0L;             /* function body */

    if (gNumOpenDocs < kMaxOpenDocs)
        newDoc = newClearPtr ((Size)sizeof (Doc));

    return (newDoc);         /* return value */

} /* allocDoc */
```

A function that doesn't return a value is declared as *void*. Here's an example:

```
void
getRGBColor (RGBColor *theColor)
{
    GetForeColor (theColor);
}
```

There is no *return* statement in *getRGBColor*.

In the early versions of the C language, a function's arguments were declared as automatic variables would be, outside the parentheses, as in

```
short
openFile (fileParams, copy)
    FileParamsPtr fileParams;
    Boolean copy;
{
...
}
```

When you define a function according to the ANSI C standard, the function's argument list appears in the parentheses.

```
short
openFile (FileParamsPtr fileParams, Boolean copy)
{
...
}
```

Function prototypes

The advantage of the new ANSI standard function definition syntax is that you can use the definition itself as a function prototype—as a model of the function's name, argument types, and return value. The prototypes for the three functions we've looked at so far in this section are

```
DocPtr      allocDoc ( void );
void        getRGBColor ( RGBColor *theColor );
short       openFile ( FileParamsPtr fileParams, Boolean copy );
```

A prototype is a statement, so it needs to be followed by a semicolon. Prototypes keep you from making mistakes when calling functions. When you've selected Check Prototypes from the THINK C environment's Preferences menu, the compiler will check all your function calls for

- the correct number of arguments
- the correct type for each argument
- the correct type for the function return value

This prototype checking keeps your code free of nasty bugs. Prototype definitions have to appear before the function is either defined or used.

To manage function prototypes, we create a separate include file (with the extension .h) for each source file in a project. The include file contains the prototypes for the source file. We use a *Pr* suffix with the include file's name to flag the include file as a prototype file. For example, if the source file is named DocUtil.c, we name the prototype file DocUtilPr.h. We then include DocUtilPr.h in DocUtil.c and in any other source file that uses a routine from DocUtil.c.

4

MACINTOSH APPLICATION FUNDAMENTALS

In this chapter, we'll create our version of every programmer's first, the program Hello World. We'll modify the program, call it Hello Mac!, and use it to address some fundamental concerns common to all Macintosh application development—screen organization, Macintosh events, and Toolbox Manager initialization.

Macintosh programs have a characteristic interface: Overlapping windows and pull-down menus, the point-and-click metaphor, and the visual file system are standard features in every application. They give your programs an edge over those with line-oriented interfaces.

The Hello World Example

Every C programmer's first exposure to a complete program is Hello World. Here's the THINK C user's manual version of Hello World in its entirety:

```
#include <stdio.h>

main ()
{

    printf ("hello, world\n");

}
```

This trivial first program illustrates the fact that every program has to have a *main()* function, the program entry point.

Hello World is a complete C program. If you wanted to run it, you would type it into a source file, create a new project, and add the source file and the ANSI library to the project. When you ran the program, your screen would look something like the screen in Figure 4-1.

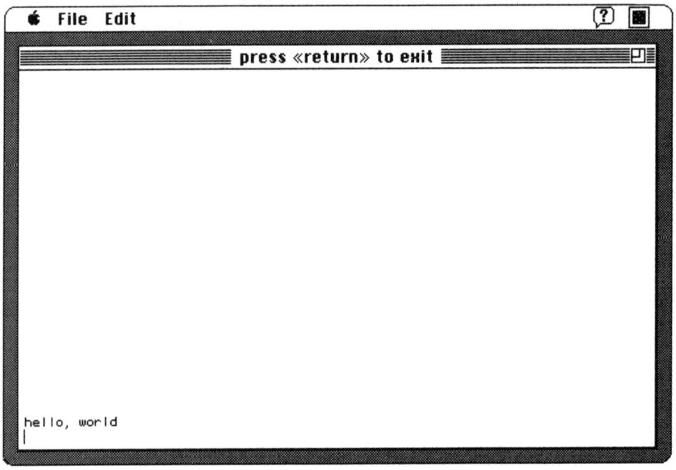

Figure 4-1. *The Hello World example program in THINK C.*

Unfortunately, this example program doesn't look or function the way a Macintosh program should. The window on the screen in Figure 4-1 is a product of the THINK C stdio library. This window, titled "press <<return>> to exit," is created for you when you issue a call to the library function *printf.* When *printf* returns, the application beeps at you until you press Return. You'd be hard-pressed to call this an example of a stand-alone application.

To create a stand-alone Hello World that works the way you expect a Macintosh program to work, you need to use the Macintosh Toolbox in place of the stdio calls.

THINK C's stdio Library

THINK C's console routines, provided in the stdio library, are the source of the primitive window management routines used in the Hello World example. These routines open a single window that emulates a character terminal's screen. Console I/O is based on the character streams *stdin* and *stdout.* UNIX aficionados will appreciate that stdio functions like *printf* work in this screen. Using THINK C's stdio is easy: Add the library to the project (by using the Add command from the Source menu), and include the header file stdio.h in your source file. The THINK C user's manual contains a tutorial on using this library.

Before your Mac can say "hello," it needs a window and an associated grafPort in which to put the greeting. And before you can create a window, you need to initialize the application's QuickDraw globals. Here's the Macintosh way to say "hello":

```
main ()
{
    WindowPtr   theWindow;
    Rect        windowRect;
    EventRecord eventRec;

    // initialize managers
    InitGraf (&thePort);
    InitWindows ();
    InitFonts ();
    InitCursor ();

    FlushEvents (everyEvent, 0);

    // create window
    SetRect (&windowRect, 40, 40, 340, 240);
    if (theWindow = NewWindow (0L, &windowRect,"\p",
                    true, dBoxProc, -1L, false, 0L))
    {
        SetPort (theWindow);
        MoveTo (20, 30);                // move pen

        TextFont (1);                   // text attributes
        TextSize (12);
        TextFace (0);
        DrawString ("\pHello, Mac!"); // why we're here

        // wait for mouse-down
        while (!GetNextEvent (mDownMask, &eventRec));

        DisposeWindow (theWindow);    // kill window
    }

    ExitToShell ();

} /* main */
```

This is a program you'll actually want to enter and run, so start up THINK C.

Creating the Program

When you start up THINK C without naming a project, a dialog box prompts you to open a project. When you click the New Project button in this dialog box, you see the dialog box shown in Figure 4-2 on the next page.

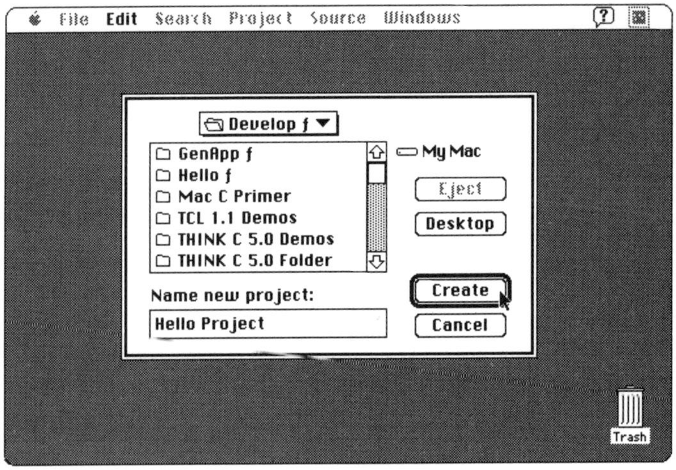

Figure 4-2. *THINK C's New Project dialog box.*

Type the name *Hello Project* in this dialog box, and click the Create button. THINK C creates a window that looks like the one in Figure 4-3.

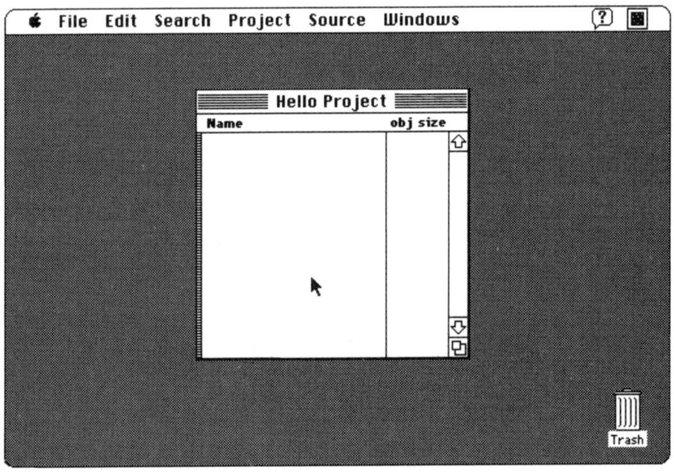

Figure 4-3. *The empty project window.*

Now open a new document by choosing New from the File menu, and type in the source code shown on page 71.

When you've finished typing in the source code, choose Save As from the File menu and type *Hello Mac.c* as the file name.

Choose Add from the Source menu. When THINK C finishes this operation, the project window should look like the one in Figure 4-4.

Next, you need to add the MacTraps library to the project file. Choose Add from the Source menu, and navigate to the MacLibraries folder in your THINK C folder, where you should find the file MacTraps. (If you followed our installation instructions in

Figure 4-4.
The project window after adding the Hello Mac.c file.

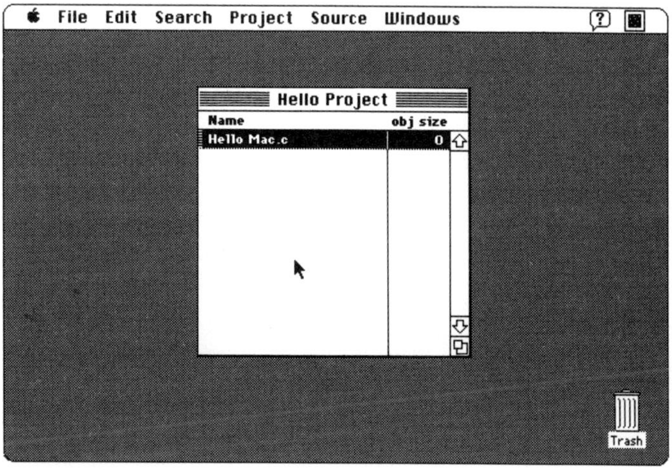

Chapter 2, you'll find MacTraps in this folder. If not, you might need to look elsewhere or reinstall THINK C.)

That's all you need to do to set up the project. Bring it up to date, which should load the library and compile the source file. (Fix any syntax errors you entered while typing in the source file.)

Run the program.

As you can see from looking at the source file, doing things the Macintosh way adds to the overhead of creating an application. This additional overhead is what makes programming the Mac both interesting and hard to learn. Even experienced C programmers will have a lot to learn—we doubt they'll recognize any of the function calls in Hello Mac! unless they've already cracked open *Inside Macintosh* and done some reading.

Most of the programming overhead in our simple example comes from creating the window in which to draw the text. On the Mac, characters are drawn by QuickDraw, the drawing part of the Mac Toolbox, which treats characters just as it does any other graphics entities (lines, circles, and so on). Drawing is possible only inside a grafPort. But before you can use a grafPort, you'll need to know a little more about the Mac's screen organization.

GrafPorts and Windows

A grafPort is a Macintosh construct that provides a "world" for a program to draw in. The coordinates of the grafPort world are defined within an imaginary grid, starting at the upper left corner of the Macintosh screen and extending in all directions from that point.

A location in this grid, the Macintosh coordinate system, is described by *Point,* which has a horizontal and a vertical component. A data structure of type *Point* is defined this way:

```
typedef struct Point
{
    short v, h;
} Point;
```

The origin of the Macintosh coordinate system is at location (*0,0*). The first value is the horizontal component, and the second value is the vertical component. Values increase as a point moves down the screen and to the right. For example, the point (*10, 20*) is 10 points to the right and 20 points below the origin.

A pixel is a screen unit that corresponds to a point. The grid values range from –32,767 pixels through +32,767 pixels in either direction, so you can imagine that there are more pixel locations off the screen than on it. The Mac Classic displays 352 horizontal pixels by 512 vertical pixels, which is only a small fraction of the area referenced by a grafPort; the standard 14-inch Apple color monitor has a resolution of 640 by 480 pixels, or 640×480 in tech-speak, still only a small part of the area you can reference with QuickDraw. Figure 4-5 illustrates the grid behind the Macintosh screen. The grafPort associated with this coordinate system is called the WMgrPort. Applications don't draw in the WMgrPort, which is the domain of Finder; rather, they use a grafPort associated with one of their windows.

Each open window has its own grafPort and might be said to "own" the grafPort. The grafPort's origin is below the upper left corner of the window, immediately

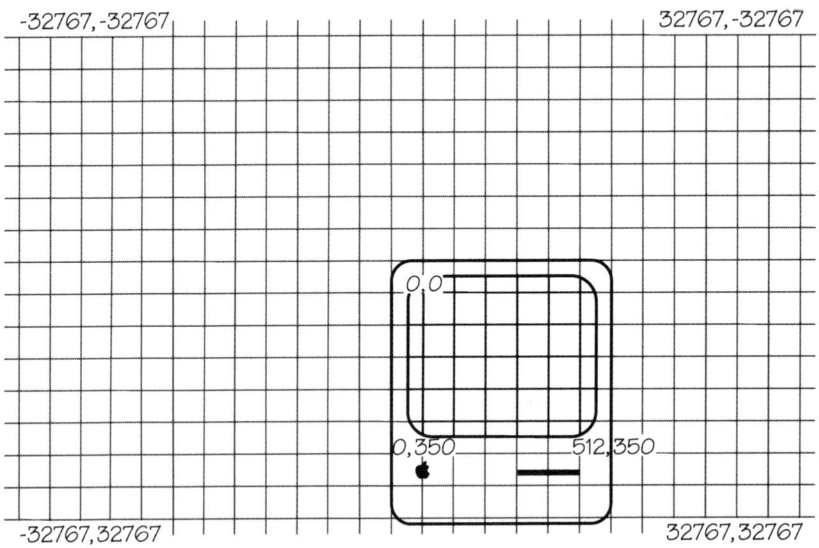

Figure 4-5.
The Macintosh WMgrPort coordinate system.

below the title bar. The grafPort has its own coordinate system, and values in its system also increase to the right and down from the origin point. We call this a "local coordinate system" to differentiate it from the WMgrPort's "global coordinate system." Figure 4-6 illustrates the relationship between these two systems.

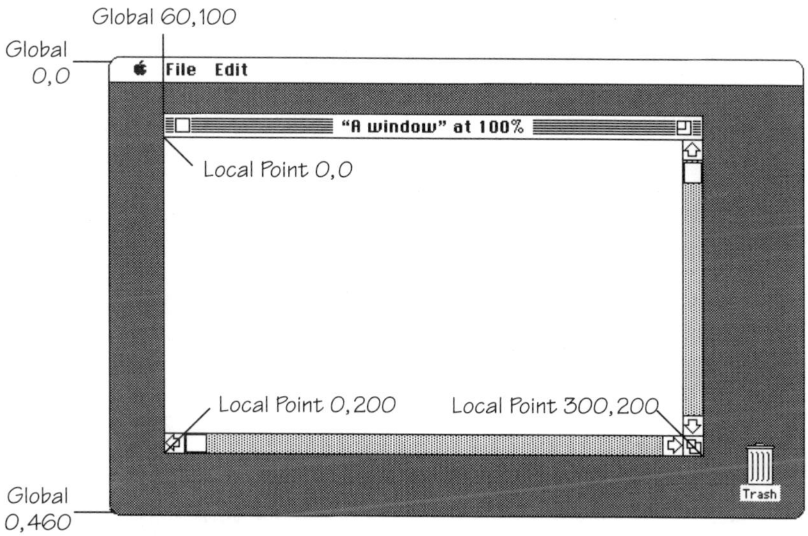

Figure 4-6.
The two coordinate systems of the Macintosh screen.

The Toolbox routine *LocalToGlobal* converts point values in the local coordinate system of a window to those of the global space. The companion routine *GlobalToLocal* works conversely, converting point values in the global system to local point values.

These conversion routines accept the address of a *Point* structure. Here's an example of their use:

```
Point p;

GlobalToLocal (&p);
LocalToGlobal (&p);
```

Notice that the points are passed by reference—that is, their addresses are taken with the ampersand. This is done so that the Toolbox routines can change the actual values of the passed variables.

Creating a Window and a GrafPort

Where there's a window, there's a grafPort (often called a "port," in programmer's slang). GrafPorts are rarely created by themselves—usually they're created automatically when a window is created. We show the definition of a *WindowRecord*, the foundation of a window, on the next page.

```
typedef struct WindowRecord
{
    GrafPort            port;
    int                 windowKind;
    char                visible;
    char                hilited;
    char                goAwayFlag;
    char                spareFlag;
    RgnHandle           strucRgn;
    RgnHandle           contRgn;
    RgnHandle           updateRgn;
    Handle              windowDefProc;
    Handle              dataHandle;
    StringHandle        titleHandle;
    int                 titleWidth;
    struct ControlRecord ** controlList;
    struct WindowRecord * nextWindow;
    PicHandle           windowPic;
    long                refCon;
} WindowRecord, *WindowPeek ;
```

Notice that the first member of the *WindowRecord, port,* is a grafPort.

The Window Manager is the part of the Macintosh Toolbox that contains the routines that create and work with Macintosh windows. We'll use the Window Manager call *NewWindow* to create a window, which creates a *WindowRecord.* By referencing *port,* we can reference the grafPort we'll be drawing in.

Passing Parameters to Toolbox Routines in THINK C

One common concern in using a language such as C on the Pascal-based Mac is how to match the Pascal function-calling convention. In languages such as C and Pascal that maintain a stack-based parameter-passing mechanism, there are two methods of passing function parameters, or variables. Passing a variable "by value" means that a copy of the variable's contents is passed to the called function. Because it is passed a copy, the called function is free to change the value of the variable without consequence in the caller. Passing by value gets expensive, both in time and in memory, when the variable is a large data structure. A Pascal compiler consequently tries to optimize time and memory by passing all parameters that are more than 4 bytes in size "by reference." When a variable is passed by reference, the variable's address is placed on the stack, and no copy of the data is made. In C, because the called function gets the address of the variable in the caller, any changes made will be reflected in the value of the variable when the function returns (in C only—Pascal safeguards against this "side effect").

Fortunately, the compiler manages the stack for you, but it's your job to get the types of the parameters correct. Here's a rule of thumb that usually works: If the size of the parameter is more than 4 bytes, pass it by reference. In other words, pass its address. The rationale behind this thinking is that if an address is 4 bytes, passing by reference limits the maximum size of a stack parameter. This approach places a burden on you, the programmer, because you need to know something about the data structures of the parameters of the Toolbox routines that you use.

Of course, every rule has an exception, and here's the exception to our rule of thumb: Whenever you find a Toolbox procedure-definition parameter that has a *VAR* in front of it, pass the address of the variable. Do this because some functions are designed to modify the contents of the variables passed to them. Pascal has a mechanism called a "variable parameter" specifically for this purpose, and the modifier *VAR* is placed before the name of the variable in the definition of the function to signify that the parameters are modifiable.

A point is 4 bytes, so normally you'd pass it by value, as in

```
Point mouseLoc;

if (PtInRect (mouseLoc, &portRect))
...
```

Notice that the point *mouseLoc* is passed by value, and that the rectangle *portRect* is passed by reference—that is, we pass its address. The point is passed by value because it is 4 bytes, but a *Rect* structure is larger than 4 bytes and is therefore passed by reference. Now consider the Event Manager routine *GetMouse*, defined this way:

```
Procedure GetMouse (VAR mouseLoc: Point);
```

This changes the way you'd pass a *Point*:

```
Point mouseLoc;
...
GetMouse (&mouseLoc);
if (ABS(mouseLoc.h - oldMouseLoc.h) >= kMouseLimit)
...
```

C and Pascal

The Macintosh Toolbox routines are designed to be called from a Pascal program, and *Inside Macintosh* documents all the routines as if you were using Pascal, not C. Experienced C programmers probably adjust quickly to the differences, but beginning C programmers might think that, just as they've begun to learn one language, they need to learn another.

C and Pascal are very similar because they share a common ancestry. They have similar data types: integers, reals, and characters. They share the ability to structure data: Pascal data structures (called records) can be and are mimicked by C data structures. And the two languages have similar control structures, so a C program can be ported to a Pascal program, and vice versa.

In the case of *GetMouse*, the *VAR* modifier calls for passing by reference. *GetMouse* returns the current mouse position in this variable and therefore needs the address to which it will write this information.

C has a built-in feature, called function prototyping, whereby the compiler will check a function's parameter types. To use prototypes, you must first tell the compiler to check for them. You'll find the option in the Compiler Flags section. You also need to declare prototypes for each of your functions, but you don't need to write prototypes for the Toolbox routines that you use in your program—they're built into THINK C. All of our projects use prototypes. For the small amount of up-front effort required to use them, they really pay off in time otherwise spent finding parameter type errors. We strongly recommend that you use them.

Here's the prototype declaration of *NewWindow*, which describes how you would call it from an application:

```
WindowPtr NewWindow (Ptr wStorage, Rect *boundsRect, Str255 title,
    Boolean visible, short procID, WindowPtr behind,
    Boolean goAwayFlag, long refCon);
```

You might first notice that this function has eight parameters. Each one is important. You can get the complete story on each parameter from *Inside Macintosh*. All the Toolbox calls used in this chapter are described in Volume I. We don't have the space to describe each Toolbox call in this book, but we'll make a few comments about *NewWindow* that apply to using Toolbox calls.

Who Allocates the Storage?

The first *NewWindow* function parameter, *wStorage*, is a pointer to some memory to be used for the *WindowRecord*, the data structure associated with the window. We're given the opportunity to allocate this memory ourselves for reasons that are not worth going into here—we'll discuss the heap and fragmentation in Chapter 5. But *Inside Macintosh* tells us that if we pass a null pointer (the value 0×00000000L) for this parameter, the Window Manager will allocate the memory for us.

This is a common convention in the Window Manager, the Dialog Manager, and other parts of the Toolbox: You pass either the address of some allocated memory or a null pointer. In our simple example, it will suffice to let the Window Manager allocate the memory for us.

Passing by Reference

The second argument to *NewWindow* is a rectangle that specifies where to place the window in global space. Because of Pascal parameter-passing conventions, you must pass this rectangle by reference, as was mentioned earlier.

Pascal Strings vs. C Strings

The title field is defined as a *Str255* type, also known as a Pascal string. *NewWindow* expects a string pointer in this argument, but Pascal and C differ in their string formats. The first byte of a Pascal formatted string contains the length of the string and is followed by the string of characters. A traditional C string, like those described by Kernighan and Ritchie, consists of the characters followed by a terminating *0*. These two formats are illustrated in Figure 4-7.

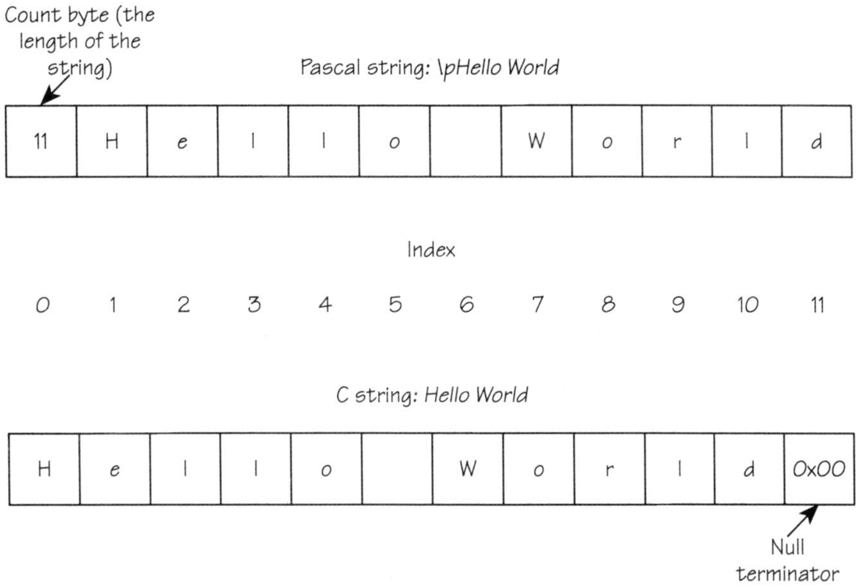

Figure 4-7.
The formats of Pascal strings and C strings.

The designers of THINK C were considerate in that they invented a notation for quickly specifying Pascal string constants: A string that begins with the token *\p* is created as a Pascal string. For example, *\pUntitled* is compiled into the Pascal string that *NewWindow* will interpret as the Pascal format of the string. A traditional C string is defined between double quotes—"*Untitled*" for example.

Creating a Window

We've excerpted the code from Hello Mac! that creates the window. The first call, to *SetRect*, initializes the *Rect* structure that defines the window's rectangle. A *Rect* structure is defined this way:

```
typedef struct Rect
{
    short top, left, bottom, right;
} Rect;
```

This window rectangle is specified in global coordinate space, so it will be 40 pixels from the top and 40 pixels from the left edge of the screen, and it will be 300 pixels wide by 200 pixels high.

```
SetRect (&windowRect, 40, 40, 340, 240);
if (theWindow = NewWindow (0L, &windowRect,"\p", true, dBoxProc, -1L,
                false, 0L))
```

Again, a rectangle is larger than 4 bytes, and to follow Pascal calling conventions, we therefore have to pass *windowRect*'s address.

After the call to *SetRect*, we've placed the call to *NewWindow*, within an *if* statement's conditional expression. *NewWindow* will return a nonzero window pointer if it was successful in creating the window, and we can draw in the grafPort only if the window was created, which is why the program tests the pointer value.

Notice the programming style here. The Macintosh programming world has adopted a convention in which a Mac construct begins with a capital letter and has a capital letter at the beginning of each important consonant sound (*WindowPtr*, *SetRect*, *NewWindow*, and so forth). For clarity, we'll always begin the function names and variable names that we write with lowercase letters so that you'll know at a glance which functions are Toolbox calls and which ones are defined in the source code.

Which GrafPort to Draw In?

All drawing in a window is specified in the local coordinate system. But, because multiple grafPorts can be open on the screen, where does the drawing appear?

QuickDraw draws to the current grafPort. The QuickDraw routine *SetPort* assigns the current grafPort. You pass *SetPort* a pointer to the window that you want to be current, as in

```
SetPort (theWindow);
```

The Pen and the Port Rectangle

Each grafPort has a "pen," which is actually an abstract concept that defines where the next drawing action will appear in the port. Before you can draw text, the program has to locate the pen at an appropriate place in the window. You use the *MoveTo* routine to set the pen to an absolute position in the grafPort. The statement

```
MoveTo (20, 30)
```

moves the pen to point (*20, 30*). Remember, this refers to the point in the window, in the local coordinate system, not to the screen point.

The *GrafPort* data structure contains information that QuickDraw uses to control drawing. We repeat the definition of a *GrafPort* on the next page, with short descriptions of its many fields.

```
typedef struct GrafPort
{
    int device;                 // 0 if on screen
    BitMap portBits;            // RAM used for this port
    Rect portRect;              // portRect
    RgnHandle visRgn;           // visible region
    RgnHandle clipRgn;          // clipping region
    Pattern bkPat;              // background
    Pattern fillPat;            // pattern used for fills
    Point pnLoc;                // current pen location
    Point pnSize;               // current pen size
    int pnMode;                 // current pen transfer mode
    Pattern pnPat;              // current pen pattern
    int pnVis;                  // current pen visibility state
    int txFont;                 // current font number
    Style txFace;               // current font style
    int txMode;                 // current font transfer mode
    int txSize;                 // current font point size
    Fixed spExtra;              // amount to add to every text space
    long fgColor;               // foreground color (pen color)
    long bkColor;               // background color
    int colrBit;                // used internally
    int patStretch;             // used internally
    Handle picSave;             // used internally
    Handle rgnSave;             // used internally
    Handle polySave;            // used internally
    QDProcsPtr grafProcs;       // grafProcs
};
```

A member of the *GrafPort* structure named *portRect* describes the port's rectangle in local coordinates. You can get the width and height of the grafPort from these coordinate values.

Recall from earlier in the chapter that the first member of the *WindowRecord* is a *GrafPort*, and, in fact, on the Mac a *WindowPtr* is actually defined as a pointer to a *GrafPort*, so you can get the port rectangle this way:

```
Rect  portRect;

portRect = theWindow->portRect;
```

Let's say that you want to draw the string in the middle of the window. You could use the *portRect* and the string width of your string to calculate the starting pen position for the *DrawString*, which draws the text at the current pen position. The QuickDraw function *StringWidth* returns the pixel width of a string.

The function *sayHey()*, shown on the next page, calculates the point at which it will draw an arbitrary string centered in a window and then draws it.

```
sayHey (WindowPtr theWindow, StringPtr theString)
{
    Rect              windowRect;
    Point             penLoc;

    /* get the center of the window */

    // first, point to our window
    windowRect = theWindow->portRect;

    // next, calculate the horizontal center
    penLoc.h = (windowRect.left + windowRect.right) / 2;

    // now calculate the vertical center
    penLoc.v = (windowRect.top + windowRect.bottom) / 2;

    /* offset the pen's horizontal location by one-half
        the string width */
    penLoc.h -= StringWidth (theString) / 2;

    MoveTo (penLoc.h, penLoc.v);

    DrawString (theString);

} /* sayHey */
```

Changing the Font

What if you wanted to write "Hello" and "Mac!" in different fonts? A *GrafPort* maintains values for the current font, font size, and face. *DrawString* always draws text using these current values. To draw each word of the string Hello, Mac! in a different font, you'd have to split the string in half, changing fonts with *TextFont* after drawing the first word. The code would look something like this:

```
TextFont (1);      // font 1 is the application font (Geneva)
MoveTo (penLoc.h, penLoc.v);

DrawString ("Hello, ");

TextFont (0);      // font 0 is the system font (Chicago)

DrawString ("Mac!");

...
```

You might wonder why *MoveTo* was called only once in this last example. Don't you need to relocate the pen before drawing the second word? Actually, *DrawString* moves the pen for you. When it draws a string, it moves the pen to a location following the last character. In other words, the pen always has a location at which it will perform its next action; you need to move the pen only when you want it to draw in a different location.

Exploring Other QuickDraw Graphics Entities

Now that you have a window and you know something about a grafPort, you can modify Hello Mac! to draw any QuickDraw entity you like.

Lines are the simplest objects to draw. *LineTo* draws a line from the current pen location to a specified point. *LineTo* moves the pen to the specified point after it draws the line. The following statements draw a 50×50-pixel square:

```
MoveTo (10, 10);
LineTo (10, 60);
LineTo (60, 60);
LineTo (60, 10);
LineTo (10, 10);
```

In addition to lines, QuickDraw supports six other kinds of graphics "primitives": rectangles, rounded rectangles, arcs, ovals (circles), regions, and polygons. It also supports five "grafVerbs," Apple's word for operations that you can perform on these primitives: *Frame*, *Invert*, *Erase*, *Fill*, and *Paint*. For example, you can have an oval that is painted, a region that is filled, or a rectangle that is inverted.

You create the name of the QuickDraw routines that draw the primitives by matching a grafVerb with a primitive, as in *FrameRect*, *InvertArc*, *ErasePoly*, *FillOval*, *PaintRgn*.

The routine paramenters differ, depending on the primitive you're using. Refer to *Inside Macintosh,* Volume I, Chapter 6, for more detail.

Events, or When to Go Away

You've seen what it takes to create the window and draw the string. The last part of Hello Mac! terminates the program. You might have read that the Macintosh uses an event-driven operating system. This means that when a user clicks with the mouse, types a character, inserts a disk, or generates some other "event," somehow the program is notified with a data structure for that event and reacts to it.

The Macintosh understands many events—each corresponds to a real-world happening. Hello Mac! looks for one kind of event—a mouse click—before returning control to the Finder.

Events are "posted" to the event queue by the Macintosh operating system. We're not concerned with the event queue mechanism—applications should always detect new events by using the routines of the Event Manager.

Hello Mac! calls the Event Manager procedure *GetNextEvent* in a loop to see whether a new event has been posted. (See the sidebar "The Correct Way to Wait for an Event.") *GetNextEvent* accepts two arguments: an event mask and the address of an *EventRecord* structure. The event mask tells *GetNextEvent* which events you're interested in. If *GetNextEvent* returns a nonzero value, an event of interest is available and the routine fills an *EventRecord* structure with data describing the event. The code we're talking about is

```
while (!GetNextEvent (mDownMask, &eventRec));
```

If you want to know about all events that occur while the application is running, you pass the mask *everyEvent*. Because Hello Mac! waits for a mouse click (mouse-down), you pass the mask *mDownMask*.

The Correct Way to Wait for an Event

The correct way to wait for an event is to call *WaitNextEvent*. This procedure lets your application work with MultiFinder. Because we're not concerned with MultiFinder context switching during Hello Mac! and because it's simpler to use, we use the lower-level function *GetNextEvent*. We'll discuss *WaitNextEvent* in detail in Chapter 6.

Disposing of the *WindowRecord*

After the program receives a mouse-down, it can return control to the Finder. But before a well-mannered Macintosh application terminates, it "cleans up after itself."

When Hello Mac! created its window, it had the Window Manager allocate space for the window's *WindowRecord*. This structure is kept in memory in the application heap, and because the program is finished with the window, it should free the memory that has been used by the window. The Window Manager provides the routine *DisposeWindow* expressly for this purpose.

Note that you never call *DisposeWindow* with a null pointer, and you never call it twice with the same *WindowPtr*. If you do, you'll see the dreaded bomb alert box. This gives us an opportunity to introduce some formal computerese. We can say that the program is structured to be "well-behaved" (it doesn't crash) in the event of an "exception" (something goes wrong). If Hello Mac! can't get a nonzero *WindowPtr* from *NewWindow*, it exits. Drawing occurs only if the program opens the window successfully. Drawing in an unspecified port will also cause unpredictable results.

Hello Mac!'s last call is to *ExitToShell*, which returns control to the Finder. This call is actually unnecessary. A THINK C application calls *ExitToShell* automatically when it terminates. We include it in our programs to remind you that execution of the program will halt when *ExitToShell* is reached.

Initializing the Program

Before any program can run, you need to set up the Toolbox managers that the program will use. Hello Mac! requires initialization of QuickDraw and the Window and Font managers as shown on the next page.

```
// initialize managers
InitGraf (&thePort);
InitWindows ();
InitFonts ();
InitCursor ();
```

The program initializes QuickDraw with this call:

```
InitGraf (&thePort);
```

The variable *thePort* is actually an external variable declared in the THINK C file QuickDraw.h this way:

```
GrafPtr     thePort;
```

It is defined in the MacTraps library. This variable is a QuickDraw global, part of the application's Macintosh environment. We'll talk more about QuickDraw globals in the next chapter, but for now you should know that you can use this variable anywhere in your application, whenever you need to get at the current grafPort, as in

```
currentWindowRect = thePort->portRect;
```

That's your first Mac application. We recommend that you use it to play with QuickDraw. Consult *Inside Macintosh,* Volume I, Chapter 6. Then try to use some of the graphics described in the chapter. Discover how simple it is to be a graphics programmer when you have a good platform to work on.

When you've had enough of Hello Mac!, go to the next chapter to find out how a Macintosh program should use memory.

The Programmer's Switch

Remember that little plastic bar that came with your Mac and looked like some kind of high-tech paper clip? It's called the programmer's switch. We recommend that you install it. Think of it as a panic button. Actually, it has two buttons. The one farthest from you switches control to the built-in ROM debugger or to the TMON or Macsbug debuggers if they've been installed. The button closest to you reboots your system. New programmers sometimes experience strange Mac behavior, such as the video's going wild or the Mac's emitting "machine gun" sounds. Such behavior occurs because the program is writing to memory that shouldn't be written to, most likely with an errant or uninitialized pointer. The video and sound phenomena occur because the program contains nonsensical information in the video or sound buffer memory. If this happens to you, don't be too concerned about damaging your Mac; simply use the programmer's switch to stop the process. Of course, if you smell smoke, you can always pull the plug.

5

MACINTOSH MEMORY MANAGEMENT

Now that you've seen how an application is put together, let's step back and examine how the Macintosh manages memory. Memory is the prime commodity of a computer. Programs need memory to store their instructions as well as data. Memory makes the Mac go 'round: You can't run a program without it.

And memory is a shared resource. The System, INITs, CDEVs, DAs, and other applications can all run at the same time as your foreground application. These programs all need RAM to hold their code and data. To get these programs to work together, your computer uses the Macintosh Memory Manager. And to get these programs to work together properly, your application program needs to follow some commonsense rules.

Application programmers aren't ordinarily concerned with the goings-on in memory. Usually, you can ignore the details of low-level actions such as the allocation of automatic variables on the stack. But when the dreaded bomb alert box appears and the source code doesn't readily reveal the cause of its appearance, your only recourse is to dig in at the machine level to see what's happening in memory. Knowing how your code and data look in RAM at runtime is the most important aspect of the black art of debugging.

In this chapter, we'll take a look at how a Macintosh application uses memory. We'll explore the stack and the heap as they relate to C programming, keeping an eye out for the pitfalls of working with data objects.

Memory Map

When you launch a program from the desktop, the Operating System allocates some of RAM to your program and organizes this RAM as shown in Figure 5-1.

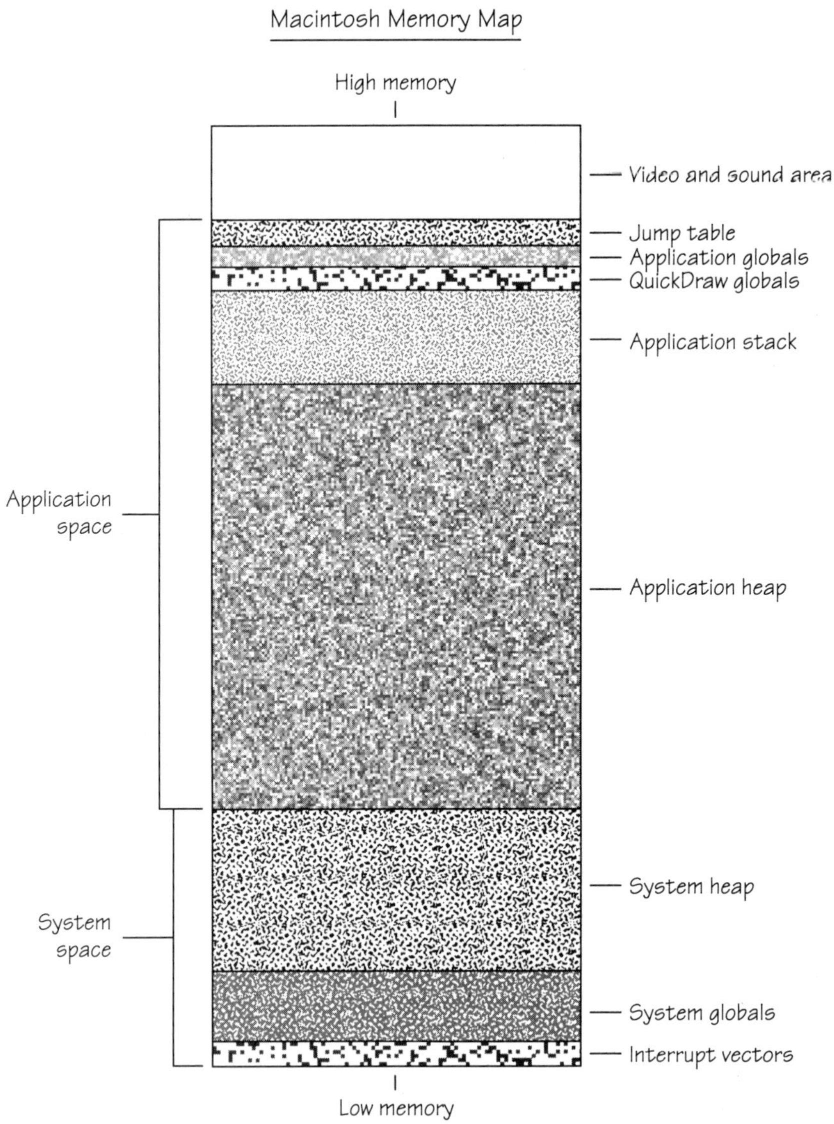

Figure 5-1.
The Macintosh Memory Map.

The "system globals" make up the lowest memory addresses. These locations hold information used by the Operating System. Programmers should use these locations sparingly, never within an application and only during program debugging. As the Macintosh OS develops, Apple often decides to change the meanings of some system globals. If your application relies on any of these changing variables, it becomes instantly obsolete with the release of a new system.

Above the system globals is the "system heap," where the OS and other critical data reside. Avoid using this section of memory completely. Imagine what would happen if some of the Operating System's code were overwritten by an errant pointer in your program.

Above the system space sits the application space, which includes the application heap, the application stack, the QuickDraw globals, your application's globals, and the jump table. We'll discuss the contents of each in a moment.

In MultiFinder and under System 7.0, you can open multiple applications. The memory map for a multiple application configuration has multiple application spaces, as illustrated in Figure 5-2 on the next page.

The lines between the system, the applications, and their components are abstract. Right now applications don't run in a protected, private area of RAM. (You'll have to wait for System 8.0 for that.) As a result, if one of the programs loaded and running in RAM has a bug, it can clobber the code of any of the other applications.

Program Code in Memory

We've already seen that source code consists of text files written in a high-level language. In memory, code consists of long lists of machine language instructions derived from source code and created by the compiler and built-in assembler. Each machine language instruction is a 16-bit, binary word that tells the machine to do something simple such as loading a value into a register, moving data from one memory location to another, or adding the contents of two data objects. We've known programmers who could read and edit machine code, poking bits here and there in RAM to fix a problem, but most people think of machine language instructions in terms of their mnemonic equivalents. The set of mnemonics for a processor is its "assembly language." A machine-level debugger such as TMON or MacNosy contains a "disassembler," which converts the binary form of an instruction to its mnemonic form, making the code more understandable. Although you can view the assembly language generated by THINK C 5.0 by selecting Disassemble from the Source menu, using a debugger is the only practical way to view machine code.

The THINK C compiler generates the machine code from your source code and places it in your project file in CODE resources. Each resource corresponds to a code segment that you define in the project window of the compiler. Each code segment is limited to 32K, so a standard-size program of 100K or so must consist of multiple code segments. The GetInfo menu selection in the THINK C environment reports the sizes of your code segments.

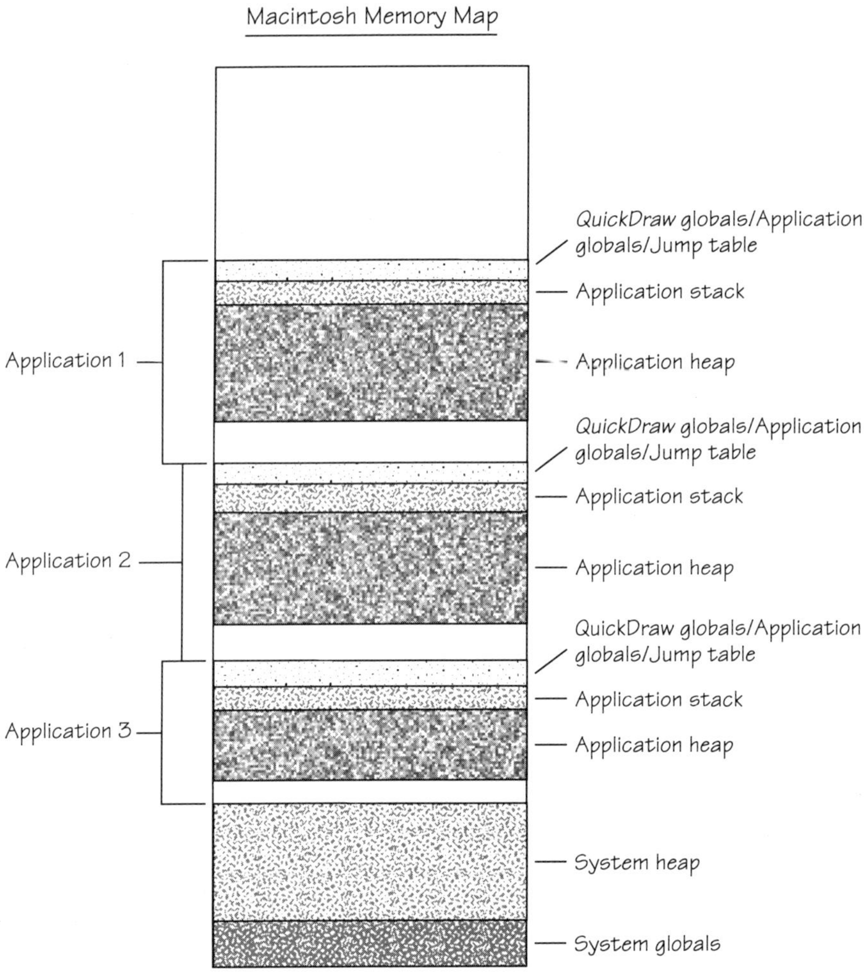

Figure 5-2.
The Macintosh Memory Map with three applications loaded.

Why is code segmentation necessary? Machine code must be in RAM while it is executing, but an entire application's code need not be resident for the program to run. With good planning, you can divide a program into multiple code segments and have it run in a limited space. Large applications manage memory by controlling which code segments are in RAM at a given time. This is how a program with 720K in code segments can run in a MultiFinder partition of 512K: Some code segments are removed from RAM when others are moved in.

Segment loading is automatic at runtime. The system moves segments in from the disk as they are needed, so you never need to worry about whether code that needs to execute is in RAM. The part of the system that manages this task is called the Segment Loader.

To save RAM, however, you might want to unload a code segment when you've finished with it, so you'll need to help the Segment Loader. The Toolbox call *UnloadSeg* marks a CODE resource as "purgeable," making it a likely candidate for replacement when another resource is brought into RAM. Some applications call *UnloadSeg* on a set of program segments each time through the event loop. Another strategy is to call *UnloadSeg* before trying to save a document. Our Generic App, presented in Chapters 6 through 8, never calls *UnloadSeg*—small applications usually don't. If you do use Generic App to create a large program, you'll want to review the information here and in *Inside Macintosh* regarding the handling of code segments.

The Jump Table

You might wonder how the Segment Loader knows to load a segment when it's needed. Whenever your program makes an intersegment function call, it does so through a structure called the "jump table." The jump table is set up by the linker during compilation and is loaded into the application's memory with the program. (The jump table information is kept in CODE #0, which is the first segment to be loaded when a program is launched. If you want more than our simple description, see *Inside Macintosh,* Volume II.)

The linker creates a jump table entry for each external function in your program. A Macintosh program never directly calls an external function. Instead, it makes a call to the last 6 bytes of the function's jump table entry. The contents of these 6 bytes differ depending on whether the segment has been loaded. If the segment for that function has been loaded, these bytes contain the address of the function in RAM and program control continues from there. If the segment has not been loaded, these bytes contain a call to *LoadSeg*, the Segment Loader routine that loads the segment and initializes all of the jump table entries for that segment before control is passed to the function.

All intersegment function calls involve the overhead of passing through the jump table, but this is a small price to pay for the efficiency of a segmented code map. Nevertheless, careful organization of applications larger than 32K can result in significant performance improvements. You wouldn't want to have two related functions that are always called in sequence separated in two different program segments, for example.

Because CODE #0, where the jump table resides, is a segment, your program's jump table is limited to 32K. In a large program with a lot of functions, you might find yourself approaching this limit if you don't make use of static functions. These functions, declared with the *static* keyword, are called only from the module and therefore from the segment in which they're defined, so they don't need a jump table entry. Use static functions to save jump table space.

Program Data in Memory

Code has to share memory with data. The data of a running program is a dynamic collection of values kept in known locations of RAM. The program reads and writes to a memory location by means of an address. To access a value in RAM, the program loads the contents of a 32-bit address register with an address and uses an instruction to fetch or to store the value.

An addressing mode defines how a particular processor uses a combination of its registers and their values to access RAM. The 68000 family of processors support more than a dozen addressing modes. The ins and outs of these addressing modes are primarily of interest to assembly language programmers, but if you plan to do any serious development, you are eventually going to need to get down and use a low-level debugger. Understanding what's going on at the machine level is critical to getting at the heart of a problem. Although the ultimate authority on 68000 machine organization is Prentice Hall's reprints of the Motorola MC68000 family user manuals, we can go into a few basic facts about these processors here.

Machine Organization

The Macintosh processors have eight 32-bit address registers, named A0 through A7, and eight 32-bit data registers, named D0 through D7. The address registers, shown in Figure 5-3, are used for address calculations and for access to values in RAM. The data registers, also shown in Figure 5-3, are used as scratch space for arithmetic calculations. Register access is faster than RAM access, and clever use of register variables in your C program can dramatically speed up a sluggish application.

Some of the registers have special purposes on the Mac. Address register A7, for instance, is used as the stack pointer, and A6 as the frame pointer. We'll look more closely at those two registers in a moment. Register A5 points to your application's global variables. OS routines use register D0 and sometimes D1 to return values.

Memory is organized with its beginning at address 0 and its maximum possible address at 4,294,967,295, which corresponds to the value $2^{32} - 1$. Addresses are usually specified in hexadecimal notation, so the "address space" of a 32-bit machine is 0x00000000 through 0xFFFFFFFF. Note that until System 7.0, the Macintosh used only the least-significant 24 bits of an address, limiting the Macintosh's address space to 16 megabytes.

A variable begins at an address and occupies 1 or more of the bytes that follow. The number of bytes that a data object occupies depends on its type. All types other than *char* and *unsigned char* are aligned on even-numbered addressing boundaries. Structures and unions can be larger than you might think because they can be padded (have additional bytes added) so that the next data object begins on an even-numbered addressing boundary. If you're looking at data objects in RAM, you'll see that there are no visible boundaries between consecutive variables. To know where one object ends and another begins, you need to know the sizes of the basic types. We've shown some of the sizes in Chapter 3; Figure 5-4 on page 94 contains a complete list. You need to know the data type sizes as well as you know the multiplication tables or the alphabet.

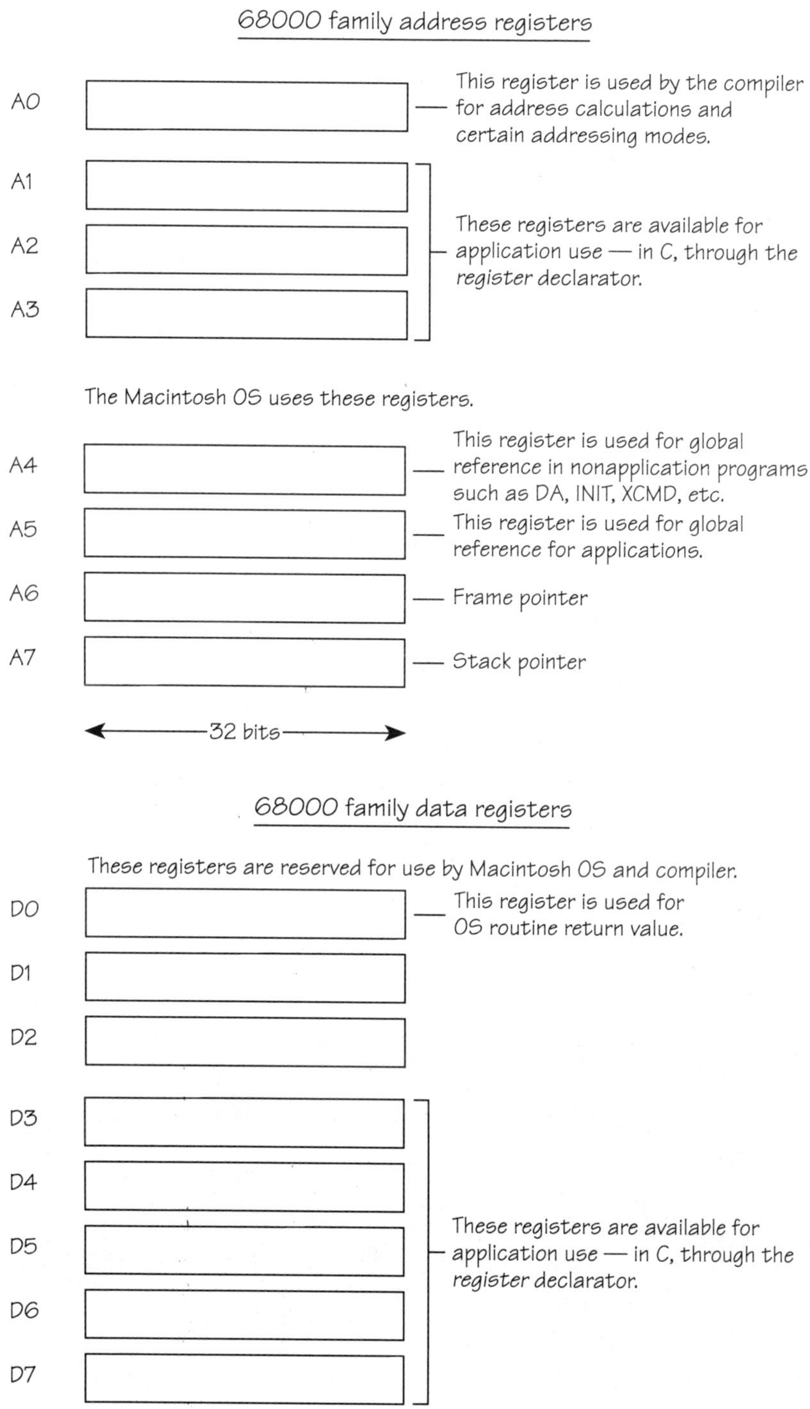

Figure 5-3.
The 68000 family address and data registers.

C Type	Mac (Pascal) Type	Size in Bytes
unsigned char	Byte	1
int	Integer	2 or 4
short	Integer	2
long	Longint	4
float	—	4
double	Extended	10
Size	Size	4
Fixed	Fixcd	4
char*	Ptr	4
char**	Handle	4
char [256]	Str255	256
unsigned char	Boolean[1]	1
Boolean[2]	Integer	2 or 4

[1]Pascal language defined (Toolbox) [2]C language defined (application)

Figure 5-4.
Sizes of fundamental C and Macintosh data types.

Scope of Variables

Some variables are long-lived; others last for only the duration of a function call. The "scope" of the variable is the length of time it contains valid data. A global variable persists: It is initialized when the program is loaded, and space for it is reserved in the application heap until the program is exited. A variable declared inside a function—a local variable—exists for only the life of that function. A local variable is not initialized when it is created; its value is unknown. You must initialize a local variable before using it. Not doing so is the source of a common C bug.

Another programming bug arises from using a variable outside its scope. The *foo()* function, shown in Figure 5-5, copies a null-terminated string of characters (a string ending with a byte whose content is *null* or *0*) and returns a pointer to the copy.

```
char *
foo (char * sourceStr)
{
    register char *p;
    char  destStr [BUFSIZ];

    p = destStr;
    while (*p++ = *sourceStr++);

    return (destStr);
}
```

Figure 5-5.
The foo() *function is a string copy utility.*

foo() Under the Microscope

The *foo()* function (a typical, unenlightening name for a generic function) has a simple job: When it is passed a pointer to a null-terminated character string, it copies the string and returns a pointer to the copy. To this end, *foo()* uses two local variables: *p*, a character pointer; and *destStr*, the destination buffer declared to be *BUFSIZ* bytes long. We've directed the compiler, through the use of the *register* keyword, to use one of the three available 680X0 address registers for *p* and then to assign the address of our buffer to it. Take a look at the assignment

```
p = destStr;
```

In C, the name of an array represents the address of its first character if you don't use square braces in the expression. If you don't choose to make use of this shortcut, another way to get the address of the first character is with this assignment:

```
p = &destStr[0];
```

Using this form, you can point to the nth item in an array, as in

```
short n;
...
p = &destStr[n];
```

But don't forget to initialize *n* so that you don't point off into who-knows-where and come up with garbage.

The copying of the string occurs inside the *while* statement. When a *null* value (*0*) is assigned to the buffer, the test fails and the loop exits. The function completes execution by returning a pointer to the first character—again, by using the name of the buffer but without the square braces.

Notice that we use a register variable for the pointer. This is simply to speed things up. The copying loop executes about four times faster than it would if we didn't use the register pointer. And notice the use of pointer arithmetic (*p++*) to step through the two strings. The semicolon after the *while* statement means that the loop has no loop-body; all execution is performed inside the *while* test clause. The brevity of this assignment exemplifies tight C code:

```
*p++ = *sourceStr++
```

The **sourceStr++* gets the next character from the string and then increments the pointer, and the **p++* assigns the character to the destination string and then increments the destination pointer.

We can't take credit for these constructs. As you read on, you'll discover the origin of this code.

The *foo()* function has a serious flaw: The destination buffer is defined *inside* the function, as a local variable. The function returns a pointer to a buffer that ceases to exist as soon as *foo()* returns. This function really needs to be passed a pointer to the destination buffer, which is declared in the caller. We show the fix in Figure 5-6. And while we're at it, let's call *foo()* by its real name.

```
char *
strcpy ( char * destStr,
         char * sourceStr )
{
    register char *p;

    p = destStr;
    while (*p++ = *sourceStr++);

    return (destStr);
}
```

Figure 5-6.
The strcpy() *function is passed a pointer to the destination string.*

Notice that *strcpy()* returns a pointer to one of its arguments; it therefore knows the address of this string. You might ask, "Why would a function return a pointer to a variable that was passed to it as a parameter?" The answer is, "So that you can write one-statement programs that look like LISP programs," as in Figure 5-7.

```
printf ("%s", strcat (strcpy (aStr, "Hello"),
    strcat (strcpy(bStr, ","), strcpy (cStr, "World"))));
```

Figure 5-7.
Hello World redux.

The Stack

Automatic variables come into and go out of existence with a function because they're created on the application stack. A stack, sometimes called a push-down list, is a LIFO, meaning Last In, First Out—the way it receives and gets rid of data. The stack grows and shrinks as data objects are *pushed onto* and *popped off* it. Access to the objects is from the top of the stack. The stack mechanism is often represented by the child's toy shown in Figure 5-8.

The top of the stack is maintained in register A7. The stack base starts in high memory and grows downward, so register A7's value decreases as items are added to the stack. In the normal sequence of a running program, one function calls another, which in turn calls another. The calling order proceeds according to the program's design. Programs use the stack to keep track of this flow.

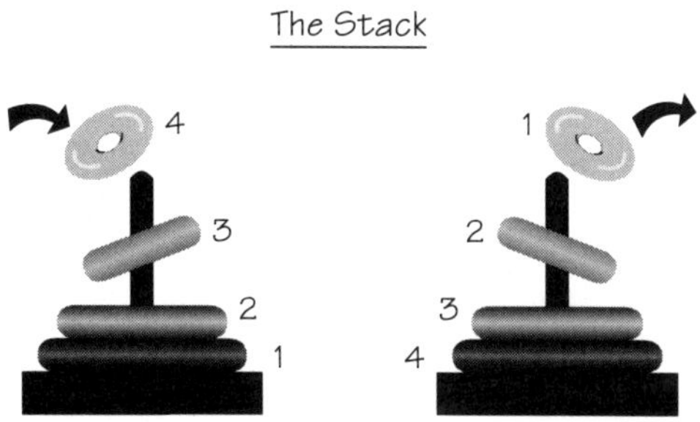

Figure 5-8.
Data objects are pushed onto a stack and popped off a stack in last-on, first-off order.

A quick note on terminology: If function *foo()* calls function *bar()*, function *foo()* is the "caller" and function *bar()* is the "called function," as shown in Figure 5-9.

```
foo ()
{
    ...
    bar (arg1, arg2);
    ...
}

void
bar (short arg1, arg2)
{
    short var1, var2;
    ...
}
```

Figure 5-9.
Another foo() bar() *example.*

The stack is used to store the data for each function call. To illustrate this, we'll use the *foo() bar()* code fragment. Let's say that *bar()* is about to be called from *foo()*. Just before *bar()* is called, the parameters *arg1* and *arg2* are pushed onto the stack.

C and Pascal Calling Conventions

C compilers push parameters in last-to-first order (*arg2* before *arg1* in our example), and Pascal compilers push their parameters first-to-last. The calling conventions of the two languages have other differences. Look up "calling conventions" in the index of the THINK C user's manual to find out more.

Next *foo()* calls *bar()* with a JMP instruction, which pushes the return address in *foo()*. When it's finished, *bar()* uses this return address to return to *foo()*. Then *bar()* allocates space on the stack for its local variables with a LINK instruction. Figure 5-10 illustrates the stack before and after a function call.

The collection of stack objects—the function's parameters, the return address, and the automatic variable space—is called the current "stack frame." Register A6 points to the stack frame, so it's called the "frame pointer." All of the function's local variables are accessed as offsets from A6.

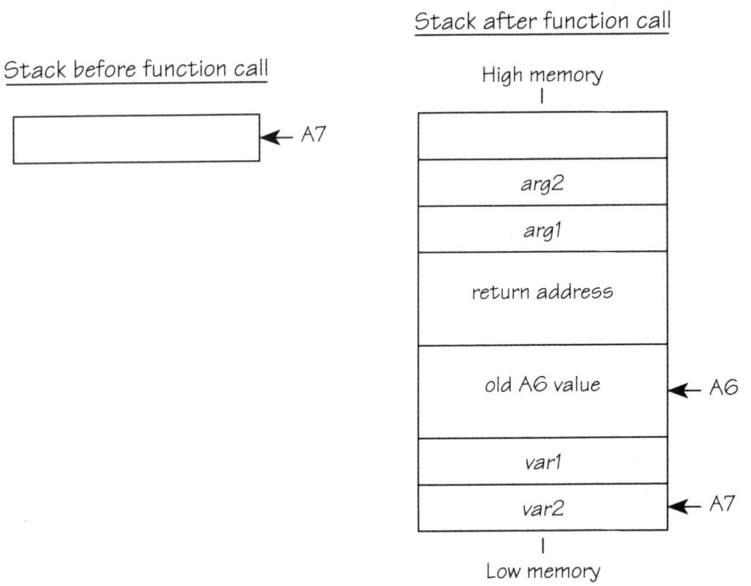

Figure 5-10.
The stack before and after a function call.

Just before the function returns, it calls *UNLK*, an assembly language instruction which sees that the frame pointer's value reverts to its previous value. At this point, all references to local variables are gone; the value of A6 no longer points to a function's locals. This is why local variables have a scope limited to their function's lifetime: The stack frame in which they reside disappears after the function returns.

The Heap

The stack mechanism is rigidly structured, and the stack's contents are limited to function-call–related data. The heap contains a varied collection of data objects. The Mac actually has at least two heap zones, one for the system and the other for an application. The system heap is hands-off as far as your application is concerned. It contains the Operating System code, fonts, DAs, INITs, device management data, and other esoteric matters important to the health of your Macintosh environment.

The application heap is yours to use as you need to, but step lightly: This heap contains your application resources, including the code segments of your applications. Many a bomb alert box appears as the result of writing over a CODE resource in the heap. We'll refer to the application heap zone simply as "the heap," but remember that multiple heap zones can reside in RAM, especially if you have loaded more than one application. The following discussion can apply to any one of the application heap zones.

A heap consists of blocks—groups of contiguous memory locations—that are accessible to your program indirectly, through the Macintosh Memory Manager. Heaps come in three types: "free," "nonrelocatable," and "relocatable." You must "allocate" a block of memory in the heap before you can use it, in a process analogous to renting a locker at the bus station: Only one application at a time can use a particular block. Likewise, you deallocate a block when you've finished with it so that another part of your program can use that block of memory.

A free block is a block that isn't in use. When an application starts to run, most blocks in the heap fall into this category. The pool of free blocks makes up the free space reported by the Memory Manager function *FreeMem*.

You allocate the free blocks to your application using the Memory Manager function *NewPtr* or *NewHandle*. Either function accepts a parameter that specifies the size, in bytes, of the block you need. When your application is finished with the block, you call either *DisposPtr* or *DisposHandle* to free the block. (Apple left the "e" off "dispose," by the way—that's not a typo.) Using either *DisposPtr* or *DisposHandle* returns the block of memory in RAM to the free pool.

A nonrelocatable block is allocated in the heap at a location that never changes. You allocate one of these blocks with *NewPtr*, which returns a pointer to the block. If you are familiar with the library function *malloc()*, you will recognize its similarity to *NewPtr*. Nonrelocatable blocks are undesirable. The Macintosh Memory Manager must sometimes allocate a large block of memory in the heap, and nonrelocatable blocks can get in the way.

Relocatable blocks are preferable. You allocate one of these blocks with *NewHandle*, which returns a handle to the block. A handle is a pointer to a master pointer, a *char*** data type in C. A relocatable block can move around in the heap. Unlike a sedentary nonrelocatable block, a relocatable block is moved by the Memory Manager when the Macintosh is trying to allocate a large block of memory in the heap. Don't misunderstand: Blocks in the heap aren't moved around for the fun of it. The Memory Manager moves blocks around only when it needs to in order to allocate a large block of memory.

When a program calls *NewHandle*, the Memory Manager looks for a run of contiguous free blocks until it has enough memory to meet the request. Sometimes it needs to move blocks out of the way in order to find the space it needs. The problem with nonrelocatable blocks is that they cause a logjam in the heap—the Memory Manager can't move them and has to restart its search for free blocks on the other side of the logjam. Figure 5-11 on the next page illustrates this problem, called "heap fragmentation," which limits the possible size of a block. The potential size of a block is limited to the size of a free block run in the heap. In a fragmented heap, this size can be much smaller than the total available memory. Relocatable objects help the Memory Manager avoid the problem because the Memory Manager can move them out of the middle of long runs of free blocks. Use *NewHandle* instead of *NewPtr* whenever possible.

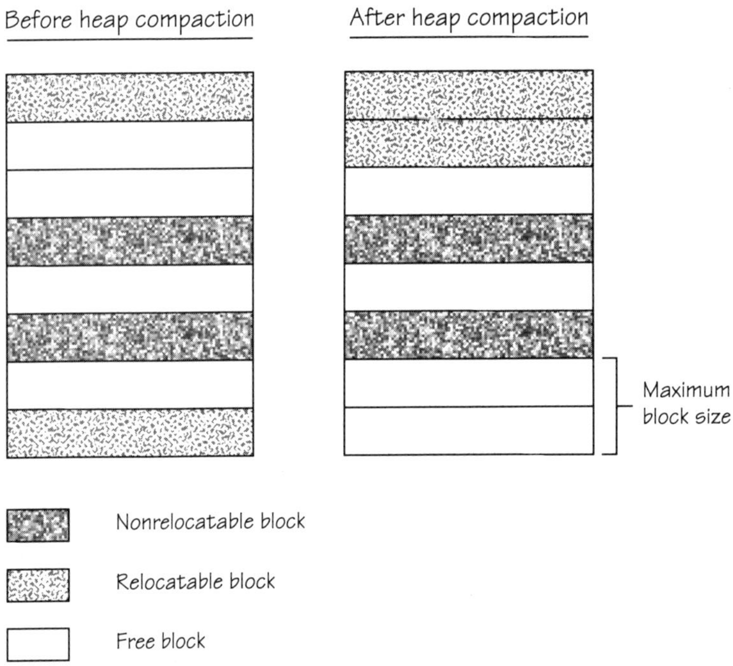

Figure 5-11.
The heap before and after compaction by the Memory Manager. Because of the nonrelocatable blocks in this heap, the maximum block size is limited to only half the amount of free memory.

Avoiding Heap Fragmentation

Nonrelocatable blocks aren't bad in and of themselves; their role in fragmenting the heap is what makes them undesirable. The description of *NewPtr* in *Inside Macintosh,* Volume II, tells us that *NewPtr* tries to allocate a nonrelocatable block to the lowest possible location in the heap. If you can preallocate all of your application's nonrelocatable blocks before allocating any relocatable blocks, the nonrelocatable blocks will be at the bottom of the heap, where they can't possibly fragment the heap. Preallocate your application's nonrelocatable blocks in its initialization routine.

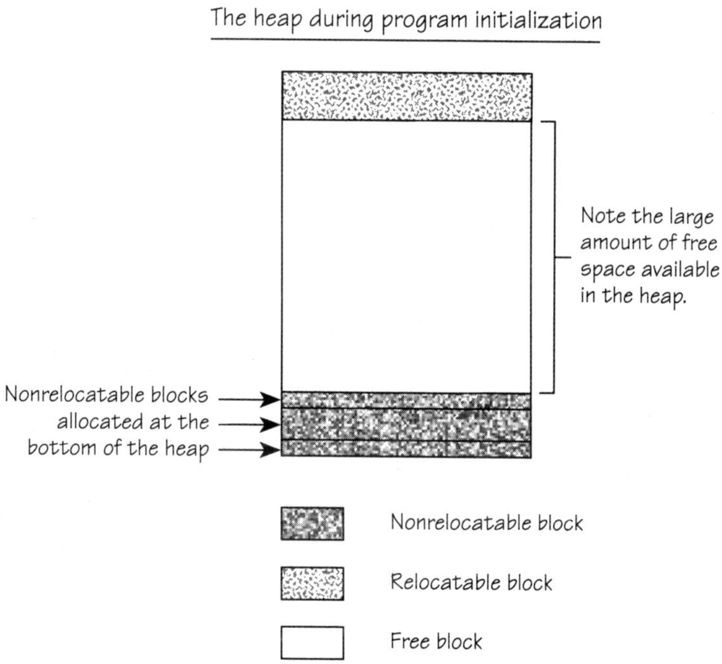

Figure 5-12.
Preallocating the nonrelocatable blocks.

A pointer to data in the heap won't always be valid if the data is in a relocatable block. How does an application reference the data in a relocatable block? Apple's solution involves a pointer to a pointer to the block. The Operating System maintains a bank of "master pointers" in the heap. Every time your application requests a relocatable block, the Memory Manager assigns the address of the block to one of these master pointers and returns the address of the master pointer to your application by means of the return value of *NewHandle.* A variable that holds the address of a master pointer is called a "handle." You saw the data type declaration for the *Handle* type in Chapter 3, but we'll repeat it here:

```
typedef char * Ptr;
typedef Ptr * Handle;
```

The Memory Manager keeps the master pointers in a nonrelocatable block and they therefore never move, so that the handle returned by *NewHandle* is always valid. If the Memory Manager needs to move the block, it changes the value of the master pointer to point to the block's new location. Figure 5-13 on the next page illustrates how the links are maintained.

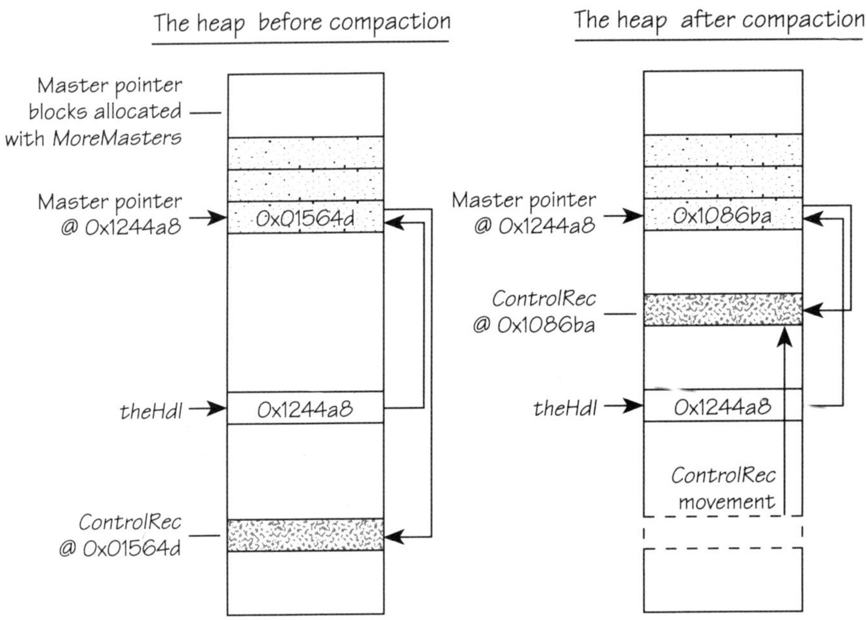

Figure 5-13.
The heap before and after compaction. In this example, theHdl *always points to the master pointer, which stays at its location,* 0x1244a8, *and points to the changing location of* ControlRec, *first at 0x01564d and then at 0x1086ba.*

An application can find its data with a "double dereference" of the handle. Let's look at an example of a double dereference.

In the example shown in Figure 5-14, we create a list structure of four *ListElm* elements. Note the double dereference of the handle to assign the value *4* to the *count*

Computerese 101

Computers have certainly enriched the English language. Take the term "double dereference." Remember the phrase "passing by reference" from Chapter 4? Recall that you pass an object by reference when you pass its address as an argument to a function call. Referencing a data object produces its address.

What is a "dereference," then? As its name implies, a dereference reverses the reference. Given an address of a data object, a dereference produces the data object—its value. A pointer holds the address of an object. Dereferencing the pointer produces the value of the pointed-to object. It should follow, then, that a double dereference of a handle would produce the data object's value because a handle contains a pointer to a pointer to the data object.

member of the *List* structure. No matter where the block ends up in the heap, we can always get to the contents with a double dereference.

```
typedef struct List
{
    short       count;
    ListElm     elm;
} List, *ListPtr, **ListHdl;

ListHandle  theList;
Size        listSize;

listSize = sizeof (List) + 3 * sizeof (ListElm);

/* allocate a list of four elements */
if (theList = NewHandle (listSize))
    (**theList).count = 4;  // here's the listSize double dereference
else
    doMemError ();
```

Figure 5-14.
An example of a double dereference.

Calling *MoreMasters*

The Memory Manager routine *MoreMasters* creates master pointers in a nonrelocatable block, so it's a good idea to create enough master pointers for your application's use early on in the program, when you're ensuring that your nonrelocatable blocks will reside at the bottom of the heap. (See the sidebar "Avoiding Heap Fragmentation.") You need to estimate the number of handles that your application is going to use and preallocate the master pointers in your application's initialization routine.

How many master pointers should you create? *Inside Macintosh* tells us that a call to *MoreMasters* creates 64 master pointers in the application. Generic App, which we introduce in the next chapter, calls *MoreMasters* four times, which allocates 256 master pointers. Because Generic App doesn't allocate much memory, these 256 master pointers should be plenty for the user interface needs of the application, such as pulling down menus and opening dialog boxes.

Our commercial application Tycho Table Maker, on the other hand, uses many relocatable blocks—at least two for each table cell—so Tycho Table Maker calls *MoreMasters* 64 times in its initialization routine, for a total of 4096 master pointers.

But the double dereference is a flaw in the memory management scheme. Think as if you were a machine for a moment, in order to realize what the CPU has to go through to get at the data in a relocatable block. Before your application can read or write any data from the block, the CPU needs to fetch the address of the master pointer from the handle variable and then fetch the address of the block from the pointer. The extra dereference every time a program accesses data on the heap can degrade an application's performance.

The code shown in Figure 5-15 allocates memory for a TextEdit record and initializes the fields of the record. This kind of code is common in Macintosh applications—creation of a data structure in the heap, followed by the initialization of the fields of the structure. With every access to the structure, the handle is dereferenced.

```
TERecord    *tep,
            **teh;
Rect        aRect;
Handle      textHdl;
...
teh = TENew (&aRect, &aRect); // allocate the TERecord (IM-I)

textHdl = NewHandle (120L);

(*teh)->hText = textHdl;      // notice the double dereference
(*teh)->just = teJustLeft;    // in every line
(*teh)->selStart = 0;         // while the TERecord structure
(*teh)->selEnd = 0;           // is initialized
(*teh)->teLength = 120;
...
```

Figure 5-15.
Allocation and initialization of a heap data structure—in this case, a TERecord.

You can improve the performance of a handle-intensive application by dereferencing the handle and putting the master pointer's value into a register variable. The code in Figure 5-16 demonstrates this technique. Immediately after the *TERecord*, *teh*, is allocated by means of *TENew*, the handle is dereferenced into the pointer, *tep*, and the pointer is used to initialize the structure.

```
TEHandle    teh;
register TEPtr    tep;

...
```

Figure 5-16. *(continued)*
Using a register pointer to the structure speeds up access to the heap.

Figure 5-16. *continued*

```
teh = TENew (&aRect, &aRect);
tep = *teh;

textHdl = NewHandle (120L);
tep->hText = textHdl;
tep->just = teJustLeft;
tep->selStart = 0;
tep->selEnd = 0;
```

Pitfalls in Using Heap Objects

We've hidden a problem in Figure 5-16 to illustrate a common hitch in this kind of optimization. The call to *NewHandle* could potentially rearrange the heap. Relocation of heap objects is the source of a wide variety of bugs: A program calculates the address of an object, calls a function or Toolbox routine that moves the object, and then attempts to use the original address, which is no longer valid.

In response to calls to the Toolbox in a user interface intensive Macintosh application, objects can be relocated within the heap without your knowledge. Display of a dialog box is a good example. Although your application might have called *GetNewDialog* and *ModalDialog* to display a dialog box, the various Toolbox Managers involved in creating, displaying, and tracking user events for the dialog box are calling *NewHandle* behind the scenes. If memory is tight, the heap is rearranged. Figure 5-17 illustrates the problem that can result, a "dangling pointer."

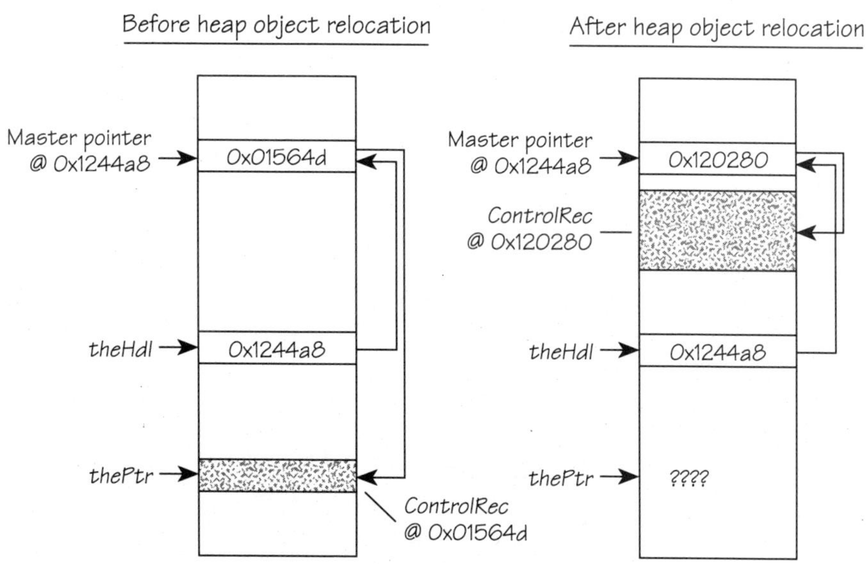

Figure 5-17.
Before and after heap object relocation. A dangling pointer.

In the first diagram in Figure 5-17, things are fine, as long as *ControlRec*, the relocatable object, doesn't relocate. In the second diagram, the worst has happened: *ControlRec* has moved in response to a Toolbox call. Note that *thePtr* still points to address 0x01564d, where who-knows-what now resides.

Not all Toolbox calls have the potential for relocating heap objects. Certain Toolbox routines—such as *OffsetRect*, *SetPort*, *FixMul*, and *InfoScrap*—perform operations that really have no reason to move relocatable objects. Another class of Toolbox routines—such as *NewRgn*, *GrowWindow*, and *TESetText*—indirectly create heap objects. How do you know which routines might move an object and which routines won't? *Inside Macintosh* lists all the Toolbox routines that have a potential for reorganizing the heap. They're listed as "Routines that may move or purge memory," which is actually a misnomer because memory doesn't really go anywhere—the objects in the heap memory are relocated. This information is available in other sources, such as Bernard Gallet's Inside Mac DA or Thom's *The Programmer's Apple Mac Sourcebook* (Microsoft Press, 1989). It's a good idea to check your code against these lists if you're going to use dereferenced pointers to relocatable heap objects.

Another instance in which relocatable blocks might move is during an intersegment function call. Remember that your application's code resides in the heap along with your data. The Segment Loader sees to it that code is in RAM when it needs to be. The process of loading a CODE resource might move some relocatable objects in the heap to make room for the new code segment.

How do you avoid the dangling pointer problem? You can live with the inefficiency of double dereferencing and always access the data in the relocatable object, as in Figure 5-18.

```
(**teh).hText = textHdl;
(**teh).just = teJustLeft;
(**teh).selStart = 0;
(**teh).selEnd = 0;
```

Figure 5-18.
Better safe than sorry? You could choose always to use the handle to access the heap elements.

Or you can use a smarter approach: Don't do anything that moves objects in the heap while you're using the dereferenced pointer. Figure 5-19 demonstrates the safe way to access a relocatable object.

```
...
register TERecord * tep;
TEHandle          teh;
```

Figure 5-19. *(continued)*
All allocation is done before *the handle is dereferenced and the pointer is used.*

Figure 5-19. *continued*

```
teh = TENew (&aRect, &aRect);
textHdl = NewHandle (120L);

tep = *teh;     // dereference after NewHandle
tep->hText = textHdl;
tep->just = teJustLeft;
tep->selStart = 0;
tep->selEnd = 0;
```

Another class of bugs results from the interaction of the Macintosh memory management scheme with C's storied portability. Because of the way the compiler is implemented, C can't guarantee when it will perform an address calculation. Let's look at this problem in detail because it bites every Macintosh C programmer at some time.

The bug occurs during an assignment from the return value of a Toolbox routine that can move a block in memory and is illustrated by Figure 5-20.

```
TEHandle          teh;

teh = TENew (&aRect, &aRect);

(*teh)->hText = NewHandle (120L);
```

Figure 5-20.
The TERecord *is created in the heap and is assigned the result of* NewHandle *directly in the object.*

It might appear that everything is correct: The handle is double dereferenced, and there is therefore no dangling pointer. But a bug occurs if the compiler generates code that calculates the heap address of the *hText* member *before* the call to *NewHandle.* Figure 5-21 on the next page illustrates the steps that the compiler could take; one produces the bomb alert box.

Contacting Symantec

A compiler does have an occasional bug, especially soon after a major release. If you have questions about THINK C or if you think you've found a problem with the compiler or one of its libraries, you can contact Symantec on the CompuServe information service. You'll get a quick answer from either Symantec or another forum member. Just type *GO THINK* at any ! prompt, and leave a message describing your problem or comment. Check back later in the day, and you'll probably have your answer.

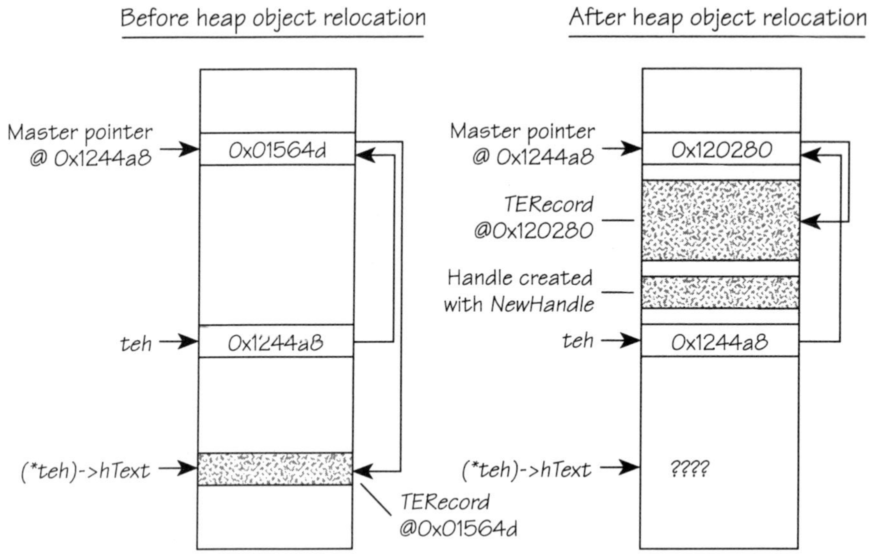

Figure 5-21.
If the compiler computes the address after the function call, there's no bug. But if it computes the address before the function call, the address could be incorrect if NewHandle *moves the* TERecord.

Is this a bug or a feature? The compiler doesn't guarantee the order of address calculation during an assignment. The language designers left this choice up to whoever implements the compiler. The Symantec compiler usually calculates the address before the function call. If you contact Symantec to report this as a bug, they'll justify their implementation by telling you what we've just told you.

Another manifestation of this premature address-calculation problem, one that has nothing to do with the compiler implementation, is demonstrated in Figure 5-22.

```
MenuHandle  theMenu;
...
theMenu = GetMenu (kMenuID);
GetIndString ((*theMenu)->menuData, kMenuStrID, kMenuStr1);
...
```

Figure 5-22.
Here's another potential bomb alert box. The address of menuData *in the heap is pushed onto the stack.* GetIndString *then relocates objects in the heap, and the address is invalid.*

Detecting the problem in Figure 5-22 requires a knowledge of the data structure you're working with. *GetMenu* returns a handle to some menu template data from the application's resource file. (We'll get to menus in the next chapter.) At the end of the data structure referenced by this handle is a string, *menuData*, which holds the menu's item strings. Because it's a string, *menuData* is passed by reference. The Resource Manager routine, *GetIndString*, reads a string from the application's resource file and loads the string into the location specified by the first argument to *GetIndString*. If *GetIndString* rearranges the heap, the address is wrong and *GetIndString* overwrites some undefined location in the heap.

You might use a temporary stack variable as a workaround for this problem. Stack objects aren't moved around the way heap objects are, so you can be sure that their addresses are stable and therefore always valid. We've used a temporary string in the code in Figure 5-23 to solve this problem.

```
MenuHandle  theMenu;
Str255      aString;

...
theMenu = GetMenu (kMenuID);
GetIndString (aString, kMenuStrID, kMenuStr1);
BlockMove (aString, (*theMenu)->menuData, (long)(aString [0] + 1));
```

Figure 5-23.
A temporary variable, aString, *is used with* GetIndString *and* BlockMove. Inside Macintosh *says that* BlockMove *doesn't move objects in the heap.*

BlockMove, which copies the string from the temporary variable to the heap object, is a general-purpose, memory-to-memory copy routine. Although this code will run without incident, it's not very efficient to make a double copy of the string simply to work around the Memory Manager's tendency to shuffle the deck. There is a way to pass the address of a relocatable object when the object might move. The easiest solution is to use the Memory Manager routine *HLock* to lock the object in the heap. This has the effect of turning a relocatable object into a nonrelocatable one. The code in Figure 5-24 demonstrates the process.

```
theMenu = GetMenu (kMenuID);

MoveHHi (theMenu);
HLock (theMenu);

GetIndString ((*theMenu)->menuData, kMenuStrID, kMenuStr1);

HUnlock (theMenu);
```

Figure 5-24.
Locking (and then unlocking) the handle.

You can pass the address of a relocatable object to a Toolbox call that will move a block in memory if you first lock the handle. But remember to unlock the handle with *HUnlock* as soon as possible.

You can use this technique of locking a block to avoid the problem of premature address calculation, as shown in the code in Figure 5-25.

```
TEHandle          teh;

teh = TENew (&aRect, &aRect);

MoveHHi (teh);
HLock (teh);
(*teh)->hText = NewHandle (120L);
HUnlock (teh);
```

Figure 5-25.
Locking the block before the address to a relocatable block is calculated.

Note the call to *MoveHHi* in Figures 5-24 and 5-25. When you create a temporary nonrelocatable object by locking the block, you'll open the door to heap fragmentation unless you first move the object out of the center to the top of the heap before you lock it. That's what *MoveHHi* does. It moves the block as high in the heap as possible. Figure 5-26 illustrates the action of *MoveHHi.*

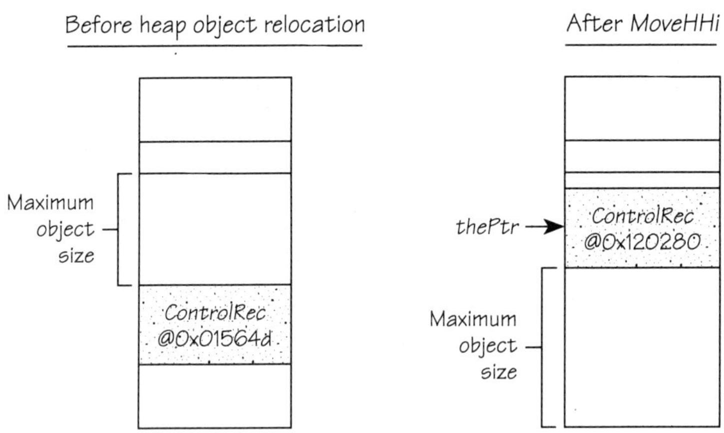

Figure 5-26.
MoveHHi.

Of course, you don't want to keep a block locked any longer than you need to. You use the Memory Manager routine *HUnlock* to unlock the block; otherwise, you thwart the very purpose of using relocatable blocks.

Locking a handle is no panacea. You want to lock the block only when necessary. We've summarized the cases in which it's necessary to lock a relocatable block:

- You run the risk of a dangling pointer.
- You assign the value of an intersegment function call to a relocatable heap object.
- You assign to a relocatable heap object the value of a Toolbox routine that has the potential to rearrange the heap.
- You pass the address of a relocatable object as an argument to an intersegment function call.
- You pass the address of a relocatable object as an argument to a Toolbox routine that has the potential to rearrange the heap.

Now you know the circumstances under which the heap is rearranged. You don't need to lock a block every time you assign one of its fields. You probably won't be returning pointers to local variables anymore, either.

We hope that you haven't misunderstood this chapter's message. We're not advocating assembly language programming. Rather, we're out to make you a more effective C programmer. An awareness of what's going on "under the hood" will not only improve your coding sessions but will reduce your debugging time as well.

But that's enough poking around at the underside of a program. Let's create a real program so that we can see these problems and solutions in practice.

6

INTRODUCTION TO THE GENERIC APPLICATION

Whether it's pasta or prescription drugs, nearly every product seems to come in a generic version these days. This chapter introduces the Generic Application—Generic App for short—a complete, stand-alone application that provides a basis for just about any Macintosh program.

Generic App is an application shell that performs the fundamental Macintosh program tasks: initializing the Macintosh interface, monitoring user input, and managing multiple documents. It's generic because it can be used as a starting point for almost any programming project.

We'll take up this generic Macintosh application in three stages. In this chapter, we'll look at the first phase, which we call miniGeneric—the simplest application. We'll use miniGeneric to describe the Macintosh's event-driven operating system, to introduce Macintosh resources, and to examine how an application reads menu selections.

In Chapter 7, we'll explore Macintosh window management with a multiwindow application we call multiGeneric. Finally, in Chapter 8, we'll extend the shell to demonstrate how an application window can display and scroll text and graphics.

Before we leap into the details of Generic App, let's take a look at how Macintosh software is organized. This overview will help you organize your programs.

Stratified Software

Macintosh software is organized in levels, like Dante's Inferno. This layering of software, shown in Figure 6-1, brings order to the chaos of a large application.

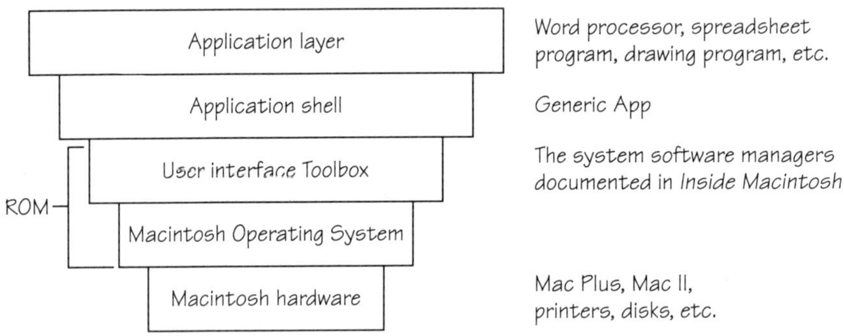

Figure 6-1.
The Macintosh software hierarchy.

At the very bottom of the software hierarchy, the Macintosh Operating System (OS) mediates the boundary between hardware and software—managing memory, supervising input and output, and processing interrupts. Above the OS sits the User Interface Toolbox, which provides the routines for standard Macintosh interface objects such as windows and menus. Together, these two levels make up the ROM, or system software.

The two layers of ROM are further divided into managers that group the system routines according to function. Within these managers lie the procedures that are called from an application to do Macintosh-specific chores such as opening a file or a window and reading a control or a menu.

The application resides in levels above the ROM software. Good application software is usually organized into two levels—one for the application shell and one for the application proper.

ROM Software

The two layers of ROM software deserve a closer look because one good way to approach a new programming environment is to examine the features that it supports. The Macintosh segmentation of system utilities into managers provides for an orderly tour of the features supported by the Mac.

User interface Toolbox managers

The user interface Toolbox is the most interesting layer of the system software. QuickDraw, TextEdit, the Window Manager, the Dialog Manager, and the Toolbox Event Manager are all on this level. Every time your application opens a window, puts up a dialog box, or reads a menu, it is calling at least one of these manager routines, and as you become more experienced in programming the Macintosh, you'll begin to learn the routines by heart. Figure 6-2 diagrams the relationships among several managers at the user interface Toolbox level and their relationship to the File Manager at the Operating System level.

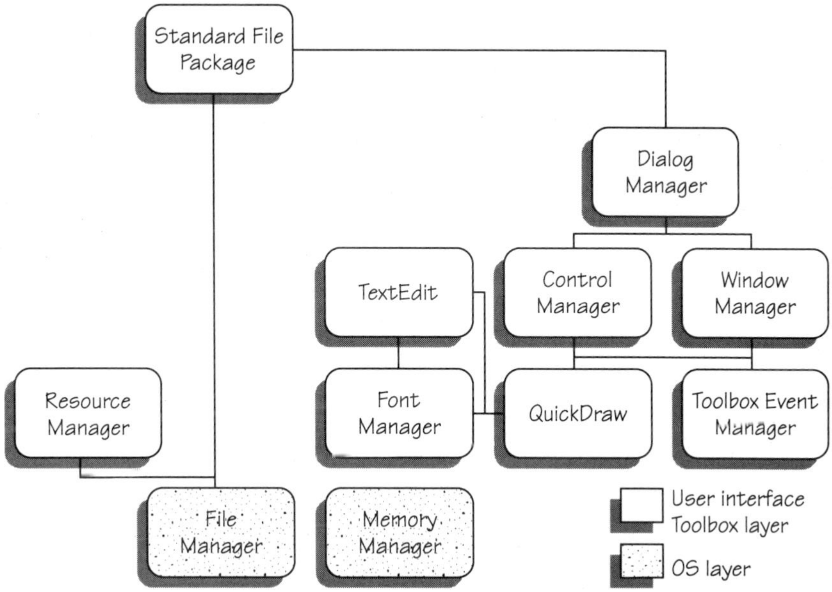

Figure 6-2.
Important managers of the user interface Toolbox level.

Operating System managers

The Operating System level routines are a bit more esoteric. A typical OS manager is the Device Manager. It provides access to standard devices such as a printer or a disk drive through a structure called a device control entry or DCE. Other OS managers include the Memory Manager, the System Error Handler, and the OS Event Manager. Figure 6-3 on the next page diagrams the interaction of several OS managers with the Macintosh hardware.

If you do system programming, you'll become familiar with the routines and data structures peculiar to some of the OS managers. If you write a disk driver, for instance, you'll become expert with the File Manager, the Device Manager, and the Disk Driver but will probably learn little about the Serial Driver.

An application programmer needs to know about the Memory Manager and certain OS utilities but usually ignores the details of the OS level. Indeed, that's why the software hierarchy is in place: The details of the technology are localized to the level.

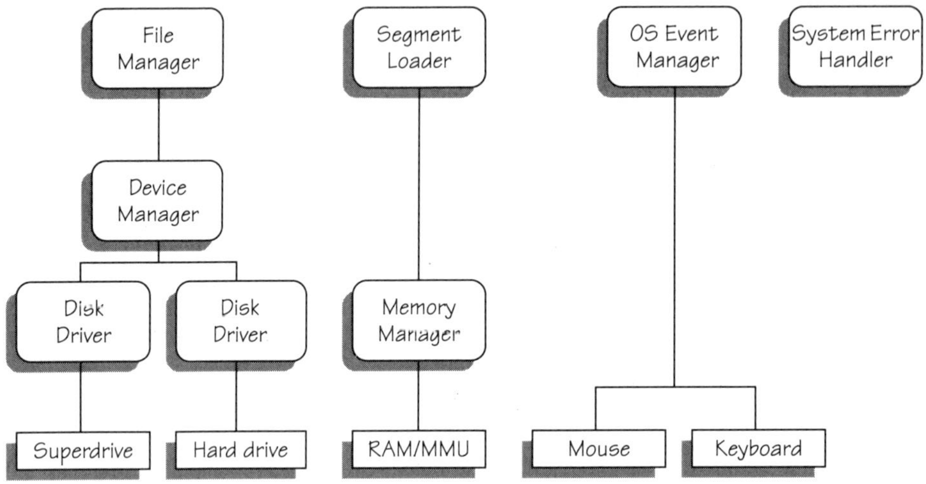

Figure 6-3.
Operating System software interacting with the Macintosh hardware.

The Shell Level

Above the ROM software level, the application programmer is in charge of the layering. We chose the next layer of our hierarchy to be the application "shell." A shell is the supporting structure of an application, supplying the application's event processing and window management.

Whatever your programming background and focus, your first task as a Macintosh novitiate is building the shell. Once you've built the shell, you can use it over and over again—for every application that you write in your long and illustrious career as a Macintosh programmer. It's been said that each programmer really writes only one program in his or her career. Generic App is the foundation for that program.

The application proper actually begins in the next higher level—at the level we've called the application layer. In a word processing program, the application layer contains the modules that process text. The interface, which consists of windows, scroll bars, and facilities for mouse and keyboard input, is supplied in the shell layer.

We're borrowing the shell concept from object-oriented programming (OOP) texts, where the idea is more formalized. In OOP, programs are made up of objects that encapsulate data and code. In the pure light of OOP thinking, the shell and the application are separate objects, each with its own independent set of data and code. As we add application-like features to Generic App in Chapters 7 and 8, and later in the chapter on Browser, you'll get a better feel for how the shell code differs from the application feature set that we add to it.

Let's look at miniGeneric, the simple phase of our shell.

What Does miniGeneric Do?

Functionally, miniGeneric is very simple: It manages the Apple, File, and Edit menus, and it supports two windows. The main window contains text, and the secondary window is for the About box, where the program's logo and version information are displayed. The About box can overlap the main window. When the About box is closed, the main window needs to be refreshed.

Figure 6-4 shows the miniGeneric screen, with the About box in front of the main window. The Apple and File menus are fully functional, but the Edit menu is present only to support any Desk Accessories that might need it, in accordance with Apple's User Interface Guidelines.

Figure 6-4. *The miniGeneric screen.*

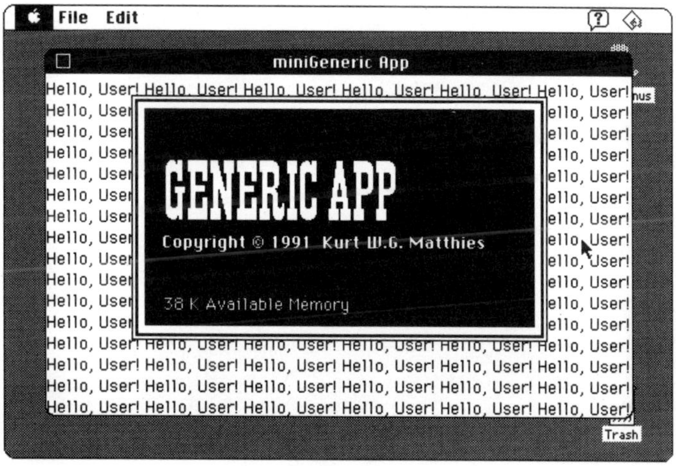

Our shell meets all the requirements for a minimum application: The user can open and close the main window and the About box and quit the application, all by using menu selections.

A user's selection reaches the application as an event. Selecting a menu item with the mouse causes an event of one kind to be generated at the system level. Using a command-key equivalent causes another kind of event to be generated.

Macintosh programs are event-driven. Most of the time, a Macintosh program is idle, waiting for a new event to process. Events are the result of real-world occurrences such as a keypress or a disk insertion. The OS layer processes the interrupts associated with the real-world occurrences, bundles up all the information about the event into an *EventRecord* structure, and makes the event available to the application.

When the application receives the event, the program's logic switches control to a function that deals with that type of event. We call this processing "event parsing."

Consider the diagram in Figure 6-5. The miniGeneric application, limited to its shell duties, is interested in only mouse and keyboard events. These real-world occurrences translate into the Macintosh events mouse-down, key-down, activate, and update. When miniGeneric gets an event of interest, it passes control to the corresponding routine—*doMouseDown*, *doKeyDown*, *doActivateEvent*, or *doUpdateEvent*.

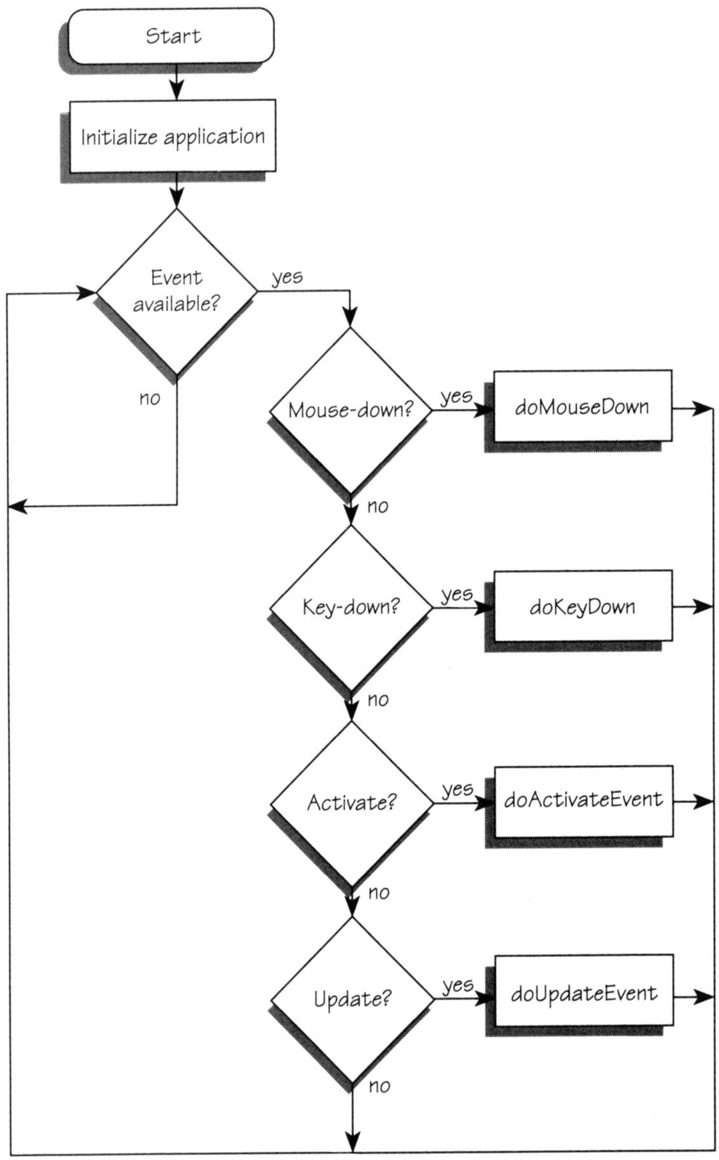

Figure 6-5.
miniGeneric's main event loop.

When the user selects a menu item or selects the command-key equivalent for the item, the application reacts. Figure 6-6 shows the top of the Apple menu, which invokes the About box, and miniGeneric's File menu, which contains three items.

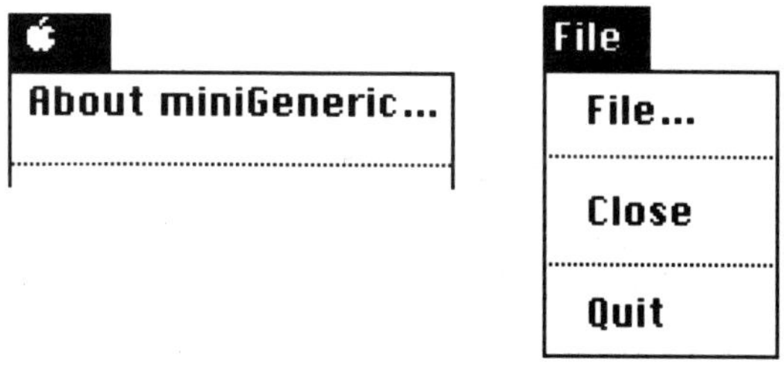

Figure 6-6.
The About miniGeneric item in the Apple menu and the miniGeneric File menu.

Figure 6-7 shows what miniGeneric needs to do to process menu selections.

Menu	Item	Action	Action Function
Apple	About	Display the About box	*doAboutBox*
File	Open	Open the window	*doOpen*
File	Close	Close the window	*doClose*
File	Quit	Quit the application	*doQuit*

Figure 6-7.
Processing miniGeneric menu selections.

The first step in application building is designing the framework to manage each event and its origin.

A Roadmap of Generic App

The complete source code for miniGeneric is in the folder miniGenApp f, found on the disk that comes with this book. The folder contains a project file, the folder miniGenApp Src with 10 source files, the folder miniGenApp Hdr containing the project's header files, and the project resource file, miniGenAppπ.rsrc. The files that make up miniGeneric are shown in Figure 6-8.

File Name	Location	Purpose
miniGenAppπ	Project folder	Project file
miniGenAppπ.rsrc	Project folder	Project resource file
Shell.c	Src folder	Main entry point, event parsing

Figure 6-8. *(continued)*
The miniGeneric source files.

Figure 6-8. *continued*

File Name	***Location***	***Purpose***
AppInit.c	Src folder	Application initialization routines
MenuUtil.c	Src folder	Menu utilities
WindowUtil.c	Src folder	Window sizing, movement, scrolling
DialogUtil.c	Src folder	Dialog box hook procedures
AboutBox.c	Src folder	About box rendering
MiscUtil.c	Src folder	A catch-all file
DocUtil.c	Src folder	Document management
FileUtil.c	Src folder	File I/O utilities
Display.c	Src folder	Drawing functions for application
xxxxPr.h	Hdr folder	Prototypes—one for each .c file
AppConstants.h	Hdr folder	Application constants (*#defines*)
AppGlobals.h	Hdr folder	Application global declarations
AppTypes.h	Hdr folder	Application type definitions
MenuConstants.h	Hdr folder	Menu constant definitions
Version.h	Hdr folder	Compiler environment definition

The miniGeneric application is a much larger project than our Hello Mac! example was. The C source code for Hello Mac! was in one file; the code for miniGeneric is organized into 10 source files and 15 header files. Why is the program split up? Here are the main reasons:

- To isolate independent "modules" within the program. A module is simply a source file in which functions are defined. Modules should be aptly named. The module DialogUtil.c, for example, contains dialog box management utilities. WindowUtil.c contains windowing routines.
- To organize the program code logically. Shell.c contains the main event loop and utilities. When the user chooses a menu item, program control passes to one of the routines in the file MenuUtil.c. Therefore, if you wanted to add another menu, MenuUtil.c would be the logical place to do it. If you added to the program helter-skelter, the program would become what is colorfully described as "spaghetti code" because it would snake and tangle all over the disk. The key to organizing modules is to create a file structure and be faithful to it. miniGeneric's file organization is appropriate for small applications and is adaptable to programs of up to 100,000 lines.
- To keep to a minimum the amount of code that must be recompiled and relinked when making the frequent small changes and adjustments that are part of the development cycle. Minimizing the amount of code that must be recompiled and relinked saves time during the development cycle and makes the code amenable to the use of source code control techniques, a topic we'll examine in passing in the next chapter.

- To retain control over the program's code segmentation. The code of all executable programs is segmented. A code segment is an atomic unit of code, loaded into RAM automatically when one of the functions in the segment is called during program execution. In THINK C, we have control over which modules are in each segment. Using a segmentation strategy is important when you're trying to fit a large program into a small space.

There's an art to distributing the functions among the source files, and many factors come into play. Routines usually group naturally. The trick is knowing where to draw the line. For example, an application draws its window contents in response to an update event. We put *doUpdateEvent()*, the function that responds to an update event, in the file Shell.c, but put *drawDocContents()*, the function that does the actual drawing, in the file Display.c. In this case, the line is drawn when the application does the actual drawing. Sometimes, when the dividing line is not so distinct, you'll use other criteria to determine where a function fits in your modular organization.

Another consideration when creating code modules is the "scope" of a function, which defines where the function can be called. In C, the scope of a "static function" is limited to the source file in which it's defined. A static function can be called only from the routines defined in its own module. Declaring a function as static isolates the function from other, non-similar, functions. Thoughtful use of static functions can therefore facilitate a layered approach to software design.

A "static variable" serves to hide data from external modules. A static variable is accessible from everywhere in the module in which it's defined—any function in the module can use it. But a static variable is hidden from external functions. So when deciding the location of a function, consider whether it needs to access a static variable. If it does, you need to put the function in the static variable's module.

Static Functions

A static function is created by putting the *static* keyword before the function name in the function's body definition. Let's look at two function prototypes for Generic's functions *doMenu()* and *doFileMenu()*, both defined in the file MenuUtil.c. The first function, *doMenu()*, is declared without the *static* keyword, and rightfully so—it's called from the functions *doMouseDown()* and *doKeyDown()*, both in another module, in the file Shell.c.

```
void            doMenu ( long menuResult );
```

The second function, *doFileMenu()*, is a static function. It's called only from *doMenu()*, which resides in the same file, in MenuUtil.c.

```
static void     doFileMenu ( short itemNumber );
```

Static Variables

Here's a small code fragment from the mythical file Foo.c that demonstrates static variable syntax:

```
static TEHandle    sCurTextHdl;    /* static variable */

    /* createText--this is a sample function */
void
    createText (Rect targetRect)
    {
        sCurTextHdl = TENew (&targetRect, &targetRect);
        ...
```

Because *sCurTextHdl* is a static variable, any function in Foo.c can access it, as the function *createText()* does in the example. Functions in other modules are unaware of the existence of *sCurTextHdl*, and the compiler will generate an undefined symbol message if you try to reference *sCurTextHdl* from another module.

Now that you have an idea of how and why functions are distributed in the 10 source modules, we'll take a look at what's in Generic App and at the event mechanism—how Generic App processes events.

The Main Event

Without input, a computer is a useless hunk of hardware. A computer application needs to know when its user is pawing the keyboard or twiddling the mouse button. The Event mechanism of the OS layer translates these real-world occurrences initiated by the user into a data structure available to the application—into the *EventRecord* data structure whose declaration we show in Figure 6-9.

```
typedef struct EventRecord
{
    int         what;
    long        message;
    long        when;
    Point       where;
    int         modifiers;
}EventRecord;
```

Figure 6-9.
The EventRecord *data structure.*

An *EventRecord* is created for each mouse-down, keypress, disk insertion, Appletalk message received, or other occurrence. The table in Figure 6-10 shows the possible Macintosh event types.

	Event Type	Description
No events	nullEvent	Nothing happening. A null event is what you get when there is no other event available.
Mouse events	mouseDown	Mouse button down.
	mouseUp	Mouse button was released. Cannot happen without a mouse-down.
Keyboard events	keyDown	A key was pressed.
	keyUp	A key was released.
	autoKey	A key is being held down.
Window Manager events	updateEvt	The window has a nonempty update region. Part of the window needs refreshing.
	activateEvt	A window has come to the front or has just left there.
External device events	diskEvt	A disk was inserted.
	networkEvt	An AppleTalk message was received.
	driverEvt	This depends on the driver and is rarely used by applications.
Application-defined events	app1Evt	User defined.
	app2Evt	User defined.
	app3Evt	User defined.
	app4Evt	MultiFinder suspend/resume. A task was switched from foreground to background, or vice versa.

Figure 6-10.
Macintosh event types.

When the computer detects a real-world occurrence, the OS Event Manager creates an *EventRecord* using the interrupt data and links the record to the application's event queue. This queue, maintained by the OS, is where unprocessed events reside in chronological order. Generic App doesn't access the queue directly. Instead, it calls *WaitNextEvent*, the Event Manager routine that returns the data for the next event and removes it from the queue.

When the application receives the event, it examines the event type and passes flow of control to its function that handles that particular kind of event. Figure 6-11 on the next page illustrates the process.

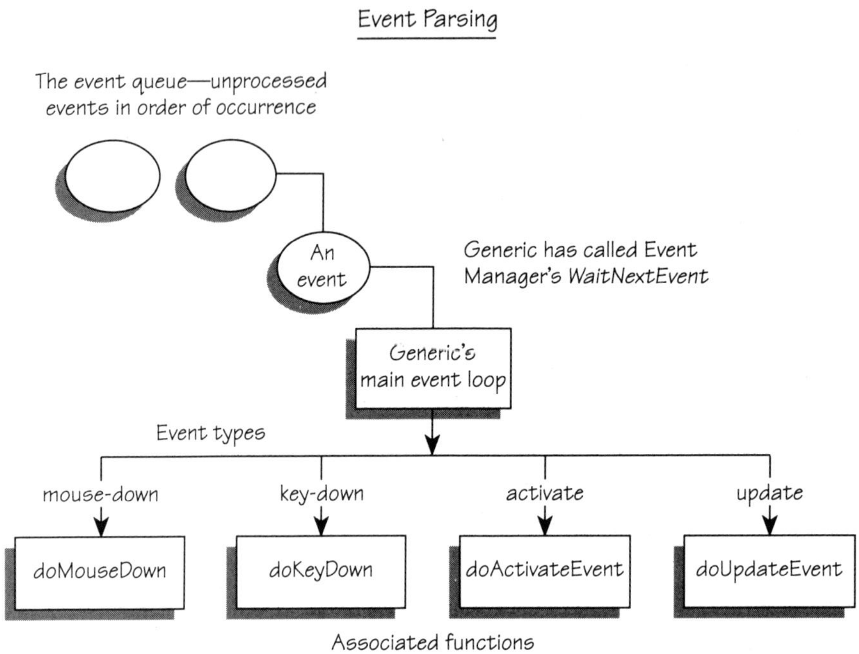

Figure 6-11.
Parsing a real-world occurrence.

Event parsing goes on in Generic's main event loop, shown in Figure 6-12. The entire loop is in the function *main()*, which is found in Shell.c. Note the four event types that Generic is interested in: mouse-down, key-down, activate, and update.

```
EventRecord                 event;
long                        sleepTicks;
Boolean                     result;

sleepTicks = 10L;

/* infinite loop */
while (1)
{
    result = WaitNextEvent (everyEvent, &event, sleepTicks, 0L);
    if (result)
    {
        switch (event.what)   /* parse event type */
        {
```

Figure 6-12. *(continued)*
Generic App's main event loop.

Figure 6-12. *continued*

```
            case mouseDown:
                doMouseDown (&event);
                break;

            case keyDown:
                doKeyDown (&event);
                break;

            case activateEvt:
                doActivateEvent (&event);
                break;

            case updateEvt:
                doUpdateEvent (&event);
                break;
        }
    }
}
```

WaitNextEvent

WaitNextEvent reads the event queue and returns an event record structure. Unfortunately, *WaitNextEvent* is not documented in the standard reference, *Inside Macintosh,* but is covered in an obscure document called *Programmer's Guide to MultiFinder.* You can glean a little more information about it from a few of the Macintosh Technical Notes. The Apple Programmers and Developers Association (APDA) makes both the *Guide to MultiFinder* and the tech notes available to programmers.

We don't expect you to have a copy of *Programmer's Guide to MultiFinder* lying around, so we'll take a look at *WaitNextEvent.* Here are its arguments:

```
short WaitNextEvent ( short eventMask, EventRecord * event,
                      long sleepTicks, RgnHandle mouseRgn );
```

- *eventMask* masks "interesting" events. The masks are enumerated in the header file Events.h supplied with the THINK C package. The Generic application uses the *everyEvent* mask and then parses the interesting ones with the *switch* construct.
- *event* is the event record returned by *WaitNextEvent.*
- *sleepTicks* is the sleep variable, in ticks (1/60ths of a second). The value of *sleepTicks* approximates the amount of time the foreground application allows background tasks to run.
- *mouseRgn,* if specified, limits the area in which a mouse-down (or mouse-up) event will be reported. If you limit this region to a 10-pixel by 10-pixel square,

your user must move the mouse at least 5 pixels from the last mouse-down position before an event will be reported. We don't specify a value for *mouseRgn* in Generic, but because you might have use for it elsewhere, we demonstrate using it in Figure 6-13.

```
EventRecord         event;
long                sleepTicks;
Boolean             result;
RgnHandle           mouseRgn;
Rect                rgnRect;
Point               mousePoint;

sleepTicks = 10L;

mouseRgn = NewRgn ();  /* initialize the region */
SetRectRgn (mouseRgn, 0, 0, 0, 0);

/* infinite loop */
while (1)
{
    result = WaitNextEvent (everyEvent, &event, sleepTicks, mouseRgn);
    if (result)
    {
        switch (event.what)    /* parse event type */
        {
            case mouseDown:

                /* get the point where the mouse was clicked
                from the event record */
                mousePt.h = LOWORD (event.where);
                mousePt.v = HIWORD (event.where);

                /* build the rectangle that bounds the point by
                five pixels */
                rgnRect.left = mousePt.h - 5;
                rgnRect.right = mousePt.h + 5;
                rgnRect.top = mousePt.v - 5;
                rgnRect.bottom = mousePt.v + 5;

                /* set up the new region */
                RectRgn (mouseRgn, &rgnRect);

                doMouseDown (&event);
                break;
                ...
```

Figure 6-13.
Use of WaitNextEvent*'s* mouseRgn *parameter.*

MultiFinder and *WaitNextEvent*

Once upon a time, under Finder, only one application at a time could be loaded into the Macintosh memory. An application called two functions in its event loop: *GetNextEvent*, which pulled the next event off the event queue; and *SystemTask*, which gave Desk Accessories a cycle or two. Then came MultiFinder.

MultiFinder has made the Macintosh a cooperative, multitasking system. A new system routine, *WaitNextEvent*, has been added to allow applications to coexist in RAM. Because multiple applications are allowed, two new concepts have been introduced: the foreground task and the background task.

The foreground task is the application that receives most of the computer's resources. There is only one foreground task at any time. All of the other loaded applications are relegated to the background.

A background task gets very little of the system resources. In truth, it's at the mercy of the foreground task's giving it any time to run at all. This is where *WaitNextEvent* comes in.

Every time it's called, *WaitNextEvent* gives background tasks a little CPU time. The amount of time that's allocated to the background is controlled through the value of the *WaitNextEvent* routine's *sleepTime* parameter. If you want to be downright unneighborly and not allow background tasks any CPU time, set *sleepTime* to *0* (actually *0L* because *sleepTime* is of type *long*). A more generous and reasonable value to start with is *20*. If you find that your foreground application is not getting enough cycles, decrease the *sleepTime* value. Note that Generic uses a variable for *sleepTicks* instead of a hard-wired constant. This approach lets you change the value from the debugger while the program is running, so that you can see how the value affects the program's responsiveness.

The System Clock

The *sleepTime* parameter of *WaitNextEvent* is specified in units of the Macintosh system clock, called the "tick counter," which ticks 60 times a second. The value of this counter is at the location named by the global variable *Tick* (at address *0x016A*) and contains the number of 1/60ths of a second that have gone by since the system was booted. Here's a simple function to read the *Tick* value:

```
long
readTicks ()
{
    return (*((long *)0x016A));
}
```

The value *0x016A* is cast to a pointer to *long* and dereferenced to return the 4-byte value at location 16A.

The miniGeneric shell, like virtually all Macintosh programs, spends most of its time in the main event loop. Each time through the loop, it checks to see whether a new event has occurred by testing the return value of *WaitNextEvent.*

The miniGeneric shell is interested in only a fresh *EventRecord*—one that is received when *WaitNextEvent* returns a nonzero value. The *EventRecord* contains the what, when, and where associated with the event. The contents of the record vary according to the kind of event, which is returned in the *what* field of the record. A consolidated list of the possible *EventRecord* values, based on event type, is shown in Figure 6-14.

		Message	**When**	**Where**	**Modifiers**
	nullEvent		Ticks since startup	Mouse location at event	
Mouse events	mouseDown		"	"	button state
	mouseUp		"	"	
Keyboard events	keyDown	character code key code	"	"	Option, Shift, Command keys
	keyUp		"	"	
	autoKey		"	"	
Window Manager events	updateEvt	pointer to window	"	"	
	activateEvt		"	"	Activate/ Deactivate
	diskEvt	drive number result code	"	"	
	networkEvt	handle to parameter block	"	"	
	driverEvt	varies	"	"	
Application-defined events	app1Evt	?	"	"	
	app2Evt	?	"	"	
	app3Evt	?	"	"	
	app4Evt		"	"	MultiFinder suspend/ resume

Figure 6-14.
EventRecord *contents by event code. Events are grouped by type on the left, and the fields of the event record appear along the top. If a cell is blank, the value of the field is undefined for that type of event and can be ignored.*

The Macintosh OS and the user interface Toolbox are constantly evolving. Just because an *EventRecord* value is undefined now doesn't mean it will always be undefined. For example, before MultiFinder, the *app4Evt* event type was not assigned and was free to be used by developers as they wanted to use it. MultiFinder came along and used this event to signal applications that are switching in and out of the foreground. Apple is very good about warning programmers (by means of the tech notes) when they anticipate a change that might affect existing programs, but they're not perfect.

Macintosh Technical Notes

Macintosh Technical Notes are Apple's way of providing supplemental, timely information on the state of the art in hardware and software. They're written by folks at Apple's Developer Technical Support group and contain information ranging from tips and tricks (as in note #007 on some great debugging techniques) to a totally new way of doing things (as in note #158 that deals with MultiFinder and *WaitNextEvent*). There are hundreds of these gems. We'd be lost without them, and if you're a serious developer, you need them too. You can get them from Apple's APDA, or you can download them from AppleLink. Apple Associates ($500 per year) get them from Developer Tech Support as a part of the service. Apple has released a HyperCard Tech Note stack, and this is great for quick lookups, but the notes come out faster than Apple seems to be able to keep the stack updated. (And you'll need a lot of hard disk space unless you buy the CD-ROM version.) For $25 a year, APDA will mail you each release—about six sets per year. Write to this address:

Apple Programmers and Developers Association
Apple Computer, Inc.
20525 Mariani Avenue, M/S 33-G
Cupertino, CA 95014-6299

The phone number is (800) 282-APDA, or you can try AppleLink: APDA.

Adding Menus to an Application

Events are only half the story. Once an event is detected, the application needs to respond to it. Generic is interested in four types of events. Two of them, activate and update events, are products of window selection and display. (We will discuss these two types of events in the next chapter.) The other two, key-down and mouse-down events, involve a menu selection. But before a menu can be used, it must be created. Let's look at what it takes to create menus for an application.

Menus are created from menu description templates, or "resources," stored in the application's resource fork. Most commercial applications define their menus by means of templates in the resource fork. Menus can also be compiled into the program—hard coded, as programmers say—but we discourage this practice. The advantage of using a resource to create menus is that you can change a menu's items without modifying the source code. This approach is often taken as part of the effort to "localize" a commercial application—that is, to give it foreign-language menus, dialog boxes, and message strings. With resource-based menus, sophisticated users have been known to add keyboard shortcuts to menus by using the resource editor ResEdit.

We use ResEdit to create all of our resources, including menus. There are other ways to create templates (and we describe them here in a sidebar), but ResEdit uses a Mac-like user interface and is probably your best bet for creating resource templates.

Use ResEdit to look at the existing menu templates in the project's resource file, miniGenAppπ.rsrc on the source disk for this book. Resources, as we'll see throughout the book, are a great way to organize an application's interface features.

A resource is identified by its "resource specification," made up of a four-character key called the resource type, and a resource number, as in MENU #1. We'll use the hash mark to identify the resource number. Here, we're interested in the MENU resources.

In miniGeneric, the Apple Menu is MENU #1, the File Menu is MENU #2, and the Edit Menu is MENU #3. Of course, the #3 refers to resource 3.

Menus contain menu items, one per line, which are numbered from 1 to *n*, top to bottom. Figure 6-15 shows a sample menu with item numbers.

In the Apple menu, Item 1 is the About item, and the rest of the items are the Desk Accessories, added to the menu with a special call.

Macintosh Resources and Menus

Resources are vital to any Macintosh program. Indeed, a correctly designed program should define in the application's resource fork all menus, dialog boxes, alert boxes, icons, pictures, and text strings that the application will display. That way, any changes you need to make, such as developing a Spanish version of your program, are confined to the resources and don't affect the program code.

The problem with resources is that Apple has given us two not-quite-finished ways of dealing with them. The traditional method, the one we use in this chapter to create menus, is to use ResEdit, a funky little what-you-see-is-almost-what-you-get editor that lets you manipulate the resources in a file directly (even after the program has been compiled). You can create some resource items directly, seeing them as the user will see them, and then drag them to the appropriate places. You create other resources by painfully filling in a series of TextEdit boxes. If you make one mistake (and you probably won't see it because there's no visual feedback that shows you how your finished object will look), you're liable to mess up your program to the extent that it crashes. Using ResEdit to add command keys, hierarchical menus, and

Figure 6-15.
A generic menu. Notice that item 4 is a dotted line.

The File menu, shown in Figure 6-16, has five items, three of which are selectable—the Open, Close, and Quit items. The two dotted lines are Items 2 and 4, but they are disabled and therefore not selectable.

Figure 6-16.
The File menu.

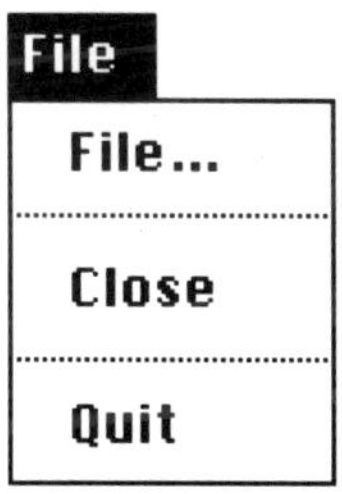

other options is a real pain. The latest version of ResEdit, 2.1, has better editors for many of the resources.

Apple's second method is to use Rez, one of the tools in the Macintosh Programmer's Workshop and in Think C 5.0. Rez lets you create resources by describing them in a structured text file. In some ways, this is the preferred method because you get maintainable source code for the resources that can easily be passed along to others, either on paper or as a file.

Next best in our opinion is Prototyper from Now Software. Forget Prototyper as a creator of generic application code, but it's a real help as a resource maker. In its menu section, though, adding new selections to the end of a menu is not a particularly intuitive process, and cut and paste functions simply aren't available—you'll have to move things manually, one at a time, if you change your mind about where to put them. Prototyper's interface could use some improvement. It doesn't always work exactly as you might expect. (Try tabbing between TextEdit boxes.) Nevertheless, Prototyper is well worth the effort you'll invest in learning to use it, especially if you're interested in seeing what the menu and dialog features of your program will look like before you commit them to code.

The Edit menu isn't used in miniGeneric, but we supply it for the Desk Accessories that need it. The menu is standard, with an Undo item separated by a dotted line from the Clipboard items Cut, Copy, Paste, and Clear.

Creating the File Menu Template

We'll use ResEdit 2.1 to create the File menu. If you are new to ResEdit, follow along step-by-step.

1. Start up ResEdit 2.1.
2. Move through ResEdit to get to your miniGenApp f.
3. Create a new file: Press Command-N and enter the name *miniGenAppπ.rsrc*. (You enter the π by pressing Option-P.)
4. Create a new MENU resource: Choose Create New Resource from the Resource menu (or press Command-K), and choose MENU from the list that appears.
5. Create the menu title: Type *File* in the edit box, and press Return.
6. Create the first menu item: Type *New* in the edit box, and then add a keyboard equivalent for this item. Select the edit box Cmd-Key, and type *N*. Press Return.
7. Create the second menu item, a dotted line: Click the button labeled *separator line*, and press Return.
8. Create the third menu item: Type *Close* in the edit box. Now add a keyboard equivalent for this item. Select the edit box Cmd-Key, and type *W*. Press Return.
9. Create the fourth menu item, a dotted line: Click the button labeled *separator line*, and press Return.
10. Create the fifth menu item: Type *Quit* in the edit box. Now add a keyboard equivalent for this item. Select the edit box Cmd-Key, and type *Q*. Press Return.
11. Renumber the menu as 2: Select Edit Menu & MDEF ID from the MENU menu. Enter *2* in the edit box marked Menu ID, and then close this dialog box.
12. Close all windows by clicking in their close boxes. To save your work, click Yes in the dialog box that appears, and then quit ResEdit.

You've just completed a 12-step program for creating the File menu. Of course, we've created all the other menus in miniGeneric's resource file, which you'll find on the accompanying source code disk.

Initializing the Menu

As most applications do, miniGeneric installs its menus at initialization and treats them as static structures throughout the life of the program. In AppInit.c, the function *setUpMenus()* initializes and installs the menus. The *setUpMenus()* code is shown in Figure 6-17.

```
/*  setUpMenus--sets up the application menus */
setUpMenus ()
{
    /* create Apple Menu */
    gDeskMenu = GetMenu (kAppleMenuID);
    AddResMenu (deskMenu, 'DRVR');
    InsertMenu (deskMenu, 0);

    /* create File menu */
    gFileMenu = GetMenu (kFileMenuID);
    InsertMenu (fileMenu, 0);

    /* create Edit menu */
    gEditMenu = GetMenu (kEditMenuID);
    InsertMenu (editMenu, 0);

    DrawMenuBar();

} /* setUpMenus */
```

Figure 6-17.
Menu initialization code.

The menu template data is stored in the resource file. *GetMenu* reads the template and returns a *MenuHandle* to the menu data, now in memory.

All of an application's menu handles are maintained in an internal data structure, the *MenuBar*, which makes them available to the user by means of the Menu Manager routine *MenuSelect*. Usually, you'll never directly change the *MenuBar* in your application. Instead, you'll use Menu Manager utilities to add and subtract menus from the *MenuBar*. The routine *InsertMenu* adds menus to the *MenuBar*, and its complement, *DeleteMenu*, removes them.

miniGeneric's *MenuHandle* variables are global, and all globals in our programs begin with a lowercase *g* to remind us that they're globals and should be treated with respect. The *gDeskMenu* variable is the Apple menu handle, *gFileMenu* is the File menu handle, and *gEditMenu* is the Edit menu handle.

In *setUpMenus()*, *GetMenu* reads the template of the specified menu and creates an in-RAM menu data structure for the menu in the application heap. *GetMenu* returns a handle to the structure. The constants *kAppleMenuID*, *kFileMenuID*, and *kEditMenuID* are defined as *1*, *2*, and *3*, respectively, in the file *AppConstants.h*. They define the resource numbers for these templates. Creating the File and Edit menus is easily understood, but creating the Apple menu requires a small trick because this menu will contain a list of the currently installed Desk Accessories.

The good news is that we don't need to know the details of currently installed Desk Accessories to add them to the Apple menu. Note the call to *AddResMenu* when creating the Apple menu. This routine asks the system to look for currently installed Desk Accessories and adds their names to the menu. *AddResMenu* does this by collecting all resources of a particular type (in this case, DRVR), sorting them by name, and placing them in the menu in question. The only detail that you need to remember in this case is that Desk Accessories are DRVR type resources.

Reading the Menu Selection

When the application detects a mouse-down event in the menu bar, *MenuSelect* automatically takes care of all the menu display and selection chores associated with a menu selection. When *MenuSelect* completes the update of the display, it returns with the menu and item number selected as a long word made up of a high word and a low word—more about that in a moment. We call this "reading" the menu.

The *doMenu()* code in Figure 6-18 demonstrates how to choose an action based on a menu selection. The *doMenu()* function is called, with the result returned by *MenuSelect.* The high word of this argument—the top 16 bits—contains the menu ID of the selected menu. If this value is *1,* the Apple menu has been selected; if it is *2,* the File menu has been selected; if it is *3,* the Edit menu has been selected. The bottom word passed to *doMenu()*—the lower 16 bits—contains the selected item number in the selected menu. The *doMenu()* function uses the Toolbox macros *HiWord* and *LoWord* to extract these high and low words from the long word.

```
/* doMenu--handles menu selections */
void doMenu (long menuResult);
{
    short     menuID, itemNumber;

    menuID = HiWord (menuResult);          /* menu number in high word */
    itemNumber = LoWord (menuResult);      /* item number in low word */

    switch (menuID)            /* which menu is it? */
    {
        case kAppleMenuID:
            doAppleMenu (itemNumber);
            break;

        case kFileMenuID:
            doFileMenu (itemNumber);
            break;

        case kEditMenuID:
            doEditMenu (itemNumber);
            break;
```

Figure 6-18. *(continued)*
Menu selection parsing.

Figure 6-18. *continued*

```
    }  /* end switch */

    HiliteMenu (0);
}   /* doMenu */
```

The menu selection parser is a two-stage switch. The first stage determines which menu was selected from the *menuID* variable and passes the *itemNumber* to the selected function for that menu. The second stage, illustrated by *doFileMenu()* in Figure 6-19, determines the item number selected and calls the action procedure for that selection.

```
/* doFileMenu--switches menu choice to appropriate function call */
void
doFileMenu (short theItem)
{
    switch (theItem)
    {
        case kNewItem:
            doOpenDoc ();
            break;

        case kCloseItem:
            doCloseDoc (FrontWindow ());
            break;

        case kQuitItem:
            cleanExit (true);
            break;
    }

} /* doFileMenu */
```

Figure 6-19.
Menu item selection parsing.

Generic detects the keyboard equivalent for a menu selection by calling the routine *MenuKey* from *doKeyDown()*. Called whenever a key is pressed, *MenuKey* returns a long word, equivalent to the long word returned from *MenuSelect*. If the key was not a keyboard equivalent, *MenuKey* returns *0L*, which signals that the application should process the keystroke as input. The Generic application has no use for keyboard input that is not a menu selection, but a word processing application, for example, would add the character to the text stream.

Give Me a Break

Notice the *break* statement terminating each branch of the switches in Figures 6-18 and 6-19. Without a break, the flow of control would "fall through" and execute the next case. For an example, take a look at this variation on an excerpt from *doFileMenu()*:

```
switch (theItem)
{
    case kNewItem:
        doOpenDoc ();
                /* <--- we forgot the break! */
    case kCloseItem:
        doCloseDoc (FrontWindow ());

    ...
```

When the user selects New from the File menu, control flows to *doOpenDoc()*, but because we forgot the break, when *doOpenDoc()* returns, *doCloseDoc()* is called. The bug manifests itself as the window opens and then immediately closes. Leaving the break out of a switch branch is a common mistake of both beginning and experienced coders. You've been warned.

Putting It All Together

If you've already compiled and run the application, you know that you've written yet another Hello World. Is this *déjà vu*? Sure, but you now have a genuine event processing platform. Check it out. While running miniGeneric, open a Desk Accessory and drag it in front of your main window. Now close it. Notice how the application automatically updates the window. What you've got there is a real Macintosh update engine. With a few changes, it'll be ready to support multiple documents. In the next chapter, we'll talk about this update mechanism and create some real document windows that respond to all sorts of variations in size and location. In the process, we'll transform miniGeneric into multiGeneric, a multidocument application shell.

7

A SHELL THAT MANAGES MULTIPLE DOCUMENTS

In Chapter 6, we saw how our miniGeneric application—or any Macintosh application—uses events to detect user-initiated, real-world occurrences. The application parses events in its main event loop and passes control to the action routine appropriate for the event type contained in the *what* part of the *EventRecord.* Because good programming practice dictates putting related functions into modules, we began in miniGeneric to split our application into source code modules.

In this chapter, we'll develop a more complex application by giving miniGeneric the ability to control multiple document windows. To keep our projects straight, we'll call this chapter's project multiGeneric. For the most part, miniGeneric will change very little in its evolution into multiGeneric, although two of the modules—DocUtil.c and WindowUtil.c—will change dramatically. Most of the information we present in this chapter will result in a rewrite of an affected module or in additional functions within an existing module. This is one of the joys of modular programming around a generic base: You rarely have to make changes to all the existing code in the generic base; instead, most of your programming is limited to rewriting an existing module to change its features or capabilities or adding new functions to the existing modules.

That's the good news. As we get deeper into the subtleties of the Macintosh system software, we'll run into some bad news as well. For example, Apple didn't make handling multiple documents—and the memory management tasks associated with handling multiple documents—easy for first-timers, and it's only fair to warn you that there are some very technical passages in this chapter. We can't do much about that—windowing is a complex topic. Remember, though, that we're building a generic application base that you can reuse—you need to write this code only once. For subsequent applications, you can reuse the concepts and the windowing code that we'll work through here. That's what the "generic" principle is all about.

The multiGeneric Application

The origins of our ultimate Generic App are in miniGeneric. We organized the project into modules and then fleshed out those modules to perform the duties of a minimum application. The next step will be to add multiple-document management—hence, the name multiGeneric. A final step, one we'll take in the next chapter, will be to concentrate on how a document's contents require changes in the shell.

By the time you reach the end of this chapter, you'll have two Generic Apps: one with single-document window ability and one with multiple-document window ability. By the time you reach the end of the next chapter, you'll have three. Which application should you use as the universal application starting point? Both miniGeneric and the scrolling Generic we present in the next chapter are teaching tools. You're unlikely to use either as a base for future projects. The real, universal Generic is multiGeneric, the application shell we describe in this chapter as we unravel the mysteries of multiple documents and windows in a single application.

Source Code Control

The code for multiGeneric contains the same source modules that miniGeneric used. This new version of our generic application requires changes that affect windowing and document management, so we modify the files WindowUtil.c and DocUtil.c extensively. Other modules are changed more subtly, and some require no changes. Instead of isolating the code permutations that migrating from miniGeneric to multiGeneric would call for, we've opted for the purposes of this book to replace the project in its entirety. On the disk that accompanies this book, you'll find a folder containing all the source code modules for multiGeneric. If you have a utility like DocuComp (or the file comparison utility that ships with THINK C), you might want to run a comparison on the source code modules of miniGeneric and multiGeneric.

Although the three projects in the three chapters provide a vehicle for teaching the basics of Macintosh application building, we can also use the evolution of Generic to shed light on an important aspect of the development process: source code control. Before we get into the windowing mechanism, let's address this important topic.

If you've made your own enhancements to miniGeneric, you'll probably want them to be included in multiGeneric. How do you integrate the code for the two versions? Managing multiple versions of a product that uses the same set of source modules is a common programming task.

What the programming world needs is a good source code control system (SCCS), a set of utilities that manage the various versions of a file within a project. Such programs keep track of changes made to a source file, maintain the previous versions, and log when and where changes are made. We've used some of these programs in UNIX and VMS environments, and others are commercially available for microcomputer development platforms, including MPW. We've yet to see an SCCS that is easy to use and that meets more than merely basic needs.

Team development efforts cause most complications in source code management. More than one programmer might need to work on the same file at the same time, sometimes within the same function. Unless the SCCS is flexible enough to allow multiuser access, bottlenecks occur and productivity drops. We've yet to see an SCCS that doesn't limit productivity.

That is why source code is usually controlled without the use of a fancy SCCS. Common sense, organization, and working discipline are used to the same end. Keep an audit trail of what changes are made and by whom. Use a file comparison program to isolate changes in two source files during integration. Such simple techniques supply all the utility that's needed to manage the most complex job. After all, the human brain is the best source code control system available.

Source code control could serve as the topic for another complete book, so we won't spend much more time on it here. During the development of Tycho Table Maker, our three-person development group used the simple system for marking changes to the source code that we'll summarize shortly. We suggest that you adopt a similar strategy now, before you have thousands of lines of code to keep track of. Our method is not particularly elegant and doesn't represent the last word on management of source code changes, but it's a start. It kept us from making a few disastrous missteps along the way to commercial release of our product.

A System for Tracking Changes to Source Code

When you integrate changes into an existing project such as miniGeneric, your job is easier if you know where the changes are. The why and what of the change is often obvious from the change itself, especially if you're liberal with comments, but merely finding the change is sometimes a problem. The trick is to meticulously mark changes as you make them. Always. With no lapses. This is a rigorous undertaking requiring great discipline and a little more time, but it's well worth the effort.

Most commercial developers will recognize the technique we use, which looks something like this in practice:

```
/* ### kwgm 11.20.90--change made to fix bug in frammis loop */
#if 0
    /* old frammis loop here */
#else
    /* new, bug-free code here */
#endif
/* ### kwgm 11.20.90 */
```

We delimit the change with two comment strings. Use a string that makes the change easy to search for. We use a triple hash mark, ###, in the opening and closing comment strings. Choose a string that is not a commonly used code construct.

The opening change comment contains the date the change was made (and the time if you frequently find yourself in marathon programming sessions), the initials of the person making the change (important if you're working in a group), and a note of any length describing the change and the reason for it.

The entire change consists of these elements:

- The opening comment string
- An *#if 0* statement to remove the old code from the compilation stream
- The old code
- An *#else* statement at the end of the old code
- The new code
- An *#endif* statement to terminate the conditional compilation
- A balancing closing comment string to mark the end of the change

It's important to leave in the entire old code passage. This gives you something to return to if your change doesn't test out and also provides a reference for integration. Indeed, using the style we show here, you can easily substitute a variable in the *#if 0* statement, define it at the beginning of your program, and have your program compile using the old code. You need to be able to return to your old code, especially if you make a batch of changes at once. After you've tested the new code, you can delete the old code from the working file, but you should always keep a backup copy. Leaving the old code in the source file takes up room on your disk, but it doesn't add any size to your program if you follow our suggestions. The old code is ignored during compilation.

If you use this system, you can integrate changes from a working copy of a source file into your archive copy with the help of the search command in the editor. Here's the process:

1. Open both copies of the source file (the changed file and the archive file), find the change delimiter string (###) in the changed file, and select the old section of code, not including the *#if 0*. Then use Command-E to add the old code selection to the search string.
2. Next, select both the old block of code and the new block of code and copy it to the Clipboard by using Command-C. This block contains the opening comment string, the old code, the new code, and the closing comment string.
3. Now select the archive document, use Command-F to search for the original code block, and note that the entire block is selected.
4. Finally, use Command-V to paste the changed code into the archive file.

Every time you or someone else on your team adds new code to an existing source file—even so-called bug-fixing code—you increase the likelihood of installing more bugs in the program. That's right—fixing bugs often adds more bugs. And there will inevitably be times when you'll wish you had heeded the old adage, "If it ain't broke, don't fix it!" You'll want to rip out a new block of code, replace it with the old, and start again. It's for those times that you keep backups.

Disks are cheap. Take advantage of that. And buy a good backup program. Back up the entire project folder at the end of a development session, even if you've changed only a few lines. This might sound wasteful, but it's not. If a catastrophe should befall your primary version, you can be up and running with the old code in the time that it takes to restore the project folder.

This organized approach to tracking changes to the source code is actually a mindset you should adopt for all your development efforts. It's a "divide and conquer" point of view. A computer program rapidly grows into a complex piece of work. The trick to getting your mind around it all is to keep it divided into small, digestible pieces. If you understand the pieces and how they're put together, you'll be able to understand the whole.

Windows and Documents

Let's return to the matter at hand: multiGeneric. The task of managing multiple windows can quickly become overwhelmingly complex. Before you begin to pound out the C code, you need to consider how the application will keep track of its windows and their related data. This is a function of document organization. A document is an abstraction that encompasses the complete collection of data associated with a window, including the data's display and file information and the in-memory structures associated with processing the data. A document therefore encompasses more than merely the window's data.

The two words, window and document, are often used synonymously by developers when they refer to windows. This is a confusion of terms that arises from use of the desktop metaphor to describe the objects on the Macintosh screen. One of the on-screen objects is called a window and is described by a *WindowRecord* data structure. A window is manipulated by calls to the Macintosh Window Manager.

The definition of a multiGeneric *Doc* data structure, which we've excerpted from the file AppTypes.h, is shown in Figure 7-1:

```
typedef struct Doc
{
    WindowRecord    theWindow;    /* window data structure */

    /* document management */
    ushort  type,                 /* document type */
            attributes;           /* document attributes */
    short   index;                /* index of open window list */
```

Figure 7-1.
The Doc *data structure.*

(continued)

Figure 7-1. *continued*

```
    /* display management */
    Point   curScroll,          /* current scroll position */
            maxScroll,          /* maximum scroll position */
            docExtent;          /* size of contents */

    /* file linkage */
    short   volRefNum,          /* volume reference number of
                                   open file */
            openFileRefNum;     /* file reference number of
                                   open file */
    char    fileName [33];      /* file name */

    /* contents */
    Handle  contentHdl;         /* document data */

} Doc, *DocPtr;
```

Windows and documents have a one-to-one relationship in an application. You won't find one without the other. The *Doc* structure in Figure 7-1 contains five different kinds of information:

- The *WindowRecord* of the associated window.
- The document type and the document attribute flags that serve to classify a document. The purpose of this information will become evident when the document contains data.
- Display management information. The variables associated with display management contain data used to maintain the scrolled position of the document's contents.
- The associated file system data.
- A handle to the document's contents.

We deliberately chose a *WindowRecord* as the first element of the document so that we could pass the address of a document structure, a *DocPtr*, to the Window Manager routines this way:

```
DocPtr        theDoc;

SelectWindow  (theDoc);
```

Most of the Window Manager routines, such as *SelectWindow()*, require the address of a *WindowRecord*—that is, a *WindowPtr* argument. Because the *WindowRecord* is the first member of the *Doc* structure, a pointer to a *Doc* looks exactly like a pointer to a *WindowRecord*, at least for *sizeof WindowRecord* bytes, which are all the Window Manager routines are interested in.

This provides for a convenient syntactical shortcut, and, although it would make a strict Pascal programmer shudder, it is acceptable to pass a *DocPtr* to a system routine that expects a *WindowPtr* as an argument. This kind of organization eliminates the need to use a variant record mechanism, called a "union" in C, or having to explicitly cast a *DocPtr* to a *WindowPtr*. The pointer is already in the correct format. The alternative would be to pass the *WindowPtr* explicitly, this way:

```
DocPtr    theDoc;

SelectWindow (&(theDoc->theWindow));
```

Because the addresses are identical, however, there's no need for the computer to perform the extra address calculation.

Opening New Windows

A window and its document are created when a mouse-down is detected on the New command of the File menu. multiGeneric's flow of control passes from *doMenu()* to *doFileMenu()* to *createNewDoc()*, found in the file DocUtil.c. This flow of control is illustrated in Figure 7-2.

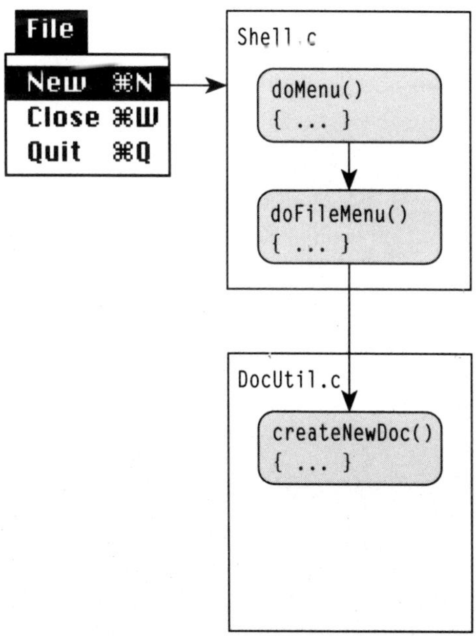

Figure 7-2.
Control flow for creation of a new document.

The routine *createNewDoc()* does the actual window and document linkage. It performs four basic tasks.

First, *createNewDoc()* calls the function *allocDoc()*, which allocates memory for the document structure. The document is created on the application heap as a nonrelocatable object. The decision to use a nonrelocatable block, one created with *NewPtr*, instead of a relocatable block created with *NewHandle*, was a tradeoff to simplify the relationship between documents and windows. All the Window Manager routines accept *WindowPtr* arguments. Because the *WindowRecord* is the first element of the *Doc* data structure, multiGeneric can pass the *DocPtr* to the Window Manager routines. You can see from the multiGeneric code on the disk that accompanies this book that this approach simplifies the code whenever multiGeneric calls a Window Manager routine.

The alternative would have been to create the *Doc* as a relocatable object. In that case, the program would have had to maintain a handle to a *Doc* structure (*DocHdl*) instead of using *DocPtr*. Then, whenever the program called a Window Manager routine that moved a block in memory, it would first need to lock the handle and dereference it to extract the *DocPtr*:

```
DocHandle        theDoc;
⋮
/* make a window manager call */
HLock (theDoc);
SelectWindow (*theDoc);
HUnlock (theDoc);
```

Opening the document is inhibited if memory cannot be allocated for the document or if the number of open windows exceeds a predefined maximum.

After memory for the document structure has been allocated, *createNewDoc()* calculates the new window rectangle so that the new window will be staggered over the existing top window, with an offset. The algorithm is something like this: If there's a top document and if that document is one created by multiGeneric, use that document's window rectangle as a starting point for the new document's window rectangle. Otherwise, use the default rectangle for the new document's window rectangle. Figure 7-3 demonstrates how multiGeneric gets the new rectangle.

After multiGeneric creates the window rectangle for the new document, it is free to create the window itself with *NewWindow*, passing it the *DocPtr* that was allocated at the beginning of the function. multiGeneric uses the *documentProc + 8* window type, a standard document window with a zoom box.

After the window is created, *createNewDoc()* adds the scroll bars. The scroll bars are not automatically a part of the window but are controls you must add explicitly with *NewControl*. The windows for multiGeneric have the usual two scroll bars: a vertical scroll bar and a horizontal scroll bar. To keep track of which is which, we tag them with the tokens *kVScrollTag* and *kHScrollTag*, which we attach to the Control Record's *refCon* field.

Finally, *createNewDoc()* titles the window, initializes the document data structures for the document, adds the document to the open document list, and makes the window visible and active.

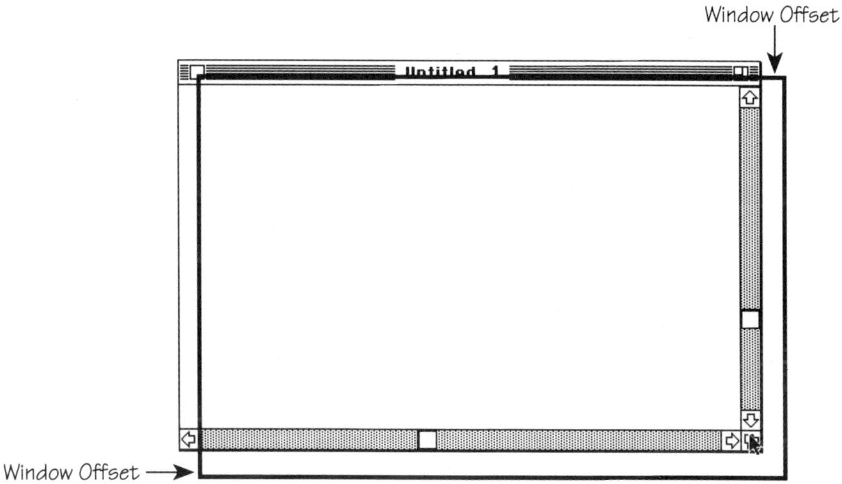

Figure 7-3.
Creating the new document's window rectangle.

Window Types and Their Origins

The Macintosh Window Manager contains a default window definition procedure (WDEF) that's responsible for several tasks, including drawing a window. WDEF supports six standard windows and a few variations on those standard themes. The fifth argument to *NewWindow* controls what kind of window is drawn. The six basic window types and the name of the constant that represents each one are shown below. The constants are included with the development system in the file WindowMgr.h.

Macintosh window types.

multiGeneric uses two global variables to keep track of the number of open documents. The variables are initialized in ApplInit.c and managed in DocUtil.c. multiGeneric uses the global variable *gNumOpenDocs* to keep track of the total number of open documents in the application at any one time. The variable's value is incremented in *createNewDoc()* every time a document is opened, and its value is decremented in *doCloseDoc()* each time one is closed.

multiGeneric uses the other variable, *gNextWindow*, to automatically name successive new documents with consecutive values (Untitled1, Untitled2, Untitled3, and so on). When all documents have been closed, *gNextWindow* is reset to *1* in *createNewDoc()*.

refCon Fields

The *refCon* fields in various Toolbox data structures, such as the *WindowRecord*, *ControlRecord*, and *ListRec* structures, are for programmer use. The fields are defined as *long*, but, because a *long* is the same size as a pointer or a handle, you can store a reference to any size data object you want. Apple engineers put the *refCon* field into the Toolbox structures so that programmers could attach related data to the structures. multiGeneric stores a token in the *ControlRecord refCon*, *contrlrfCon*, by passing the values as the last argument to *NewControl*.

The Open Document Table

The multiGeneric application uses the "open document table" to keep track of all documents that are opened in the application. multiGeneric uses the open document table to cycle through the documents, as it does in the close all documents operation, or to activate a document when the name of that document is selected from the Window menu.

The Window menu gives your user an alternate way to choose which window will be the active window, and therefore which document will be worked in. This feature is handy when the window the user wants is completely covered by other windows. The Window menu also supports Command-key equivalents for the first nine open documents.

The source file WindowTbl.c contains the routines that manage the open document table and the menu. In fact, the table and the menu are closely related.

The table itself is contained in the static variable *sDocTblHdl*, a handle to a structure of type *DocTbl*. This document table consists of an array of *DocInfo* structures and a count of the elements in the array. Each open document is represented by an element in the array. The *DocInfo* data structure contains the document pointer, the document's menu item number, and the document's Command-key equivalent, if any, called the "slot number."

Finding Global Symbols in a THINK C Project

The THINK C programming environment has a nice feature that we use all the time. If you double-click on a global variable in a source file, the environment will open the source file in which the variable is declared and move the text cursor to the first instance of the variable in the file. In multiGeneric, the file Shell.c, in which *main()* is defined, will be opened if you double-click on a global variable name anywhere in the project sources. This is because we include the file AppGlobals.h, in which the project globals are defined, at the top of Shell.c.

This feature also works with nonstatic function names. If you double-click on a function call, THINK C will open the source file in which the function is defined and find the first instance of the symbol. This is useful when you are following a new program's flow of control.

Adding to the Open Document Table

When the application successfully creates a new document, *createNewWindow()* calls the function *addToDocTbl()*, which is in WindowTbl.c. The *addToDocTbl()* function first assigns a Command-key equivalent to the document, if one is available. A bitmap of which Command-key slots have been used is maintained in the static integer *sSlotBitmap*. multiGeneric uses the least-significant 9 bits of this *short* integer to hold the slot information. If a bit is set, the slot it corresponds to is taken.

For example, if the 1, 4, 5, 6, and 7 keys are being used in combination with the Command key, the value of *sSlotBitmap* is *0x0079*, or *0000 0000 0111 1001* in binary. Figure 7-4 illustrates this value. The algorithm in *addToDocTbl()* searches for the next available slot in *sSlotBitmap* and assigns it to the new document.

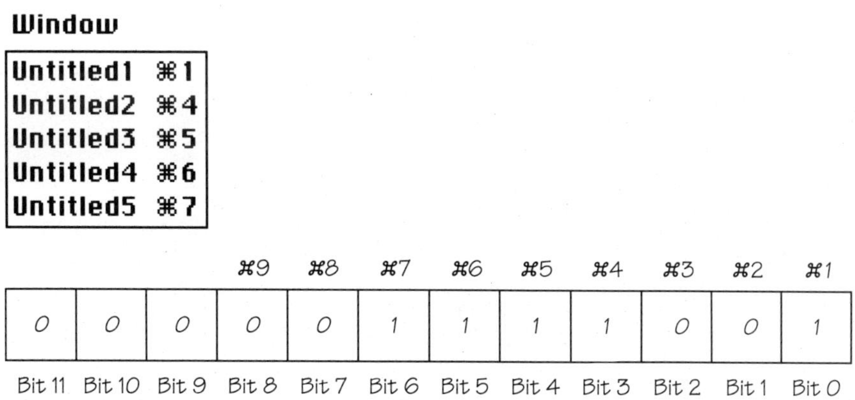

Figure 7-4.
Keys 1, 4, 5, 6, and 7 are being used in combination with the Command key. The value of sSlotBitmap *is* 0x0079.

After it assigns a Command-key equivalent to the document, *addToDocTbl()* calls *buildMenuItemStr()* to create the menu string from the window's title and the document's slot number.

Note the special processing of the file name in *buildMenuItemStr()* to avoid adding any of the Menu Manager's special token characters to the menu item string. If the character ^ were in the string, for example, the Menu Manager would interpret the next character as an ICON resource number, which would not be included as part of the menu item string. A complete list of the special Menu Manager tokens is found in *Inside Macintosh*, Volume I. The *buildMenuItemStr()* function filters out any of these special characters and substitutes the empty character.

After the menu string has been built, *addToDocTbl()* calls *InsMenuItem* to add the string to the bottom of the Window menu. The new menu item is then explicitly enabled with *EnableItem*. Explicit enabling might not always be necessary, but we've discovered that a new item is not always created in the enabled state, so we recommend that you always take this extra step.

The next step is to add the new *DocInfo* record to the document table. To conserve space in RAM, the program makes the size of the document table only large enough to hold the number of entries. For example, if three documents are open, the table consists of a count plus three *DocInfo* records. The count is a *short* integer, and a *DocInfo* record consists of 8 bytes, so the entire table is 2 + (3 * 8) bytes, or 26 bytes. If another document is opened, the table needs to be 34 bytes to accommodate the new record.

The *addToDocTbl()* function expands the table by the size of a *DocInfo* record before it assigns the new *DocInfo* data to the table. Because the table is stored in a relocatable block, *addToDocTbl()* uses the Memory Manager routine *SetHandleSize* to resize the table. This is informally known as "growing the handle." Growing the handle doesn't change the handle; it simply allocates more memory to the structure that the handle refers to. This process is illustrated in Figure 7-5.

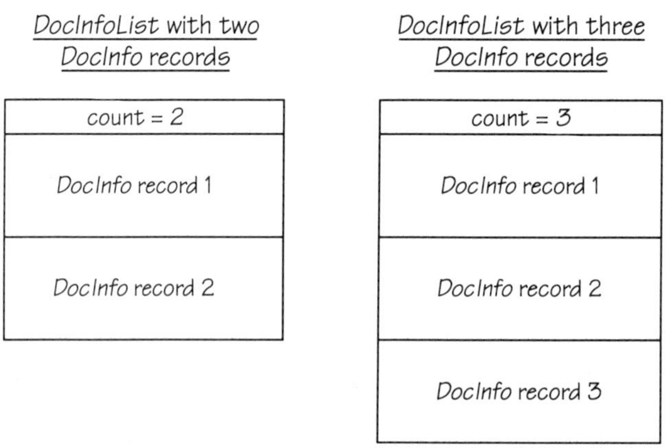

Figure 7-5.
Growth of the DocInfoList *table structure.*

After the table has been expanded, the new *DocInfo* record is initialized with its slot number, *DocPtr*, and the menu item number of the document.

The *DocInfo* record and the document are doubly linked with data: The *DocInfo* record contains the *DocPtr*, and the *Doc* structure contains the array index number of the *DocInfo* record. This double link is necessary so that multiGeneric can get to the data starting with either structure. For example, when the document is chosen from the Window menu, the *DocPtr* (*WindowPtr*) is extracted from the *DocInfo* structure and passed to *SelectWindow*. The code for this approach to the data is in the function *doWindowMenu()*, found in WindowTbl.c. And when the window is closed, as we'll see in a moment, multiGeneric needs to delete the *DocInfo* structure from the document list and therefore needs to know where the *DocInfo* structure is in the array. The *index* member of the *Doc* structure contains the window's index into the open document table.

Deleting from the Open Document Table

To delete a document from the open document table, you reverse the addition procedure. The multiGeneric application calls *removeFromDocList()* with the *DocPtr* when a document is closed. The *removeFromDocList()* function accesses the corresponding open document table entry by using the index value stored in the document. The *removeFromDocList()* function removes the menu item for the document from the Window menu by using *DelMenuItem* and clears the document's slot bit in *sSlotBitmap*, if applicable.

The last step is to remove the *DocInfo* data from the open document table. Remember that this table is stored as a contiguous array, and, if you remove an array element, you need to compact the array to remove any gaps in the table. The only array elements that have to be moved during compaction are the ones with index numbers greater than the index number of the deleted document. Figure 7-6 on the next page illustrates the process. The *removeFromDocList()* function uses *BlockMove* to compact the array.

Deletion of a menu item and its *DocInfo* record causes some data misalignment. Each *DocInfo* record contains a menu item number for a corresponding menu item. When *removeFromDocList* deletes a menu item, the menu item values of some of the *DocInfo* records—the ones with index numbers greater than the index number of the deleted record—must be decreased by one. Likewise, because *removeFromDocList()* removes an array element, the index numbers stored in documents that refer to elements of the *DocInfo* array above the deleted element also need to be decremented. The *removeFromDocList()* function performs this fix in its *for* loop.

Closing Windows

We've talked of closing open documents, but we haven't looked in detail at how to close an open window. Closing a window consists of disposing of all data associated with the document and deleting the window data structure. The *doCloseDoc()* function, found in DocUtil.c, manages this operation.

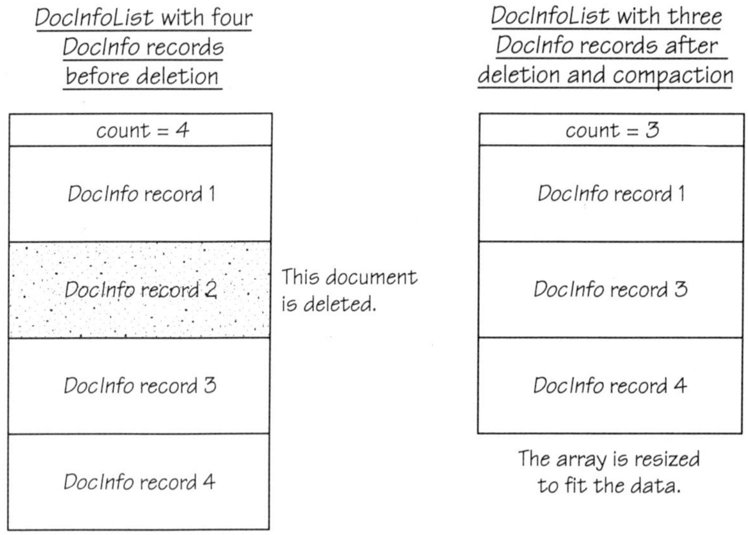

Figure 7-6.
Compacting the document table. When the user closes the document associated with DocInfo *record 2,* removeFromDocList() *moves records 3 and 4 and resizes the relocatable block down to the new table size. Note that record 1 does not have to be moved.*

The *doCloseDoc()* function first checks the validity of the document pointer. Although the document pointer wouldn't ordinarily be null, it could be if the open document list had become corrupted. Some might argue that this sort of defensive programming slows an application down, but that's a price well paid for ensuring that your user will avoid the bomb alert box.

Closing the window is a matter of disposing of the window's scroll bars with *DisposeControl*, closing the window with *CloseWindow*, disposing of the *Doc* structure with *DisposPtr*, and updating the multiGeneric internal window management variables and the open document table.

Screen Management with Multiple Windows

The main advantage of multiGeneric over miniGeneric is that multiGeneric manages multiple windows. Having more than one window on the screen at a time creates interesting demands on your application. It must provide for the user's selecting an active window—the one in which he or she is currently working. And it must redraw the screen when the user selects a new window or moves the windows around on the desktop. Depending on the positions of the windows before and after the update, usually only certain parts of the screen will need to be redrawn. Figure 7-7 illustrates these two aspects of multiple window management.

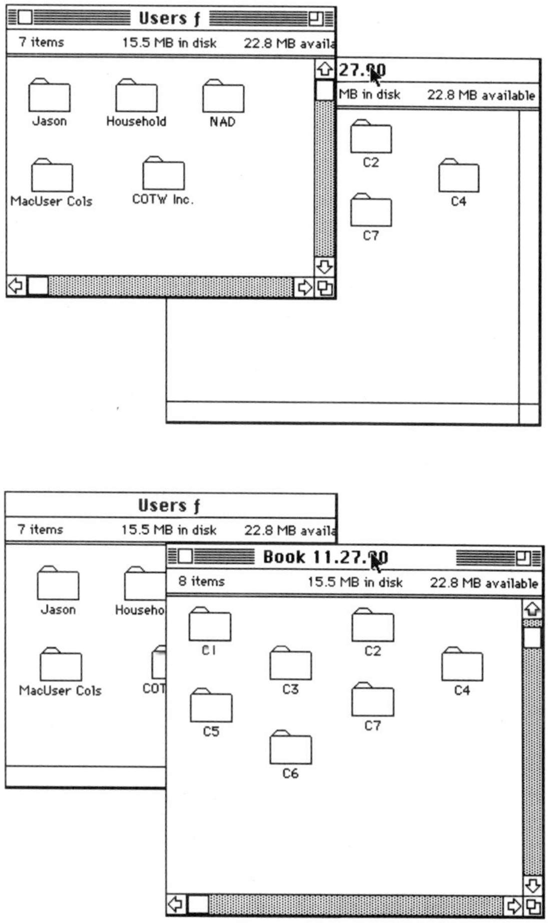

Figure 7-7. *Selecting a new active window and redrawing the screen. Users f is the active window. The user clicks in the title bar of the other window, making the second window active and Users f inactive.*

Activating a Window

When an application has multiple windows open, the user has a choice of windows to work in but is limited to working in only one window at a time—the "active" window. The user indicates which window is active by pointing and clicking or by selecting the window from the Window menu.

The active window is visually distinct from the other windows on the screen. The title bar, title controls, scroll bars, and other controls are highlighted. The activation routine is responsible for maintaining this visual difference from the other windows on the screen.

A window is activated in response to the user's selecting a new active window. The user's selection generates two events: an activate event and a deactivate event. The activate event is targeted at the new active window, and the deactivate event is targeted at the old active window.

The behavior of controls in a window must conform to the Macintosh user interface guidelines on the appearance of activated and deactivated controls. Figure 7-8 shows activated and deactivated scroll bars.

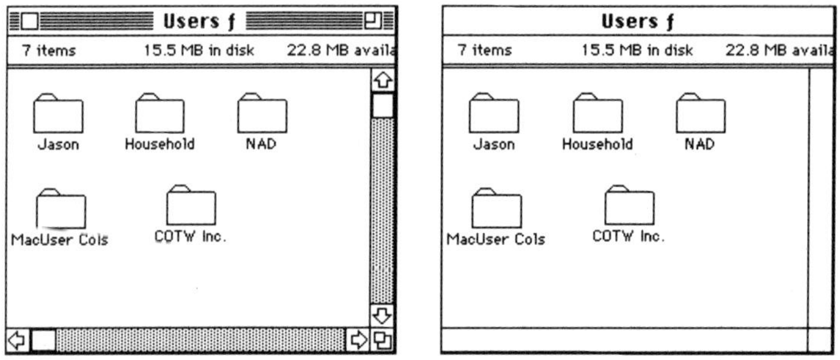

Figure 7-8. *Active and inactive scroll bars. When an inactive window is activated, the areas that should be shaded need to be redrawn.*

The user selects the new active window with a mouse-down somewhere in the window. The event-parsing mechanism passes the mouse-down event data to *doMouseDown()*, the multiGeneric routine that processes mouse-down events.

When *doMouseDown()* is called by the event data, it in turn calls *SelectWindow*, the Window Manager routine that posts the appropriate activate and deactivate events for both the new and the old active windows.

Calling *SelectWindow* causes the Window Manager to redraw the new active window's title bar. As a result, the new active window's title area is highlighted—that is, the title bar is redrawn with distinctive stripes, and the close box and the zoom box appear. Figure 7-9 illustrates the effect of calling *SelectWindow*.

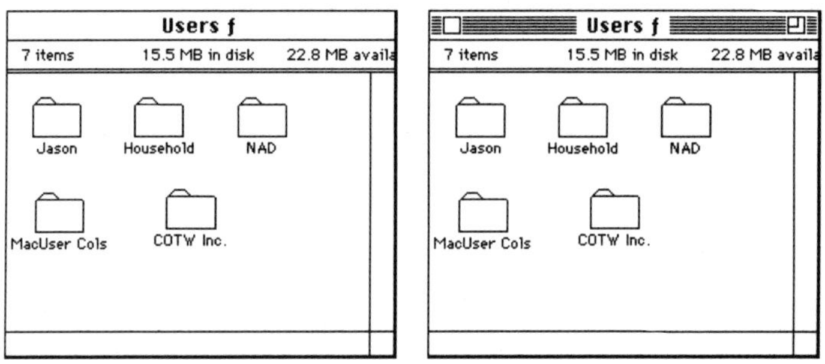

Figure 7-9. *The visual effect of calling* SelectWindow, *showing an inactive window and an active window with the close box and the zoom box.*

SelectWindow changes the Macintosh's current grafPort to the one associated with the new active window. As Chapter 4's discussion pointed out, all *QuickDraw* calls are performed in the current grafPort.

Calling *SelectWindow* also posts two events to the event queue: the deactivate event for the old active window and the activate event for the new active window. The application will process these events in the main event loop.

When the main event loop detects an activate event or a deactivate event, it calls the *doActivateEvent()* routine—found in Shell.c—by using a pointer to the *EventRecord.* Actually, both activate and deactivate events come with the same token in the *EventRecord*'s *what* field: *activateEvt.* The *doActivateEvent()* function processes both activate and deactivate events, distinguishing between the two kinds of events by testing a bit in the *modifiers* field of the *EventRecord* to determine whether the window is to be activated or deactivated:

```
doActivateEvent (EventRecord    *e)
{
if (e->modifiers & activeFlag)
    /* do activate stuff */
else
    /* do deactivate stuff */
```

The *doActivateEvent()* function is responsible for maintaining the appearance of the window's scroll bars. The Window Manager maintains a linked list of all controls associated with each window. A handle to the head of the Window Manager's list is in the *controlList* field of the *WindowRecord.* The *doActivateEvent* function traverses the list, calling the Control Manager routines *ShowControl* and *HideControl* as appropriate:

```
ControlHandle    controlHdl;

controlHdl = ((WindowPeek)theWindow)->controlList;
while (controlHdl)
{
    if (e->modifiers & activeFlag)
        ShowControl (controlHdl);
    else
        HideControl (controlHdl);

    controlHdl = (*controlList)->nextControl;
}
```

Calling *ShowControl* or *HideControl* alone doesn't show or hide a window's scroll bars. The scroll bars not only need to be activated or deactivated, but they also need to be redrawn in the highlighted or unhighlighted state. The multiGeneric application uses a routine called *invalScrollBars()* to "invalidate" the scroll bars so that they'll be redrawn during the next update event. We'll discuss invalidation at length a little later in this chapter.

If you look at the complete source code for *doActivateEvent()* on the disk that accompanies this book, you'll notice that the routine calls *HidePen* before doing anything visual like calling *ShowControl. HidePen* is a QuickDraw routine that inhibits all drawing. The *doActivateEvent()* function calls *HidePen* to ensure that drawing occurs only inside an update event, eliminating the chance that the scroll bars will be drawn twice.

Without *HidePen*, the calls to *ShowControl* and *HideControl* would cause an immediate redrawing of the scroll bars. If the controls were then to be completely redrawn during the next update event, they would be drawn twice, causing an effect that is aesthetically unpleasing and computationally inefficient. In a Macintosh program, you put off all drawing for as long as possible. This rule of thumb we call the *mañana* principle.

Note that the call to *HidePen* is balanced with a call to *ShowPen* at the end of the routine. Without the balancing *ShowPen* call, nothing further would appear on the screen.

We've mentioned invalidation, update events, and the *mañana* principle. Now it's time to examine how, when, and why the window contents are drawn. In the next section, you'll see how the processing of update events, in which redrawing is localized, is handled. But first, you'll need to know about window regions.

Window Regions

A "region" is a QuickDraw data structure that describes any arbitrary shape, although for our purposes a region is usually rectangular or made up of rectangular components. Regions are important in the discussion of windows because of their relationship to window update events.

A window formally has three regions:

- The "structure region" contains the title bar, which contains the close box and the zoom box; and the window frame, which is the black rectangle that outlines the window. The Window Manager draws these elements automatically when your program calls *SelectWindow*. Generally, you can ignore what happens in the structure region.
- The "content region" is where the application draws—below the title bar and inside the frame. The scroll bars are included in the content region, making it the application's responsibility to draw them.
- The "update region" is a dynamically changing subregion of the content region. It contains all the accumulated window area that needs to be redrawn. Figure 7-10 shows the structure region and the content region.

Drawing and the Update Process

The multiGeneric application is structured so that drawing in a window is limited to the window's update region. Area is added to or subtracted from the update region in one of two ways: Window Manager routines automatically add window space to the region (to the area under a top window that has just been closed, for instance); or other system routines allow the application to add area to or subtract area from the update region. Figure 7-11 shows the update region left behind by a recently closed About box.

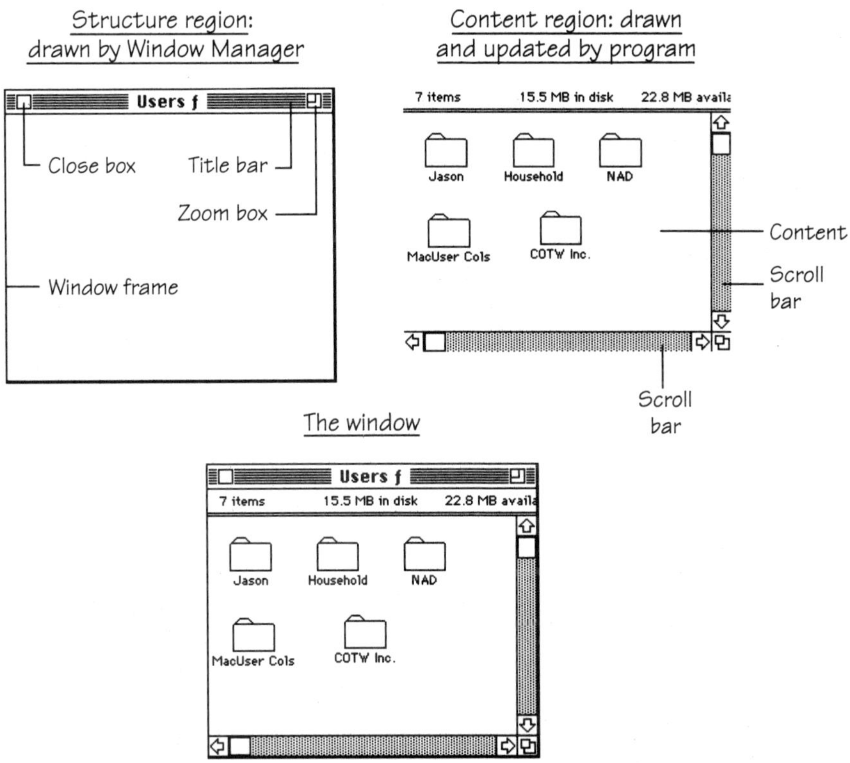

Figure 7-10.
Window regions include the structure region and the content region, which make up the window.

Figure 7-11.
The update region left by a closed About box.

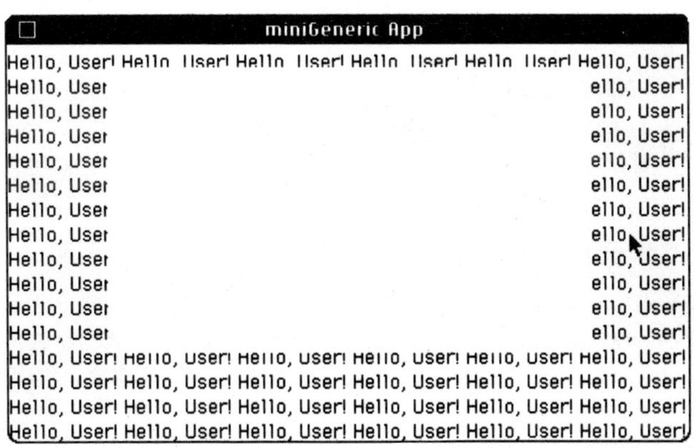

The application's need to redraw some of the screen is determined by the status of the update region. When this region is nonempty in one or more of an application's windows, the Window Manager posts an update event for the application.

When multiGeneric detects an update event in the main event loop, it calls the routine *doUpdateEvent()*, found in Shell.c, which causes drawing in the necessary parts of the window.

When the main event loop receives the update event, it passes the *EventRecord* received from *WaitNextEvent* by reference to *doUpdateEvent()*. The *EventRecord* contains all data necessary to respond to the update event.

An update event is specific to a window. The application might receive an update event for each open window that has a nonempty update region. The Window Manager passes a pointer to the window of interest in the *message* field of the *EventRecord*.

If a Desk Accessory is open in front of the application, the application gets the update event for the DA. This is important: Your application is responsible for passing the update event on to the DA. The application must therefore determine whether the event is targeted at one of its windows or at the DA.

To this end, an application checks the *windowKind* field of the *WindowRecord* to determine whether the event is for one of the application's windows. If the value in this field is greater than or equal to *1*, the window is an application window and the event should be handled by the application. If the value of the *windowKind* field is less than *0*, the window is a Desk Accessory window and updates should be handled by the DA.

After *doUpdateEvent()* determines that the event is for one of the application's windows, the routine saves the old grafPort and then sets the current port to the one associated with this window. This step is necessary because an update event can be generated for an inactive window. Remember, all drawing occurs in the current grafPort.

The heart of the update process begins with a call to *BeginUpdate*. *BeginUpdate* takes advantage of the fact that QuickDraw, which is responsible for rendering everything on the screen, limits its drawing to the visible region of the current grafPort. *BeginUpdate* changes the visible region of the window's grafPort to match that of the update region of the window. Thus, when the application draws, its drawing is limited to the update region.

Before drawing the window contents, *doUpdateEvent()* erases the window's update region, by means of the grafPort's visible region, to clear any extraneous screen elements that might be in the region.

Finally, *doUpdateEvent()* makes the calls that draw the window's scroll bars and contents. When drawing is complete, the call to *EndUpdate* restores the port's *visRgn* and clears the window's update region. Figure 7-12 illustrates the entire update process.

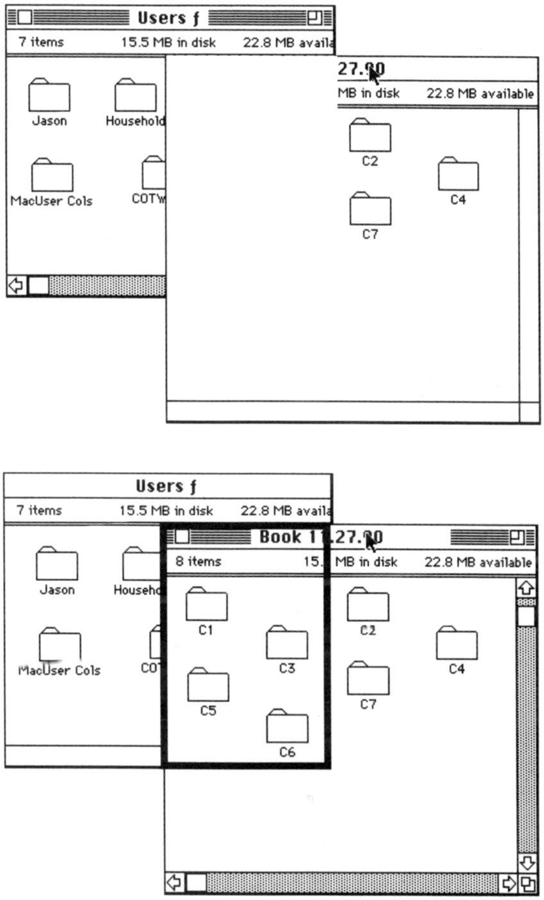

Figure 7-12. *The Macintosh update process. An update event is posted for the new front window. The update routine calls* BeginUpdate *and erases the update region. The update routine then draws the new update region, shown in the heavy-bordered rectangle.*

As we've mentioned before and will mention again because it's so important, all drawing is done inside this update routine. Limiting drawing to the confines of an update routine ensures that only the window's update region is redrawn and that double drawing doesn't occur.

By now you should understand that you shouldn't redraw parts of the screen as soon as they need it. And you've seen that the update region is where you keep track of the areas of the screen that need to be redrawn. But you've not yet seen how to add areas to a window's update region by means of the invalidation process.

Invalidation and the *Mañana* Principle

In Macspeak, an invalid area of a window is a region that needs updating or refreshing. Conversely, a valid area of the screen doesn't require a redraw. Regions of the screen destined for redrawing are invalidated by the application, making them eligible for drawing during the next update event. Invalidation of a region can be done anytime, but drawing is always deferred until an update event.

This is the fundamental canon of the *mañana* principle of Macintosh screen management: Whenever possible, put off drawing until the update process.

The Window Manager supports two pairs of routines that validate or invalidate an area of a particular window. *ValidRect()* and *ValidRgn()* both subtract area from a window's update region—that is, they validate an area; *InvalRect()* and *InvalRgn()* add area to the update region and are therefore used for invalidation. Use *ValidRect()* and *InvalRect()* when your bounding area is rectangular; use *ValidRgn()* and *InvalRgn()* when your area is more complex or when you already have a *RgnHandle* to the area.

The *mañana* principle has implications for the way in which you design an application. If you're writing a graphics program, for example, you'll need to know the bounding rectangle or region of your on-screen objects in order to invalidate them when they need to be redrawn. Figure 7-13 demonstrates the principle of invalidating an object's bounding box, or extent. Three shapes—a circle, a diamond, and a triangle—appear in a drawing program's window. If the user moves the triangle shape, both the old and the new triangle bounding boxes need to be invalidated. The old extent needs invalidation so that the area will be clear of the object and so that any object that was underneath the triangle will be redrawn. The new extent needs invalidation so that the object can be redrawn at its new location.

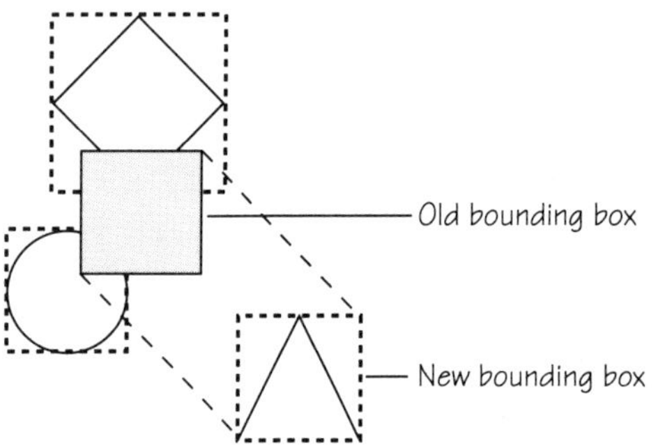

Figure 7-13.
A screen object needs a bounding box so that it can be invalidated. Bounding boxes, shown here as heavy dashed lines, are not visible on the screen. When the user drags the triangle to a new location, the program invalidates the old bounding box for the triangle and draws the new bounding box for the triangle.

Using the *mañana* principle to postpone drawing improves the look and the performance of your application because all drawing is done at the same time. Commercial applications take this one step further and draw to an off-screen grafPort. Then the entire contents of the grafPort, bounded by the update region, are blasted to the current screen. This buffering of the drawing gives the user the impression that the application is faster than it really is because all the window contents show up at the same time. This speedup is actually an optical illusion: The process is slower than it would be if the window were redrawn directly, because of the overhead involved in managing the off-screen port and transferring the screen contents to the on-screen window.

You don't need to adhere to the *mañana* principle strictly. You can make an exception, for example, when a user holds the mouse button down in a scroll bar (a topic we'll cover in the next chapter). But, in general, when you limit drawing to the update routine, you give your application that slickness that is the hallmark of Macintosh applications.

Supporting the Standard Window Manipulations

Window activation and invalidation are important features of any Macintosh application. But because multiGeneric is a multiple-window application shell, it needs to support the other window operations that are typically found in a Macintosh application. And we've added a couple of nonstandard features that will allow any application created with multiGeneric to stand out in a crowd.

The standard window manipulations—resize, zoom, and drag—are the results of mouse-down events. When multiGeneric detects a mouse-down event in its main event loop, it passes control to the *doMouseDown()* function, which determines where the event occurred and acts accordingly.

The routine does this by translating the *where* coordinate value returned in the *EventRecord* into a token representing the zone in which the mouse click occurred. The mapping of the zone is achieved with a call to the Window Manager routine *FindWindow*, which returns the token. The tokens, described in Figure 7-14, are defined in the THINK C #include file Windows.h.

inDesk	Returned when mouse is on desktop
inMenuBar	Returned when mouse is in menu bar
inSysWindow	Returned when mouse is in DA
inContent	Returned when mouse is in content region of window
inDrag	Returned when mouse is in structure region of window
inGrow	Returned when mouse is in size box
inZoomIn	Returned when mouse is in zoom box
inZoomOut	Returned when mouse is in zoom box
inGoAway	Returned when mouse is in close box

Figure 7-14.
Result codes returned by FindWindow.

multiGeneric's mouse-down parsing function, *doMouseDown()*, switches control according to the location of the mouse-down event returned by the call to *FindWindow*:

***FindWindow* returned *inMenubar*.** The mouse-down was in the menu bar. The *doMouseDown()* function calls *doMenu()*, in MenuUtil.c, which parses the menu selection.

***FindWindow* returned *inSysWindow*.** The mouse-down was in a DA window. The *doMouseDown()* function calls *SystemClick*, which passes events to the DA. No further processing is necessary.

***FindWindow* returned *inContent*.** The mouse-down was in the content region of a window. When the mouse is in the content region, the application first needs to detect whether the window is already the current window. The test compares the value of the window pointer returned by *WaitNextEvent* with that returned by *FrontWindow*—a pointer to the current window. If the window is not the current window—that is, if the pointers don't match—the window is activated with *SelectWindow*. If it is the current window, other processing might be necessary, depending on your application. We've included the function *doInContent()* to demonstrate where to direct this kind of processing.

***FindWindow* returned *inDrag*.** The mouse-down was in the window's title area but not in the close box or the zoom box. multiGeneric reacts to this occurrence in one of two ways. If the user double-clicked in the drag area, multiGeneric calls *clickZoomWindow()*, which zooms or unzooms the window. (This feature is common to both Microsoft Word and our own Tycho Table Maker.) Otherwise, the document is selected with *SelectWindow* and the mouse position is tracked for dragging with *DragWindow*.

***FindWindow* returned *inGrow*.** The mouse-down was in the size box, which appears in the lower right corner of the window. multiGeneric calls *doGrowWindow()* to track the resize process.

***FindWindow* returned *inZoomIn* or *inZoomOut*.** The mouse-down was in the zoom box. The application zooms or unzooms the window as appropriate.

***FindWindow* returned *inGoAway*.** The mouse-down was in the close box of the window. The application closes the current window. If, however, the user has pressed the Option key while clicking in the close box, the application closes all of the documents that are currently open.

As you can see by this list, the range of standard window manipulations is actually quite extensive. Once *doMouseDown()* determines the zone in which a click occurred, control is switched to a supporting routine that carries out the action. Now we'll take a look in detail at how the actions are implemented in code.

Resizing a Window

From a user's perspective, the window resizes when he or she presses the mouse button in the size box—in the lower right corner of a sizeable document window—and drags a gray outline of the window to a new size. When the user releases the mouse button, the window reappears in the new size. The window's contents shift accordingly.

Resizing the window is a two-part process: The first part is tracking the user's mouse movements and sketching the gray outline of the window border in response to the mouse movements; the second part is redisplaying the window and its contents.

The Window Manager routine *GrowWindow* performs all the tracking and sketching and, when the user releases the mouse button, returns a result that becomes the input of the Window Manager routine *SizeWindow*. *SizeWindow* changes the actual *WindowRecord* data structures to fit the new size information.

In multiGeneric, the mouse-down event is directed to the routine *doGrowWindow()* in WindowUtil.c, which manages the resize procedure. The *doGrowWindow()* function first invalidates the old scroll bar areas so that they will be erased and redrawn when the document is updated. The function then creates a bounding rectangle that limits the window to a minimum size of 48 by 48 pixels because the scroll bars start to look quite silly when the window gets smaller than that. (Without limits, windows can disappear on the desktop.)

The *doGrowWindow()* function then calls *GrowWindow* and *SizeWindow* for the resizing. After the window is resized, *doGrowWindow()* relocates the scroll bars to the right and bottom corners of the window by calling *moveScrollBars()* and then re-invalidates the scroll bars at this new location so that they'll be redrawn in the update process.

Zooming a Window

Zooming a window is much like resizing a window. The Window Manager routine *ZoomWindow* makes the actual change in window size. It's up to the application to adjust the window contents accordingly.

When multiGeneric detects a mouse-down in the zoom box, it calls *doZoomBox()* in WindowUtil.c. *doZoomBox()* calls *ZoomWindow* and then relocates the scroll bars by calling *moveScrollBars()*. Finally, this routine invalidates the entire window so that it will be redrawn in the update process.

In addition to zooming when a mouse-down is in the zoom box, multiGeneric also zooms the window when there is a double-click in the window's title area. This action is performed by the function *clickZoomWindow()*, also found in WindowUtil.c.

An examination of *clickZoomWindow()* reveals that the window structure contains a handle to a data structure of type *WStateData*. The *WStateData* data structure contains the two rectangles that the window will zoom or unzoom to. *clickZoomWindow()* compares the *userState* rectangle of this structure to the port rectangle of the window's grafPort and calls *doZoomBox()* to do the window zooming based on the comparison of these two rectangles. If the *userState* rectangle equals the port rectangle, the window is zoomed; otherwise, the window is unzoomed.

Dragging a Window

Dragging a window—that is, dragging a gray outline representing a window—is also controlled by a Window Manager routine. One call, to *DragWindow*, does it all. In fact, *DragWindow* is so simple to use that it is called right in *doMouseDown()*, without the need for an intermediate function. multiGeneric's organization puts all Window Manager–related utilities in WindowUtil.c, but the drag process is so simple that we felt it a waste of time to call *DragWindow* in an intermediate function.

DragWindow does all sketching (responding to movements of the user's mouse) and then moves the window to the location the user specifies. Because the dimensions of the window never change in this operation, we don't need to change the scroll bar locations in the window or to invalidate the contents of the window. Invalidation of the background is handled by the Window Manager.

The third argument to *DragWindow* is a constraint rectangle that limits the drag area. multiGeneric limits the drag area to the *gGrayRgnRect*, which is initialized in AppInit.c. The gray region is the combined area of all video devices attached to your Mac. If you use multiple monitors, the gray region encompasses all screens. If the gray region is the limit rectangle, the window can be dragged even across monitors.

What's Ahead

You'll find the code for multiGeneric on the source disk that accompanies this book. If you use multiGeneric as a basis for your applications and if you add more functionality to the shell, remember to comment any modifications to the source code with a search string as we recommended earlier in this chapter. In the chapters up ahead, we'll add to multiGeneric, hooking up the scroll bars in the next chapter and hooking Generic App into the file system in the last chapters, turning this shell into a bona fide application.

8

SCROLLING WINDOWS

Whether your application displays text or graphics, its document data will soon outgrow the window bounds, and you're going to have to confront the scrolling issue, as a colleague of ours did. He called to ask what Toolbox routine he could use to add scroll bars to his application's window. His assumption was that once the window had scroll bars, scrolling followed. If only it were that simple.

Scrolling a Macintosh document is truly a black art. The way a Macintosh document scrolls depends on the document contents. Text documents scroll a line at a time. Figure 8-1 illustrates this kind of scrolling.

Figure 8-1.
A Microsoft Word document scrolls one line at a time.

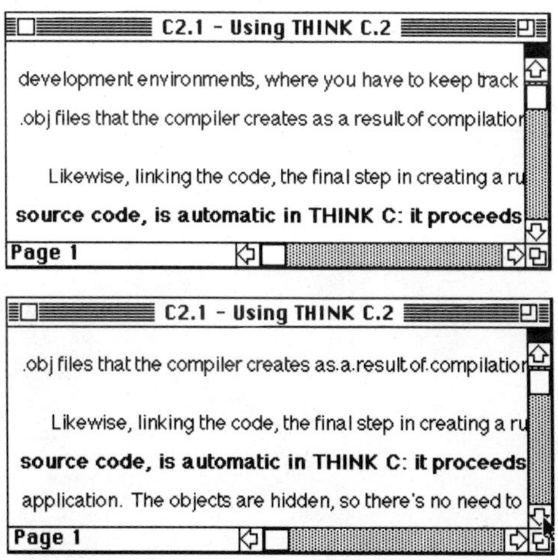

Graphical documents scroll an arbitrary number of pixels at a time, as in the floor plan shown in Figure 8-2 at the top of the next page.

Figure 8-2.
A graphical document scrolls n *(some arbitrary number of) pixels at a time.*

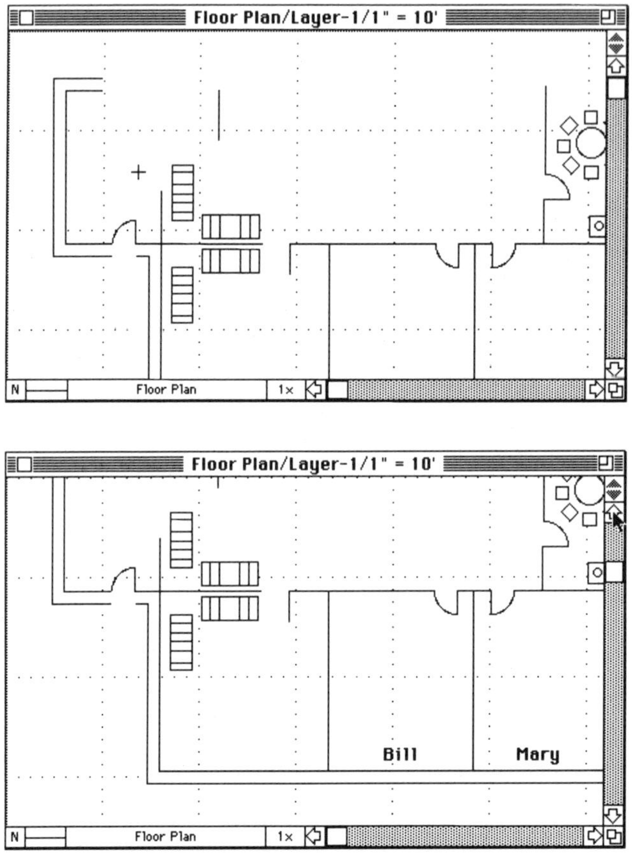

Another application, Kurt and Thom's Tycho Table Maker, for instance, might scroll one row of cells at a time, as in Figure 8-3.

Figure 8-3.
Tycho Table Maker scrolls one row of cells at a time.

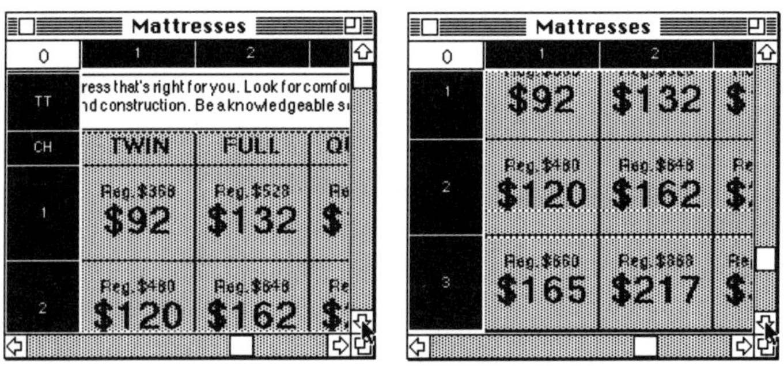

Hybrid documents made up of text and graphics—like spreadsheets or table editors—scroll based on either the text or the graphical model. Some programs—Microsoft Word is one—change their scrolling strategy mid-document when graphics or tables are encountered in the midst of text.

In this chapter, we'll develop a scrolling technique that works with both text and graphical documents. We'll modify multiGeneric into nonGeneric, an application that puts up either a text window or a graphical window, and then we'll add the scroll bars and scrolling routines to it. Again, we'll make most of our modifications to DocUtil.c and WindowUtil.c, and we'll mark the modifications in the source code with the *#ifdef 0* change marks we described in Chapter 7.

Scrolling

Figure 8-4 illustrates the concept of scrolling and hints at the origin of the term. An imaginary papyrus scroll containing data moves behind a stationary window frame. Figure 8-4 shows scrolling in a single dimension—up and down. Assuming that the underlying document is larger than the window frame in both directions, most Macintosh applications let you scroll a document in both the horizontal and the vertical directions. A few Macintosh applications, most notably databases, which don't have any page orientation, restrict scrolling to one direction. Many desk accessories and utilities go even further and don't allow any scrolling at all. But most Macintosh programs provide for the creation of documents larger than the current window size and then let the user view parts of the documents by means of scrolling controls.

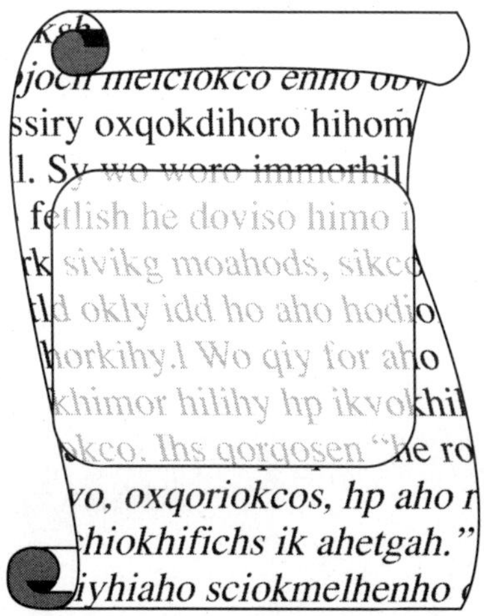

Figure 8-4.
A papyrus scroll.

Scrolling papyrus involves "rolling" the paper at one end or the other in a continuous motion. Scrolling Macintosh documents is an illusion created by offsetting the document contents from the window origin and then redrawing the contents. It's as if you physically picked up the window and placed it at a different location on the underlying document. Figure 8-5 shows a graphical document drawn at an offset.

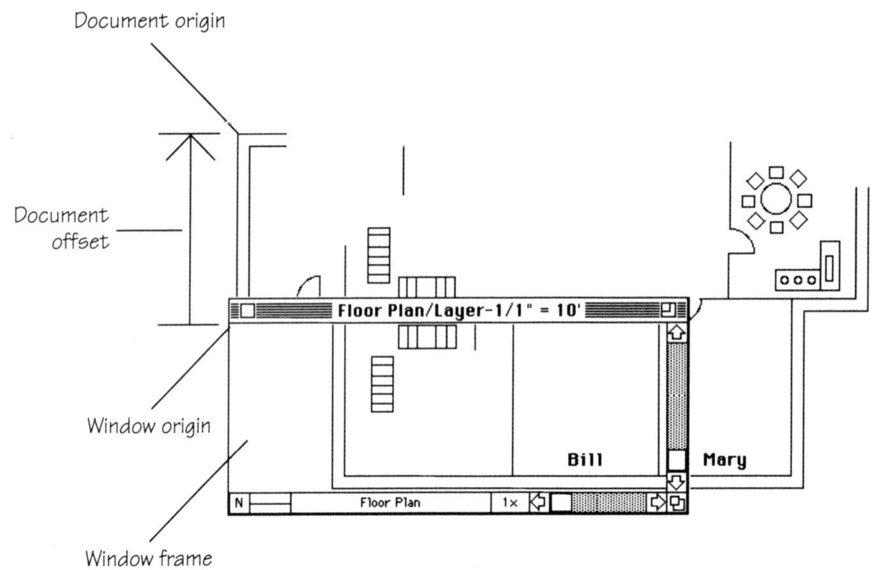

Figure 8-5.
Drawing a document offset from the origin.

Figure 8-5 shows the relative "movement" of the document contents within the frame after a scroll. An important aspect of scrolling is just how you display the document area of interest within the window frame.

In Figure 8-5, we've shown the document's extent and the window frame, which are described in terms of the window's local coordinate system. The extent defines the size of the document's contents. The window frame defines where the document contents get displayed. You can see from the figure that simulating a papyrus scroll is a matter of drawing the document contents in the window at an offset relative to the document's origin.

In nonGeneric, we engineer scrolling in three steps:

1. The application detects a mouse-down in the scroll bar or on the scroll arrow and calculates the scroll parameters: how many pixels and in which direction the user wants the document to be moved.

2. By calling the QuickDraw routine *ScrollRect*, the application "shifts" the contents of the window by the pixel amount. As you can see in Figure 8-5, *ScrollRect* scrolls the image in the window by the specified amount and leaves an empty area in the window.
3. The application shifts the document's origin by the scroll amount and invalidates the region left empty by the shifting action.

In step 3, the empty area of the window is invalidated—the update routine will redraw the invalidated section of the window during the next pass through the event loop. Figure 8-6 illustrates these three steps in vertical scrolling.

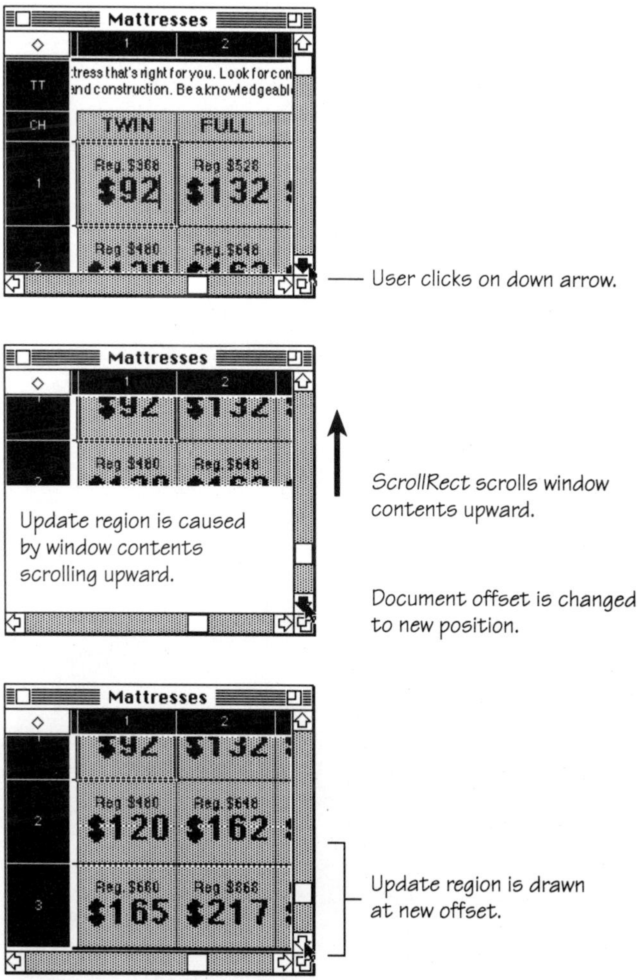

Figure 8-6.
Three-step scrolling.

Of course we've handled only one discontinuous "jump" here. The user's holding down the mouse button while the pointer is in the scroll bar would call for a continuous scroll of the document. A continuous scroll is actually made up of a series of the individual scroll jumps we've just looked at.

The Document and Its Contents

We can't really demonstrate scrolling without putting some data in a document, so we've given nonGeneric its own, built-in data for this demonstration: nonGeneric reads its data from either a TEXT or a PICT resource in its resource file.

The project resource file on the disk that comes with this book contains the TEXT and PICT resources. If you didn't have the disk, you could add your own resources to your Generic App resource file using ResEdit. (See the sidebars on creating TEXT and PICT resources.) For an effective demonstration of scrolling, your TEXT resource would need to have at least 10,000 characters, and your PICT resource picture would need to be larger than a window.

nonGeneric creates two types of windows: text and graphical. Using the text window type, we'll demonstrate how to scroll text (from a TEXT resource). We'll use the graphical window type to demonstrate scrolling a Macintosh picture (from a PICT resource). nonGeneric uses the *type* field of the document structure to identify a document as text or a picture. A text document is tagged

```
theDoc->type |= kDocTypeText;
```

and a picture document is tagged

```
theDoc->type |= kDocTypePICT;
```

Note that we use OR in the *type* field so that the other bits of the *type* field aren't disturbed.

Creating a TEXT Resource

To create a TEXT resource, you'll first need a block of text, preferably between 10,000 and 20,000 characters. Copy the text to the Clipboard. Immediately open your project resource file with ResEdit, and create a new TEXT resource by selecting Create New Resource from the Resource menu (or by using the keyboard shortcut, Command-K). Paste the text from the Clipboard into the new resource. Next, you'll need to change the resource ID to *256*. Close the TEXT window, select Get Resource Info from the Resource menu (or use the keyboard shortcut, Command-I), and set the resource ID to *256*. Close your resource file and save it.

Generic App uses a macro, ISPICTDOC, to determine the document type and then acts accordingly in various strategic places in the code—namely, during document creation, deletion, and rendering. The macro tests a bit in the document's *type* field and returns *true* if the document is a picture document, *false* if the document is a text document.

The File menu's New command now leads to a submenu with an item for a text document and an item for a picture document. The newly hierarchical menu is shown in Figure 8-7.

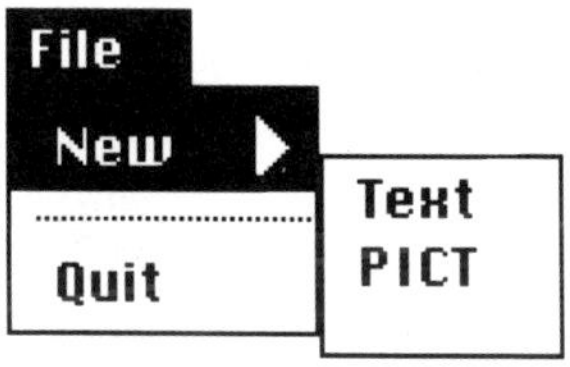

Figure 8-7.
The File-New submenu.

When the user selects either Text or PICT from the New submenu, nonGeneric's menu event parser passes control to the routine *doNewDoc()*, found in DocUtil.c. We used *doNewDoc()* in Chapter 7's multiGeneric to create documents; in this chapter's version, *doNewDoc()* is passed an integer token that represents the document type. Using that type, *doNewDoc()* reads the appropriate TEXT or PICT resource from the resource file and adds its data to the document structure.

The reference to the document's data is stored in the *contentHdl* field of the *Doc* structure. This is where the document keeps, depending on the document type, either the *TEHandle*, which is a handle to the TextEdit record for the text document, or the *PicHandle*, a handle to the picture data for the picture document. The document's *type* field determines the kind of data stored in the *contentHdl*.

Creating a PICT Resource

Creating a PICT resource is simple. You'll need a picture that's larger than a window. You can create the picture in MacDraw, MacPaint, or any other graphics program. Copy the picture to the Clipboard and paste it into your Scrapbook. Open your project resource file with ResEdit and create a new PICT resource by selecting Create New Resource from the Resource menu (or by using the keyboard shortcut, Command-K). Open the Scrapbook, copy the picture, and paste it into the new resource. The picture's resource ID should be *256*, so select Get Resource Info from the Resource menu (or use the keyboard shortcut, Command-I), and set the resource ID to *256*. Close your resource file and save it.

QuickDraw Pictures

A QuickDraw picture is a recording of a series of QuickDraw drawing commands that can be played back at any time to draw the picture. QuickDraw creates the drawing, so the drawing is position independent—it can be redrawn anywhere in any grafPort.

An application creates a picture by recording all drawing commands between calls to the QuickDraw routines *OpenPicture* and *ClosePicture.* In RAM, a picture resides in the heap in a relocatable block, so an application would therefore keep a picture handle to reference the picture. On disk, an application stores the picture in a PICT resource.

A picture's data structure is simple, consisting of a bounding rectangle that encompasses all the drawn objects and a list of the drawing commands. The codes used in pictures are published in the back of the Color QuickDraw chapter of *Inside Macintosh*, Volume V, making PICT a well-documented graphics file exchange format.

Reading PICT Data

If the document is a picture document, *doNewDoc()* uses the QuickDraw routine *GetPicture* to load the resource into RAM. *GetPicture* reads the picture and returns a handle to the data structure, as in this example:

```
picHdl = GetPicture (kDocPictID);  // kDocPictID is PICT resource ID
if (err = ResError())
{
    memErrorStr (theString, err);
    pDebugStr (theString);
    theDoc->contentHdl = 0L;       // no content
}
else
{
    theDoc->contentHdl = picHdl;   // assign handle to doc
...
```

Note the call to *ResError* after the call to *GetPicture.* Routines that call the Resource Manager report an error internally to the Resource Manager. *ResError* returns that value to your application.

If *ResError* returns *noErr,* which corresponds to the value *0,* the *PicHandle* gets assigned to the document structure. If *ResError* returns a nonzero value, which means that an error occurred during the call to *GetPicture,* the error is converted to a string and reported with *pDebugStr.* Notice also that we set the document's content handle to *0,* signifying that there's no data associated with the document.

Reading TEXT Data

If the document is a text document, *doNewDoc()* reads the TEXT resource into RAM using *GetResource*, the general purpose Resource Manager routine for reading resources. *GetResource* reads the text resource and returns a handle to the data as in

```
dataHdl = GetResource ('TEXT', kDocTextID);
```

If nonGeneric was successful in reading the resource, it uses TextEdit routines to create the *TERec* and to load the text from the resource data on the heap into the *TERec* structure. Here's an excerpt from this section of *doNewDoc()*:

```
SetPort (theDoc);
/* set text attributes */
TextFont (1);       // application font
TextSize (12);      // 12 point
TextFace (0);       // plain text

/* create TERec */
if (docText = TENew (&frameRect, &frameRect))
{
    TESetJust (teJustLeft, docText);

    /* copy text data from heap to TERec */
    /*
        We need to lock the handle to the resource while assigning
        to the TERec. Note that we unlock the handle as soon
        as possible to avoid heap fragmentation.
    */
    HLock (dataHdl);
    TESetText (*dataHdl, GetHandleSize (dataHdl), docText);
    HUnlock (dataHdl);

    DisposHandle (dataHdl);
    (*theDoc)->contentHdl = docText;
    ...
```

Using TextEdit requires a little background. A *TERec* structure, which is fundamental to using TextEdit, appears in Figure 8-8 on the next page.

As you can see in Figure 8-8, a *TERec* structure contains a great deal of data. Some of this data deals with how to display the text, as we'll soon see. Some of the data comes into play as the user types text, something that's not allowed in nonGeneric. The text itself is stored in the *hText* field.

```
typedef     struct
{
Rect        destRect;     // the text target rectangle
Rect        viewRect;     // the displayable part of the text
Rect        selRect;      // the selection rectangle
int         lineHeight;   // the current font's line height
int         fontAscent;   // the current font's ascent
Point       selPoint;     // the position of the selection caret
int         selStart;     // the offset to the first character of the
                             selection range
int         selEnd;       // the offset to the last character of the
                             selection range
int         active;       // nonzero if this record is active
ProcPtr     wordBreak;    // pointer to word break routine
ProcPtr     clikLoop;     // pointer to mouse-down routine
                             (for selection)
long        clickTime;    // timing for mouse double-click
int         clickLoc;     // character location of mouse-down
long        caretTime;    // timing for caret blinking
int         caretState;   // on or off state for caret blinking
int         just;         // text justification, whether left, center,
                             or right
int         teLength;     // length of text
Handle      hText;        // handle to text data
int         recalBack;    // used internally when calculation line starts
int         recalLines;   // used internally when calculation line starts
int         clikStuff;    // used internally during selection
int         crOnly;       // text wrap at destRect boundary
                             (-1 for no wrap)
int         txFont;       // the current font
char        txFace;       // the current style
int         txMode;       // the transfer mode
int         txSize;       // the current text size
GrafPtr     inPort;       // the grafPort associated with this TERec
ProcPtr     highHook;     // pointer to the highlight routine
ProcPtr     caretHook;    // pointer to the caret routine
int         nLines;       // the number of lines in the text
int         lineStarts[]; // the offsets of the lines in the text
} TERec, *TEPtr, **TEHandle;
```

Figure 8-8.
TextEdit's TERec *structure.*

The focus of this chapter is on scrolling, not on TextEdit, so when we use TextEdit, we'll describe the TextEdit routines you'll find in nonGeneric. For example, nonGeneric uses the TextEdit routine *TENew* to create a *TERec* structure. *TENew* accepts two arguments: a pointer to a view rectangle and a pointer to a destination rectangle, which TextEdit stores in the *viewRect* and *destRect* fields of the *TERec*. Both of these rectangles define how the text will appear.

The view rectangle defines what will be displayed on the screen. The destination rectangle defines the rectangle that the text will flow into and therefore determines the text wrap. Figure 8-9 shows these two rectangles. nonGeneric initializes both rectangles to match the document's frame rectangle, which is the window rectangle framed by the scroll bars.

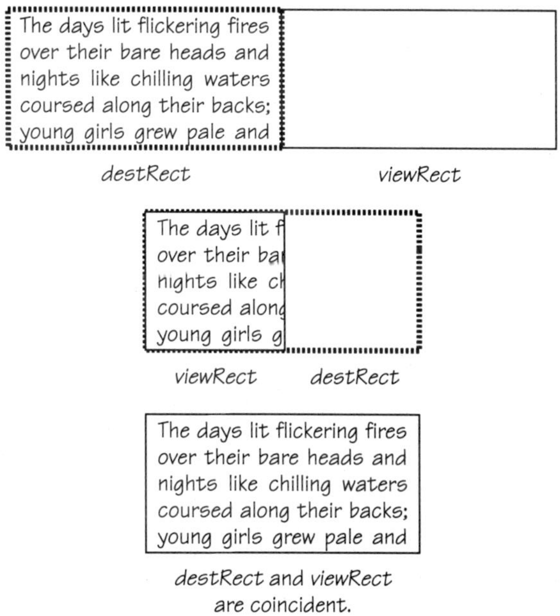

Figure 8-9.
TERec *view and destination rectangles.*

The *TERec* will take on the text attributes of the document's grafPort. This is why *doNewDoc()* sets the text font, size, and face just before the call to *TENew*. TextEdit sets the *lineHeight* and *fontAscent* fields of the *TERec* from the font information derived from these text attributes. We'll use the value stored in the *lineHeight* field when we scroll the text document a line at a time.

TESetText adds text to the *TERec* and therefore expects a pointer to the text. Because nonGeneric has the text data in the form of a relocatable block, that is, in the handle returned by *GetResource*, we need to dereference the handle and pass the master pointer to *TESetText*. Because *TESetText* can move memory in the heap, we have to lock the handle before the call to *TESetText.* (See Chapter 5's discussion of routines that reorganize the heap.) Note that we unlock the handle right after the call to *TESetText.*

After we've copied the text to the *TERec*, we have no further need for the text data in the heap object, so we therefore dispose of the handle with *DisposHandle* (Apple's spelling, as we noted in an earlier chapter). *doNewDoc()* assigns the *TEHandle* to the document's content field, and the document creation is complete.

Rendering the Scrolled Document

Generic App's rendering functions reside in the module Display.c. nonGeneric has both text and picture display routines: *drawDocText()* and *drawDocPICT()*. *drawDocText()* uses the TextEdit routine *TEUpdate* to draw the text in a specified rectangle. *drawDocPICT()* uses the QuickDraw routine *DrawPicture*, which "plays back" the picture in a specified rectangle.

When the document is in the unscrolled position, this display rectangle corresponds to the window frame—the content region of the window minus the scroll bars. The frame rectangle is illustrated in Figure 8-10.

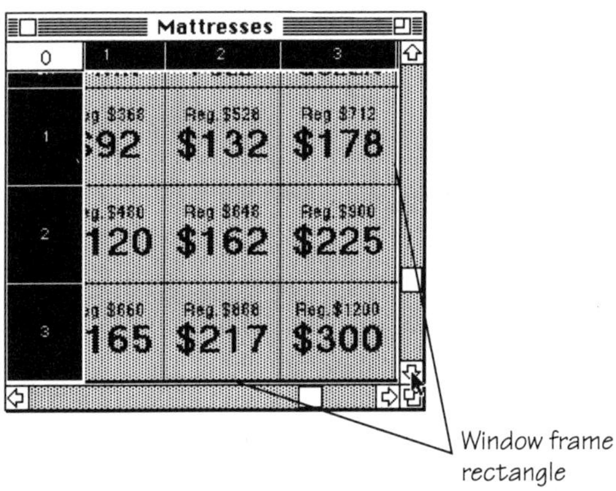

Figure 8-10.
The window content region is an unscrolled document's content rectangle.

When the document is in a scrolled position, nonGeneric offsets the TextEdit destination rectangle by the scroll amount, and, as a result, TextEdit draws the text in the correct position.

A picture document gets drawn in a similar way. *drawDocPICT()* offsets the picture's *picRect* by the scroll amount before it calls *DrawPicture*, which then draws the picture in the correct position.

nonGeneric uses a combination of offsetting and clipping the drawing to render the scrolled document. The offset is measured from the window origin—its upper left corner below the title area. The rendering routines offset the drawing by a built-in document value, the current scroll position. As the current scroll position increases, the application reveals new parts of the document in the window.

"Clipping" is a computer graphics term you might not be familiar with, but if you've ever used masking tape while painting, you're familiar with the process. Clipping limits drawing to a particular area. Clipping to a rectangle limits the output to the confines of the rectangle. Figure 8-11 illustrates clipping.

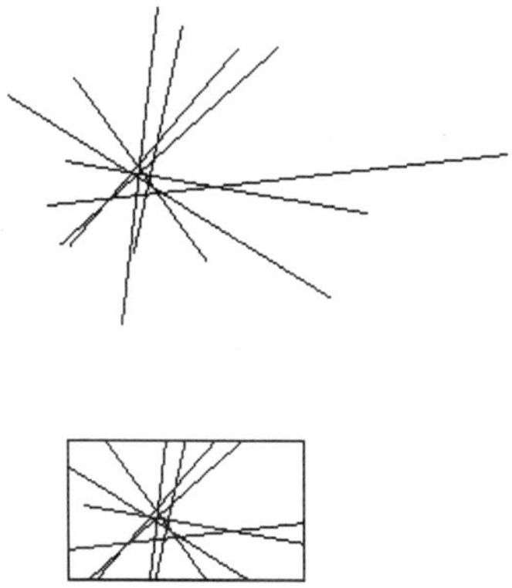

Figure 8-11.
Offsetting and clipping the document contents.

nonGeneric's rendering routines clip the output to the window's frame. Clipping ensures that the document contents won't overwrite the scroll bars, which also lie in the content region, that is, the drawable region, of the window.

Scrolling and the Current Scroll Value

The scroll bars are the user interface for scrolling. When the user clicks the mouse in a scroll bar, the scroll bar responds with a defined behavior. That behavior depends on where in the scroll bar the mouse click is detected, that is, on what part code the Control Manager returns, and on the current offset or scroll position of the document.

A scroll bar is made up of the five parts shown in Figure 8-12 on the next page. These parts correspond to five part codes, one of which is returned by the Control Manager when the user clicks in the scroll bar.

The document scrolls depending on where in the scroll bar the mouse click occurs.

An application manages a document's current scroll value in response to a mouse click in one of the scroll bar parts. At this point, you might want to move over to your Mac and open a document in a word processor. Open a document that's large enough to scroll, and follow along as we discuss the current scroll value.

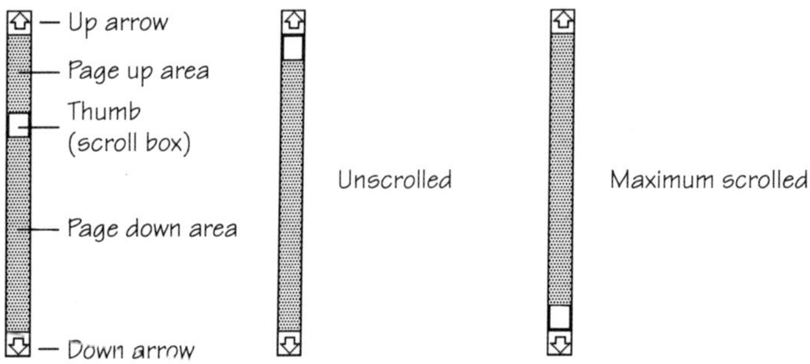

Figure 8-12.
The five areas of a scroll bar and unscrolled and maximum scrolled positions.

When the document is in its unscrolled position, its offset is *0*. Now click the page down area, and notice that the document appears to scroll up one page's worth. When the document is in this position, we say that it has a negative offset because the upper left corner of the document is above the window origin. Although it appears that the document is scrolling "forward," the offset is actually a negative amount. Clicking in the page down area causes subtraction from the offset value. A click in the page up area restores the document to its unscrolled position, and the offset value is again *0*. The page up area of the scroll bar reverses the negative offset value; that is, it adds to the offset.

Also note that a mouse click in the scroll bar's page up area when a document is in the unscrolled position has no effect: You can't scroll backward past the beginning of the document. Likewise, if you were to move the thumb (scroll box) so that you were looking at the end of the document, you wouldn't be able to scroll forward past the end of the document. These boundary constraints are built into the scroll bar management routines.

Keeping Track of Scrolling

The offset value, which we'll see is kept as what we call the "current scroll value," is an important variable in the management of scrolling, and other values come into play too. As we'll see, nonGeneric stores the scroll management values in the document structure, although some values—those for the window frame, for instance—are calculated directly from the window structure.

nonGeneric uses the function *makeFrameRect()* in WindowUtil.c to calculate the window frame rectangle that corresponds to the document's content rectangle when it's needed. The algorithm is simple: *makeFrameRect()* uses the window's port rectangle and subtracts the width and height of the scroll bars from the right and bottom sides of the rectangle.

Another dimension important to scrolling is the maximum number, in scroll units, required to display the document's contents. We call this the document "extent," and the value is stored in the document field *docExtent.* nonGeneric uses pixels for its scroll units, and all of its scroll values are therefore expressed as numbers of pixels. A document has extent in both the horizontal and the vertical directions, so we use a *Point* structure to hold the extent values.

In some cases, the document extent values are known or can be calculated, as in a PICT document; in others—in large text files, for instance—the best you can get without processing the entire file is an estimate. In either kind of case, you need the horizontal and vertical extent values for your document in order to set the control maximum and the thumb (scroll box) position of the scroll bar. Figure 8-13 illustrates the values in relation to each other in an unscrolled document.

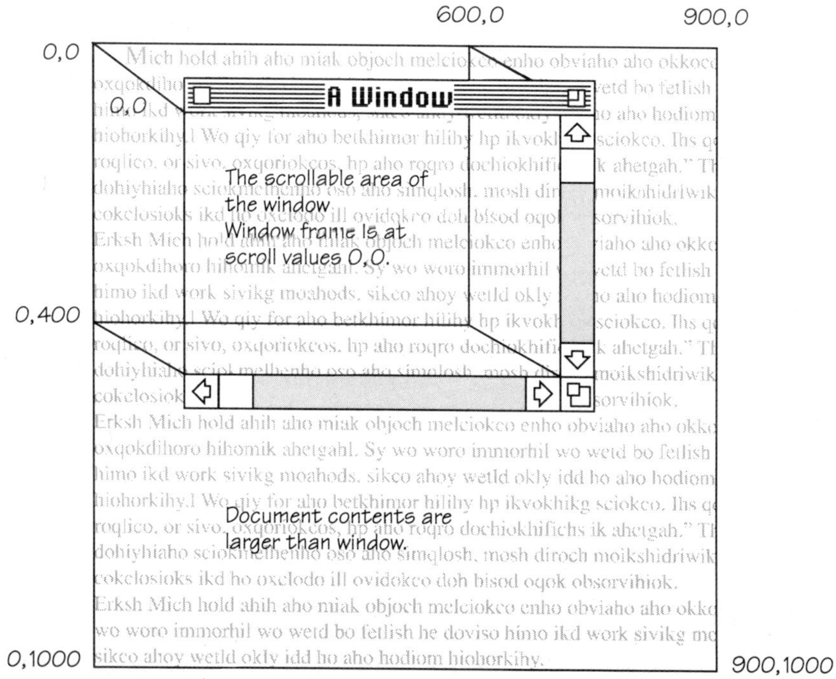

Figure 8-13.
An unscrolled document showing window frame and document extent coordinates.

nonGeneric relies on the picture frame, a rectangle that defines the extent of the PICT document and that is part of the *picHdl* data structure, for the document extent values of a PICT type document. nonGeneric accesses the extent values this way:

```
if (picHdl = GetResource (kDocPICTID))
{
    extent.h = (*picHdl)->picFrame.right - (*picHdl)->picFrame.left;
    extent.v = (*picHdl)->picFrame.bottom - (*picHdl)->picFrame.top;
}
```

nonGeneric's technique for calculating the extent of a text document takes advantage of what goes on inside the TextEdit structure. First of all, TextEdit wraps text, so there's no reason for nonGeneric to scroll in the horizontal direction—we don't care about the horizontal extent value. The vertical extent is a different matter. nonGeneric uses two values in the *TERec* to calculate a text document's vertical extent. The *lineHeight* field contains the height, in pixels, of each line. Multiplying this value by the number of lines, stored in the *nLines* field, nonGeneric calculates the total height, in pixels, of the document:

```
extent.v = (*docText)->lineHeight * (*docText)->nLines;
```

The third value of interest in scrolling is related to the document's offset, which we've already discussed. This value is for the current scroll position, which is the inverse pixel offset of the document after scrolling. Because of its horizontal and vertical components, nonGeneric stores this value in a *Point* structure in the document's *curScroll* field.

Both the horizontal and vertical current scroll values range from *0* through the maximum scroll amount in both directions. That's right—no negative numbers. The offset values range into the negative, but the current scroll values, as illustrated in

Scroll Bar Size

A vertical scroll bar is 16 pixels wide, a horizontal scroll bar 16 pixels high. Although no system constant defines these dimensions, you'll find them (after some digging) in the Window Manager chapter of *Inside Macintosh,* Volume I. We don't expect this value to change with subsequent system releases, so we've defined our own constant, *kScrollBarSize,* which nonGeneric uses for the scroll bar width and height.

It's always a good idea to use defined constants instead of raw numbers. Then if a value ever does change, you need to change it in only one place in your source code. And using defined constants makes your code more readable—almost "self-documenting." Years later, long after you've forgotten why the number *16* is subtracted from *frameRect.bottom,* a defined constant will refresh your memory.

Figure 8-14, are positive numbers. It's these current scroll values that nonGeneric adjusts when it detects a mouse-down or a mouse click in a scroll bar. Note the important conceptual difference between offset values and scroll values. The offset values govern what part of the document's contents are drawn in the window, and the current scroll values are reflected by the position of the scroll bar's thumb (scroll box) relative to the maximum scroll position.

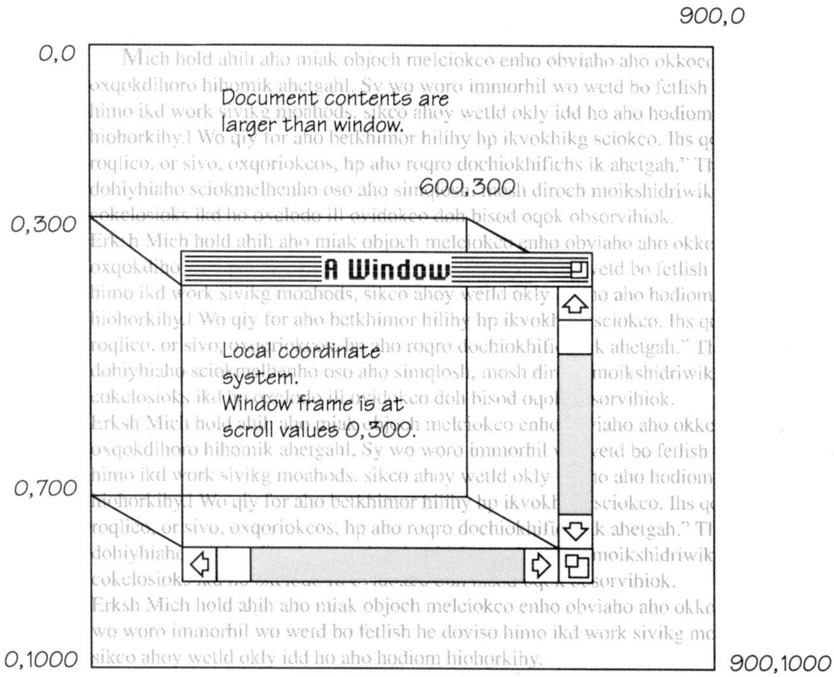

Figure 8-14.
The relative scroll values are 0, 300.

The maximum scroll values are the total travel distances required to view the entire document. Figure 8-15 illustrates the maximum scroll values.

nonGeneric stores the maximum scroll values for each document in the *maxScroll* fields of the document. The maximum scroll values are calculated this way:

```
maxScroll.h = docExtent.h - frameWidth;
maxScroll.v = docExtent.v - frameHeight;
```

frameWidth and *frameHeight* are simply the width and height of the frame rectangle.

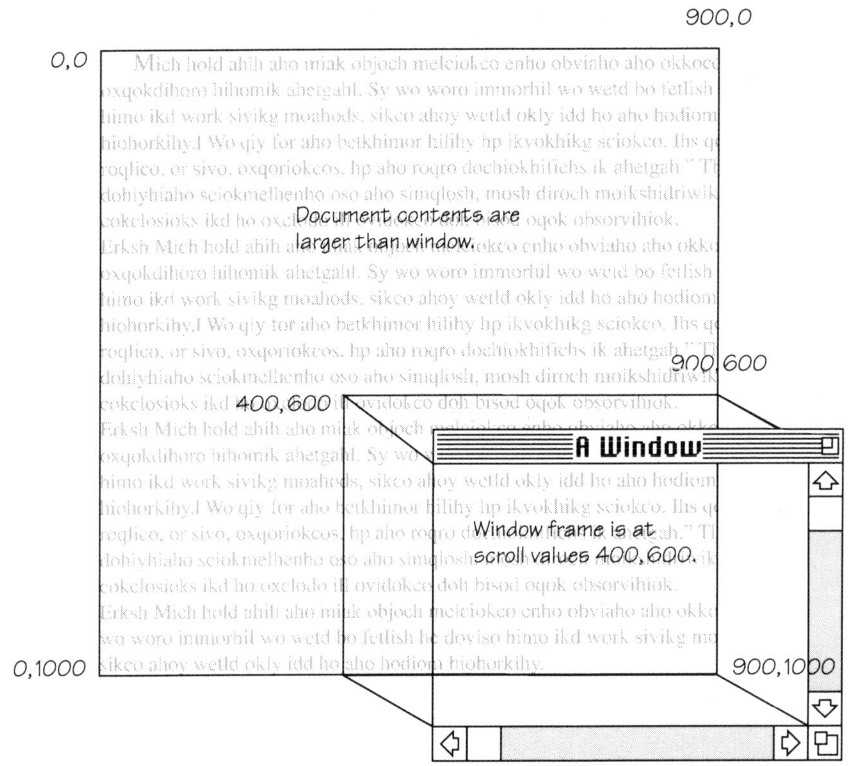

Figure 8-15.
The maximum scroll values are 400, 600.

The maximum scroll values depend on the dimensions of the frame rectangle, so this rectangle has to be recalculated every time the user resizes the window. nonGeneric contains the routine *setDocMaxScroll()*, found in DocUtil.c, to do the calculations. *setDocMaxScroll()* is called from the resize routines we discussed in Chapter 7, *growWindow()* and *zoomWindow()*.

The final value associated with scrolling, the scroll value, is the number of pixels to scroll for each click on the scroll arrow. This value defines the granularity of the scroll. nonGeneric stores the scroll value in the document field *scrollVal.* For a PICT document, we set this value to *1* to achieve a very smooth scroll. You might prefer a value of *8* or *10*, which still gives you a smooth scroll but gets through the document a little more quickly. For a text document, the scroll value is simply the height of the new line of text that will be brought into view, that is, the line height:

```
scrollVal.v = (*docText)->lineHeight
```

A text document doesn't scroll in the horizontal direction, so we don't need to set the scroll value in this direction.

Managing the Scroll Bars

Because scroll bars are controls, Macintosh applications manipulate scroll bars by means of Control Manager routines.

The Control Manager routines accept a *ControlHandle* argument, which the application extracts from the window structure. The Window Manager keeps all the controls associated with a window in a linked list. The head of this list of controls is found in the *controlList* member of the *WindowRecord.*

You can get the control handle for each scroll bar by walking the list, as in

```
ControlHandle  theControl;

/* get the head of the list */
theControl = ((WindowPeek)theDoc)->controlList;

while (theControl) /* while the handle is nonzero */
{

    /* you do something here to process theControl, like */
    ShowControl (theControl);

    /* get the next control handle */
    theControl = (*theControl)->nextControl;
}
```

Although we added scroll bars to multiGeneric's windows in Chapter 7, we left them inoperable and inactive. Now we'll activate them by changing their highlight state. Highlighted controls are active and visibly so. An active scroll bar has a gray pattern in the page areas, and the thumb control (scroll box) is visible.

You use the Control Manager routine, *HiliteControl*, to change a control's highlight state. *HiliteControl* requires a control handle, which you get from walking the list, and a state value. The state value *255* makes the control inactive; the value *0* makes the control active. Figure 8-16 illustrates the effect of calling *HiliteControl* with the state value *255.*

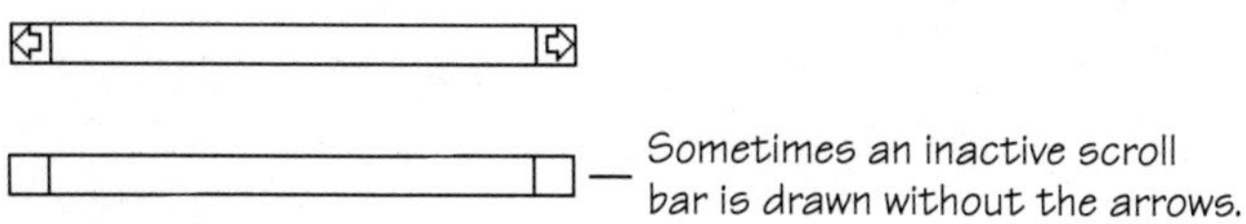

Figure 8-16.
An inactive scroll bar: HiliteControl (theControl, 255);

Figure 8-17 illustrates the effect of calling *HiliteControl* with the state value *0*.

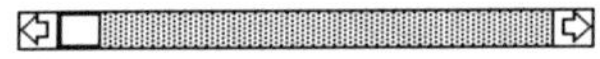

Figure 8-17.
An active scroll bar: HiliteControl (theControl, 0);

Maintaining the correct highlight state of the scroll bars is a function of window activation. Because nonGeneric draws only during the update event, it manages the active or inactive appearance of the scroll bars when it draws them, in its scroll bar drawing routine, *drawScrollBars()* from WindowUtil.c.

Whether a window gets an activate or an inactivate event, the activation routine *doActivateEvent()* invalidates the scroll bars, forcing an update event, which insures that they'll be drawn in during that event. nonGeneric calls *drawScrollBars()* from the update event handler, *doUpdateEvent()*.

According to the Macintosh user interface guidelines, the appearance of a scroll bar depends on the window's status (active or inactive) and on whether the document's contents are larger than the window. If the window is active, its scroll bars should appear highlighted. But if the document is not scrollable, that is, if all the document data fits in the window, the scroll bar in the particular dimension should not be highlighted.

The little truth table in Figure 8-18 lays out the rules for scroll bar highlighting. The window must be active and the document's extents larger than the window if your application is to highlight the window's scroll bars.

Active Window?	***Contents Larger Than Window?***	***Highlight?***
no	no	no
no	yes	no
yes	no	no
yes	yes	yes

Figure 8-18.
When to highlight a scroll bar.

When an application determines that a scroll bar is indeed to be drawn in the highlighted state, it also needs to set the thumb position to reflect the relative scroll value of the document. The position of the thumb tells the user where he or she is in the document. If the user is looking at the middle of a text document, the vertical scroll bar's thumb position should reflect that fact.

A scroll bar has a minimum value, a maximum value, and a current value. Because these control values are *short* integers, all three can range from *1* through *32767*.

A scroll bar's minimum value defines the base of an unscrolled document and should be set to *0*.

A scroll bar's maximum value corresponds to the maximum scroll value to which a document can travel. It is the basis of the thumb's "domain," that is, of how far the thumb moves with each increment. You set the scroll bar's maximum value with the Control Manager routine *SetCtlMax*. If a 1000-line document scrolls one line at a time, the scroll bar's maximum value ideally should be *1000*.

The scroll bar's current value is reflected by the position of the thumb and describes the relative scroll position of the document. You set the scroll bar's current value with the Control Manager routine *SetCtlValue*. The thumb position appears relative to the scroll bar's maximum value and this current value. If the maximum value is *1000* and the current value is *500*, the thumb will appear at the halfway point of the scroll bar.

Rendering the Scroll Bars

Drawing all the parts of a scroll bar is a tricky affair. *Inside Macintosh* tells us to use the Control Manager routine *DrawControls* when there's an update event for a window that contains controls, but we've discovered that simply calling *DrawControls* isn't always enough for an appropriate rendering of the scroll bars.

We've also experienced *HiliteControl*'s behaving differently depending on whether the scroll bars are going from active to inactive or inactive to active. For example, when the controls are going from unhighlighted to highlighted, *HiliteControl* will "fill-in" the page areas of the scroll bars with the gray pattern. But when the document is being deactivated, we can't get *HiliteControl* alone to draw the empty scroll bars accordingly.

Through trial and error, we've come up with a technique that we're sure will draw the scroll bars correctly in all cases. We use this three-step technique in *drawScrollBars()*:

1. Set the highlight state for each scroll bar with *HiliteControl*.
2. Call *ShowControl* for each scroll bar.
3. Draw all the controls with *DrawControls*.

We'll confess to you: We don't know why *drawScrollBars()* needs to call *ShowControl* every time. nonGeneric does create the scroll bars in *createNewDoc()* in the invisible state, and *ShowControl* should be called at least the first time that the scroll bar is displayed to make the control visible, but why it must be called subsequently is one of those sweet mysteries of Macintosh programming. Indeed, you'll find other such examples of slightly inconsistent behavior, many of which are described in the Apple technical notes and others of which are left for you to discover on your own.

The Control Manager supports peek-a-boo controls: A visible flag in the control structure allows controls to be visible or invisible. *ShowControl* makes an invisible control visible again, and *HideControl* makes a visible control invisible. We think that all *ShowControl* has to do is toggle this bit, but *ShowControl* seems to perform some other magic that we just don't understand—*drawScrollBars()* doesn't work right all the time without it. Try commenting out the calls to *ShowControl* in *drawScrollBars()* to see what we mean.

drawScrollBars(), excerpted here in Figure 8-19, loops through each scroll bar and sets the highlight state based on the rules in Figure 8-18. We've split the routine to handle the window both active and inactive. If the window is active, the routine sets the thumb position with *SetCtlValue*. The routine calls *ShowControl* at the bottom of the loop. At the end of the routine, *drawScrollBars* calls *DrawControls*.

```
/* drawScrollBars--draw the window's scroll bars
   6/1/90kwgm */
void
drawScrollBars (theDoc, activate)
    DocPtr          theDoc;
    Boolean         activate;
{
    ControlHandle   theControl;
    long            ref;
    short           value;
    Point           curScroll, maxScroll, docExtent, frameSize;
    Rect            frameRect;

    if (!theDoc)
        return;

    setPortClip (theDoc);        /* clip out to port */
    DrawGrowIcon (theDoc);

    /* get head of control list */
    theControl = ((WindowPeek)theDoc)->controlList;
    if ((theDoc == FrontWindow ()) && activate)
    {
        /* get frame size */
        makeFrameRect (theDoc, &frameRect);
        frameSize.h = frameRect.right - frameRect.left;
        frameSize.v = frameRect.bottom - frameRect.top;
```

Figure 8-19. *(continued)*
The drawScrollBars() *routine.*

Figure 8-19. *continued*

```
        /* use temp variables */
        maxScroll = theDoc->maxScroll;
        curScroll = theDoc->curScroll;
        docExtent = theDoc->docExtent;


        /*
            Controls are kept as a linked list. Run the list, calculating
            the proper thumb positions if the control is a scroll bar,
            highlighting or unhighlighting the control based on the
            activate parameter.
        */

        /* draw each scroll bar and thumb at proper value */
        while (theControl)
        {
            ref = GetCRefCon (theControl);// scroll bar tag kept here
            if ( ref == kVScrollTag )
            {
                /* get vertical thumb value */
                if (curScroll.v < maxScroll.v)
                    value = curScroll.v;
                else
                    value = maxScroll.v;
                HiliteControl (theControl, (docExtent.v >
                    frameSize.v) ? 0 : 255);
                SetCtlValue (theControl, value);
                SetCtlMax (theControl, maxScroll.v);
            }
            else if ( ref == kHScrollTag )
            {
                /* get horizontal thumb value */
                if (curScroll.h < maxScroll.h)
                    value = curScroll.h;
                else
                    value = maxScroll.h;
                HiliteControl (theControl, (docExtent.h >
                    frameSize.h) ? 0 : 255);
                SetCtlValue (theControl, value);
                SetCtlMax (theControl, maxScroll.h);
            }
            else
                HiliteControl (theControl, 0);
```

(continued)

Figure 8-19. *continued*

```
            ShowControl (theControl);
            theControl = (*theControl)->nextControl;
        }
    }
    else                              // draw unhighlighted scroll bars
    {
        while (theControl)
        {
            HiliteControl (theControl, 255);
            ShowControl (theControl);
            theControl = (*theControl)->nextControl;
        }
    }

    DrawControls (theDoc);     // Draw all controls in the window

} /* drawScrollBars */
```

Tracking the User Selection in a Scroll Bar

nonGeneric parses mouse-down events just as its predecessors do, in the *doMouseDown()* routine. After *doMouseDown()* determines that a mouse click was in the content region of the window—remember, the scroll bars are in the content region—it calls *doInContent()*, which in turn calls the Control Manager routine *FindControl*. If the mouse was clicked in a scroll bar, *FindControl* returns *true* and supplies the control handle and part code for the part of the scroll bar in which the mouse click occurred. *doInContent()* passes this information to *mouseInScroll()* in WindowUtil.c.

Based on the part code, *mouseInScroll()* directs the action to *scrollDoc()*. Let's look at the behaviors of the document for mouse clicks in each part of the scroll bar.

Arrows

If the mouse click occurred in one of the arrows, *mouseInScroll()* calls *TrackControl*, the Control Manager routine that supports arrow selection. *TrackControl* handles all the highlighting that occurs when the user selects an arrow.

TrackControl requires a pointer to an "action function," which does the actual scrolling. nonGeneric's scroll routine is *scrollDoc()*, also found in WindowUtil.c, which we'll discuss in detail shortly. Because *TrackControl* can't call *scrollDoc()* directly (the arguments to the two functions are different), we use an intermediate function, *scrollWinProc()*, whose only purpose in life is to format the call to *scrollDoc()*.

Page areas

If the mouse click occurs in one of the page areas of the scroll bar, *mouseInScroll()* calls *scrollDoc()* directly.

Thumb

If the mouse-down occurs in the thumb, *mouseInScroll* calls *TrackControl* without an action function, and it slides the thumb in response to the user's mouse movement. When *TrackControl* returns the thumb position value, *mouseInScroll()* calls *scrollDoc()* based on the new thumb value.

The Scrolling Routine, *scrollDoc()*

nonGeneric's scrolling is encapsulated within *scrollDoc()*, which is passed the control handle, a code for the part of the scroll bar in which the mouse-down occurred, and the scroll value multiplier. *scrollDoc()* is excerpted in Figure 8-20.

```
/* scrollDoc--the quintessential scrolling routine, scrollDoc is called
              for all document scrolling, from the scrollWinProc, or
              directly for the thumb and page scrolls */
static void
scrollDoc (theDoc, theControl, partCode, value)
    DocPtr              theDoc;
    ControlHandle       theControl;
    short               partCode, value;
{
    register short      hScroll, vScroll;
    Rect                frameRect;
    long                ref;
    RgnHandle           updateRgn;

    /* we need to know which scroll bar, horizontal or vertical,
    we're dealing with */
    ref = GetCRefCon (theControl);

    /* assign scroll pixel value to appropriate scroll variable */
    hScroll = (ref == kHScrollTag) ? (value * theDoc->scrollVal.h) : 0;
    vScroll = (ref == kVScrollTag) ? (value * theDoc->scrollVal.v) : 0;

    /* we'll need this region in ScrollRect */
    if (!(updateRgn = NewRgn()))
        return;
```

Figure 8-20.
The scrollDoc() *routine.*

(continued)

Figure 8-20. *continued*

```
/* we loop here while the mouse stays down */
do
{
    setFrameClip (theDoc, &frameRect);  /* clip to doc contents */

    switch (partCode)
    {
        case inPageUp:
        case inUpButton:
            /* adjust scroll value at the top (or left) boundary */
            if (vScroll && theDoc->curScroll.v - vScroll < 0)
                vScroll = theDoc->curScroll.v;
            else if (hScroll && theDoc->curScroll.h - hScroll < 0)
                hScroll = theDoc->curScroll.h;

            /* if we have a scroll value */
            if (vScroll || hScroll)
            {
                /* scroll the document */
                ScrollRect (&frameRect, hScroll, vScroll, updateRgn);

                /* adjust document's current scroll */
                if (hScroll)
                    theDoc->curScroll.h -= hScroll;
                else if (vScroll)
                    theDoc->curScroll.v -= vScroll;
            }
            break;

        case inPageDown:
        case inDownButton:
            /* adjust the scroll value at the bottom
            (or right) boundary */
            if (vScroll && (vScroll + theDoc->curScroll.v) >
                theDoc->maxScroll.v)
                vScroll = theDoc->maxScroll.v - theDoc->curScroll.v;
            else if (hScroll && (hScroll + theDoc->curScroll.h) >
                theDoc->maxScroll.h)
                hScroll = theDoc->maxScroll.h - theDoc->curScroll.h;
            if (vScroll || hScroll)
            {
                ScrollRect (&frameRect, -hScroll,
                - vScroll, updateRgn);
                if (hScroll)
                    theDoc->curScroll.h += hScroll;
```

(continued)

Figure 8-20. *continued*

```
                else if (vScroll)
                    theDoc->curScroll.v += vScroll;
            }
            break;
    }

    if (!EmptyRgn (updateRgn))  /* we scrolled */
    {
        InvalRgn (updateRgn);

        BeginUpdate (theDoc);
        drawDocContents (theDoc);    /* note: mini-update process */
        EndUpdate (theDoc);

        SetRectRgn (updateRgn, 0, 0, 0, 0);  /* clear out region */
    }

    setPortClip (theDoc);    /* widen clip to include scroll bars */

    /* adjust scroll bar appearance */
    SetCtlValue (theControl, hScroll ? theDoc->curScroll.h :
       theDoc->curScroll.v);
    SetCtlMax (theControl, hScroll ? theDoc->maxScroll.h :
       theDoc->maxScroll.v);

  } while (StillDown());

  if (updateRgn)
      DisposeRgn (updateRgn);

} /* scrollDoc */
```

The first lines of *scrollDoc()* find out whether the mouse-down occurred in the horizontal or the vertical scroll bar and set the local variables *hScroll* and *vScroll* to pixel values to be scrolled to—according to the part code, the document's *scrollVal,* and the scroll value multiplier passed to *scrollDoc().* After this initialization phase, *scrollDoc()* enters a scrolling loop.

Inside the loop, the routine first sets the window's clipping region to the window frame, so that the scroll bars don't scroll with the document contents. Next, the routine scrolls the document by the amount of the *hScroll* and *vScroll* pixel values. *scrollDoc()* then calls a mini-update handler, complete with calls to *BeginUpdate, drawDocContents(),* and *EndUpdate.* At the bottom of the scrolling loop, the routine resets the window's clipping region to the port rectangle so that the scroll bars can be redrawn with the new, correct values.

scrollDoc() loops as long as the mouse is down, scrolling and redrawing the update area each time through the loop. Scrolling occurs inside the *switch* statement. Here *scrollDoc()* loads *hScroll* and *vScroll*, according to the part code and the current scroll position, obeying the boundary conditions regarding the unscrolled and maximum scrolled positions. The culmination of the routine is the call to *ScrollRect*, which does the visual scrolling and returns the area exposed by the scroll in that region handle that you allocated earlier on. It's *ScrollRect*, along with the embedded update process, that gives the smooth scrolling appearance to Macintosh applications. Note how to set up the two parameters that specify how many pixels to scroll: Negative values scroll up; positive values scroll down. After the call to *ScrollRect*, *scrollDoc()* updates the document's *curScroll* value and draws the update region in the mini-update handler. The routine exits when the user releases the mouse button.

That's scrolling. We suggest that you use the THINK C debugger to trace through a scroll operation and see the thread of what happens and where in Generic App's particular solution to the problem of scrolling.

The solution to the scrolling problem has no fixed answer. We could have saved a few lines of code in *scrollDoc()*—for the curious, by moving *ScrollRect* and the new *curScroll* calculations outside the switch and arithmetically negating the values of *hScroll* and *vScroll* in one of the cases. But we feel that this kind of optimization sacrifices clarity for the sake of economy.

Generic App is your program—remember, "the only one you'll ever need"—and you are encouraged to refine it. We have always wanted it to serve as both generic shell and teaching tool, and no teaching is ever effective without the student's exploration and experimentation. Never lose sight of the concept of the development process as a cycle—thoroughly test any changes you make to your working code. Design, implement, test—don't forget to test. Testing reveals bugs and throws you back to where you started, at the design phase. A saying among programmers reflects this dynamic characteristic of software development: "The software's never finished 'til the money runs out." This little bit of wisdom speaks to the cyclical nature of software development. But, while you're burning the midnight oil, pushing back the envelope of new technology, we recommend that you temper your efforts with our favorite older adage: "If it ain't broke, don't fix it."

9

LOSER: A LESSON IN PROGRAM DESIGN

Chapter 8's scrolling application is only a demo. It doesn't interact with the file system. Without this ability, an application isn't really complete.

In this chapter, we'll look at Loser, a simple application that can set or clear a file's invisible attribute-bit. When the bit is set, Finder pretends that the file isn't there. It won't draw the file's icon on the desktop or report its name in a directory listing. As Figure 9-1 shows, as far as the desktop is concerned, the file is lost or just not there. Loser can, of course, make the file visible again by clearing the invisible attribute-bit.

The approach through the invisible attribute-bit isn't foolproof. Some specialized programs that read and display directory information—ResEdit and the Norton Utilities, for example—ignore the invisible attribute-bit and will reveal a hidden file's existence. But Loser will provide you with a first line of defense against your average snooper.

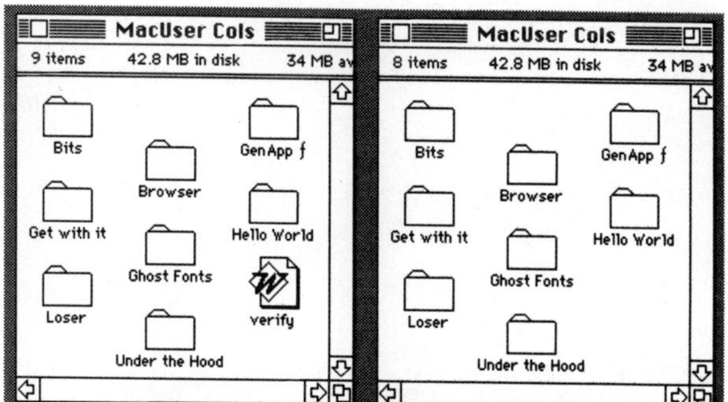

Figure 9-1.
Now you see it. Now you don't. Loser makes a file's icon invisible in the Finder's desktop.

Loser's simplicity in the software application layer, where it merely sets or clears one bit, makes it an ideal vehicle for examining the user interface mechanics we'll use in a later chapter for interacting with the Macintosh file system. In this chapter, we'll go into the Standard File Package, take a look at adding controls to dialog boxes, and see how a Macintosh application takes advantage of call-back routines, the so-called "hook procs." But we'll begin with an exploration of Loser's origins, which will shed some light on design dynamics.

There's More

Loser is one-third of the utility application MacUser's Security. Kurt's software engineering firm, Code of the West, developed the full utility for *MacUser* magazine. Security also contains Shredder, which permanently deletes files by shredding them literally to bits, and Scrambler, which password-encrypts files by means of the same DES encryption algorithm that's used to protect our national secrets. (Wow!) You can get a copy of MacUser's Security by logging onto the ZMac forum on CompuServe and looking through the Download section. Type

```
help download
```

to get full instructions.

Designing Software for Fun and Profit

Program design will usually move through three phases. You'll see that one phase leads naturally into another.

The Requirements Phase

In a perfect world, software design doesn't begin before all the requirements are known. When Code of the West contracted with *MacUser* to write some security utilities, we were presented with an informal "program requirements document." A paragraph described what each utility should do. Informality is OK. The essential characteristic of a requirements document is that it be complete.

Of course, *MacUser* asked for the moon—features that would take a year to develop. Most clients do. The problem was that *MacUser* didn't want to pay for a year's worth of work. After all, this program was to be a giveaway to promote their new online service, ZMac. The expression "Champagne taste on a beer budget" aptly describes most software clients.

In a requirements document, your client might ask for the moon—and if you're not careful you might have to deliver it. Usually, as was the case with *MacUser*, you'll negotiate with the client over what can be delivered within both the project's time frame and the client's price range. The requirements document is the platform for that negotiation.

The Functional Specification Phase

It all comes down to time and money—how long and how much—so both you and the client need to be sure of what you're getting into. It's easy to underestimate the time and money a software project will take.

In the normal flow of events, a requirements document begets a "functional specification document" that describes the whats and hows of the project. The purpose of the functional specification is twofold. This document describes the finished program's user interface and major features, and it enables you and the client to come to a mutual understanding of what comprises the deliverables.

The Preliminary Design Phase

But of even greater significance to your mental health, the functional specification provides you with a first opportunity to think about implementation details. As a direct outgrowth of the functional spec, you'll do a preliminary design. In the design phase you consider alternative strategies for meeting the program requirements—before you sit down to write a line of code—and you discover the answers to these very important questions: Can it be done? How long will it take? What will it cost?

You work out the program's structure during the design phase, as well as a rough cut of fundamental algorithms. Any device you choose for this structuring is OK—pseudocode, flowcharts, data-flow diagrams, Buhr diagrams—whatever makes sense for you and the particular project. The important thing is that you write it down. Taking the time to think the details through before committing them to code and writing them down so that you'll stay on track saves you time overall.

> **Reality Check**
>
> In our less than perfect world, requirements documents, functional specs, and preliminary designs are elegant figments of a software engineer's imagination. Most software is specified and designed in haste, on a blackboard or the back of a napkin.

Designing the Loser Interface

When we designed the Loser component of *MacUser*'s Security utility, we began with the bottom line. Essentially, Loser had to hide a file from the user. In programming terms, Loser needed to toggle the file's status between two states: visible and invisible.

How do you make a file invisible? Anything to do with the file system should lead you to the *Inside Macintosh* chapters on the File Manager. The first appears in Volume II and deals with the MFS (Macintosh file system), the so-called flat file system of the early Macintosh 128 and 512. The chapter with greater relevance to our modern Mac, on the HFS (hierarchical file system), is in Volume IV.

No matter which of these two chapters you consult, you'll discover that an "invisible bit" is associated with every file. It's a bit maintained by the File Manager, existing in the file's "Finder information block" and controlling whether Finder displays the file's icon or name in the desktop. You get access to this bit from the *fdFlags* field of the Finder information block.

We won't get into all the exact details of this stuff—nothing in the File Manager is simple, as we'll learn in the next chapter! What's important to know here is that *GetFInfo* and *SetFInfo*, a pair of routines in the File Manager, allow an application to read and set a file's Finder information block. Here's some sample code that shows how to get the value of the *fdFlags* field:

```
#define     kInvisible     0x4000

FInfo       fInfo;
Boolean     invis;

:
GetFInfo (fileName, volumeRefNumber, &fInfo);
invis = fInfo.fdFlags & kInvisible;
```

GetFInfo makes use of a file specification that consists of a file name and a volume reference number. As we'll see a little later in this chapter, Loser's user interface supplies the file specification.

Making a file invisible is simple: Get the Finder information block, set the invisible attribute-bit, and write the data structure back into the file system. Here's the code that makes a file, specified by *fileName* and *volumeRefNumber*, invisible:

```
FInfo          fInfo;
Boolean        invis;

:
GetFInfo (fileName, volumeRefNumber, &fInfo);
fInfo.fdFlags |= kInvisible;
SetFInfo (fileName, volumeRefNumber, &fInfo);
```

Notice the fragment *OR*s in the invisible bit defined as the token *kInvisible*. This code fragment is, in essence, the entire application layer for Loser. Loser's application layer is so simple that the outstanding design issue is the user interface: How does the user select the file for losing or finding?

Our first impulse was to use Finder for file selection—Mac users are familiar with the point and click selection techniques of the desktop. We thought, Wouldn't it be neat to use Finder for file selection and then hide the selected files?

It turned out that this wasn't such a neat idea after all. Finder doesn't have a programming interface yet, which means that there are no system calls a program can make to get the list of selected desktop files. Finder desktop selections are local to

Finder, and it doesn't share that data with the outside world. How does our application find out what those files are?

We were aware of another application, a utility that extends Finder's capability called Aladdin's Magic Menu, that actually uses the desktop's selected files. When we talked with Aladdin about their technology, hoping to get an insight into how they did it, they told us that the Aladdin engineer who discovered their technique did so only after many hours of rummaging around in RAM and arduous debugging—a grim prospect. Magic Menu reads the selected desktop files by reading Finder's internal data structures.

The problem with hacking in undocumented areas of the system is that your software then has to react to changes in each subsequent release of the system software, with little or no help from Apple. Aladdin's slick interface has the potential to become a maintenance nightmare.

There was another problem associated with using Finder as Loser's interface: It made sense only half the time. One of Loser's requirements was that it be able to make invisible files visible again. How would the application find invisible files?

When you're backed into a corner, the best thing to do is to keep the solution simple. Included with the system software is the Standard File Package, which presents and manages the dialog box that the user normally uses to select a file for opening. Figure 9-2 shows this familiar file selection dialog box, named the SFGetFile dialog box after the routine that invokes it.

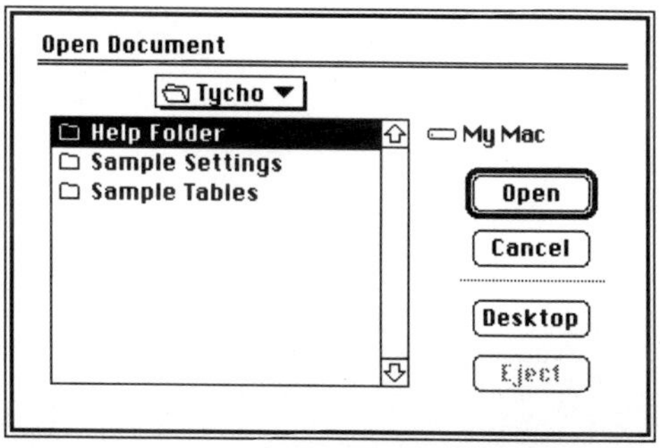

Figure 9-2.
The SFGetFile dialog box.

The other half of the Standard File Package is the SFPutFile dialog box, shown in Figure 9-3 on the next page. It's the dialog box the user sees when he or she chooses the Save As command in a File menu.

The best thing about using the Standard File Package is that its routines are already written and debugged and therefore could save you weeks of coding and debugging an interface to the file system. When you're designing software for a fixed price, time is money.

But if we were to use the Standard File Package for Loser's interface, how was that interface to be managed? Loser was to have two modes: It needed to hide ("lose")

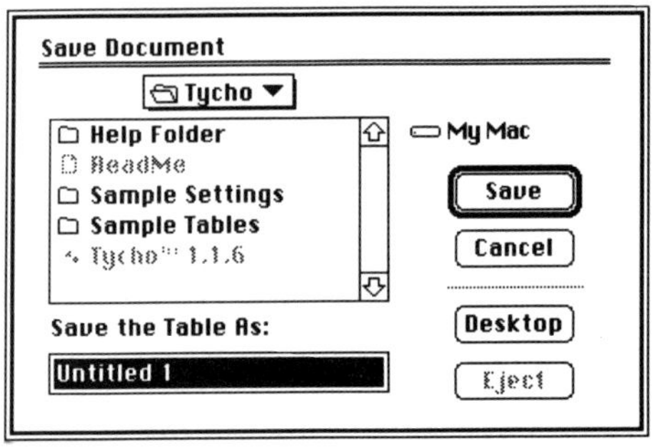

Figure 9-3.
The SFPutFile dialog box.

visible files and to find lost ones. If we added two radio buttons, named "Lose File" and "Find File," to the bottom of the standard Open dialog box, we'd make it possible for the user to view either all visible or all invisible files in a folder. To emphasize the mode selection aspect of opening a file, we decided to have Loser retitle what would normally be called the Open button as "Lose" when the user had chosen Lose mode and as "Find" when the user had chosen Find mode. Figure 9-4 shows the Loser dialog box.

Whether we could use the SFGetFile dialog box for the Loser interface hinged on two issues: Could we get the Standard File Package to display either all visible files or all

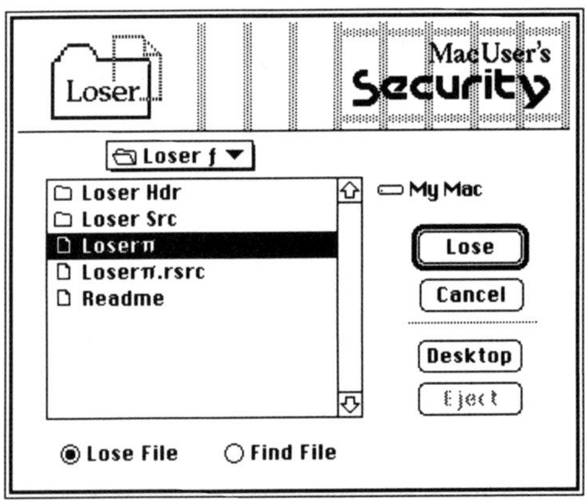

Figure 9-4.
The Loser interface.

Macintosh Packages

A Macintosh package like the Standard File Package is a collection of routines that extend the Toolbox and the Operating System. These routines reside on disk in a PACK resource. They're brought into RAM only when they're needed. Examples of other Macintosh packages are the Disk Initialization Package, which provides you with an interface for naming and initializing disks, and the Binary-Decimal Conversion Package, which you use for converting integers to strings, and vice versa.

invisible files in its list of file names? And could we add radio buttons to the SFGetFile dialog box?

The answer to both questions was yes—thanks to hooks. The Standard File Package provides a place, called a "hook," where you can install two "hook procs." ("Proc," of course, is short for "procedure.") Hook procs are also called "call-back routines," referring to the ability of a system procedure to call an application-defined function at certain times during its operation. Call-back essentially allows you to extend the features of system routines. Installing a hook proc is as simple as passing a function pointer as an argument to a system routine.

The Standard File Package will support two hook procs:

- The package calls the file filter hook proc whenever it adds a file name to its list box. This filter proc is actually a feature of the Dialog Manager (which you'll see in a moment) that the package uses to implement its dialog box interface. The Dialog Manager calls this hook proc whenever the package receives an event. The file filter proc returns a value that the package uses to determine whether to display the file name in its list box. The file filter proc therefore controls the display of the dialog box, based on the value of the file's invisible attribute-bit.
- The package calls the dialog hook proc when it receives a mouse-down event in the dialog box. Loser takes advantage of the dialog proc to manage the radio buttons. Because the package calls the dialog hook proc whenever it receives a mouse-down event in the dialog box, Loser can respond appropriately when the user chooses the Lose File or Find File button in that box.

With all our design issues addressed, we can move on to the details of Loser's implementation.

Hook Procs

Understanding hook procs is one of the keys to understanding how to get the Macintosh to do your bidding. The Toolbox provides a number of hooks that let you use call-back routines to get the most out of your application. For example, TextEdit (in System 6.0 and later) provides hooks to call your routines when it

- draws a line of text
- measures the caret's position
- calculates the end of a line
- gets a mouse-down in the text area

We'll venture to say that hooks are responsible for the overwhelming success of Macintosh software. Without hook procs, Mac programs would still look like MacPaint and MacWrite 1.0.

Using the Standard File Package

The Standard File Package simplifies much of the coding job. Its set of routines frees us from the burden of putting up a dialog box by means of the Dialog Manager routines or of having to navigate the file system.

We saw in Figure 9-4 on page 196 that Loser uses the SFGetFile dialog box, which appears when the application calls the *SFGetFile* routine. Normally, an application calls *SFGetFile* after a user has selected Open from the File menu. *SFGetFile* displays the dialog box and the list box that contains file names; interacts with the user, calling routines in the Dialog Manager directly; and returns all necessary information about the selected file. One call does it all.

The SFGetFile Dialog Box

When *SFGetFile* returns control to your application, the user has either selected a file or canceled the Open operation. The routine communicates with Loser by means of the *SFReply* record. The application passes the address of the *SFReply* record to *SFGetFile*, and *SFGetFile* fills in the values before it returns. Here's the definition of the *SFReply* record:

```
typedef struct SFReply
{
    char      good;
    char      copy;
    long      fType;
    int       vRefNum;
    int       version;
    unsigned char  fName[64];
} SFReply;
```

When *SFGetFile* returns, the *good* field of the record is *true* (the value *1*) if the user has selected the Open button, or *false* (the value *0*) if the user has selected Cancel. If *good* is *true*, *vRefNum* specifies the volume reference number of the file and *fName* contains the file name. The other fields of the *SFReply* record can be ignored. With a volume reference number and a file name, *SFGetFile* has enough information to open or, in our case, access the Finder information for a file.

Loser has those two radio buttons, so it can't use the standard *SFGetFile* dialog box or the *SFGetFile* procedure that invokes the dialog box. We have to create another dialog box, similar to the *SFGetFile* dialog box but with the addition of the Lose File and Find File radio buttons.

SFGetFile uses a dialog box template, the DLOG -4000 resource from the System file. This template contains the information that describes the dialog box. Now, you don't want to modify the dialog box in the System file—unless you want every other application on your disk to have Lose File and Find File radio buttons appended to their SFGetFile dialog boxes. The technique for appending items to a standard system dialog box calls for copying the dialog box template to your application's resource file and then modifying the copy. ResEdit is the best tool for this job. If you're interested in how it's done, see the sidebar "Creating the Loser Dialog Box" at the end of this chapter.

Now, how do we get the *SFGetFile* routine to use our new dialog box instead of DLOG -4000 from the System file? The answer is that we don't use *SFGetFile*, but rather a similar routine, *SFPGetFile*.

SFPGetFile (the *P* is for "Programmer") provides all the utility of *SFGetFile* but accepts an alternative dialog resource ID number. *SFPGetFile* accepts nine parameters, one of which is the ID number for our new dialog resource. Three of its parameters are pointers to our hook procs, defined as type *ProcPtr*. Here's the prototype for *SFPGetFile*:

```
void SFPGetFile (Point where, StringPtr prompt, ProcPtr fileFilter,
    short numTypes, SFTypeList typeList, ProcPtr dlgHook,
    SFReply *reply, short dlgID, ProcPtr filterProc);
```

The first argument, *where*, defines the coordinates of the point at which the upper left corner of the dialog box will appear. We use the *prompt* argument to print a prompt string in the dialog box. Loser passes a pointer to the file filter hook proc in the third argument. The next two arguments, *numTypes* and *typeList*, define which files will appear in the dialog box's list box. You would normally specify the file types of the files that you're interested in, but Loser is supplying its own file filter function by means of the file filter hook proc, so *SFPGetFile* won't use these arguments. We therefore pass *0* to *numTypes*. Loser passes a pointer to the dialog hook proc in the *dlgHook* argument. The *reply* argument we've already mentioned—this is where Loser passes the address of an *SFReply* record. Loser passes the new ID number of its *SFGetFile* dialog resource in the *dlgID* argument. Finally, Loser passes the address of its filter proc to the last argument, *filterProc*.

Toolbox calls, and that includes packaged routines, use Pascal calling conventions, and C and Pascal are different in their conventions. We can write a hook proc in C, but we must declare it by using the *pascal* keyword, as in

```
pascal void
foo (char a, char *b)
{
...
}
```

The *pascal* keyword is a unique feature of the THINK C environment and provides the "glue" required to manipulate the stack when calling C functions from Pascal. All of Loser's hook proc C functions are declared using this keyword.

Passing a pointer to a function is as simple as typing its name. If *foo()* is our hook proc and *bar()* accepts a *ProcPtr* argument, we pass the address of *foo()* to *bar()* in this way:

```
bar (foo);
```

The File Filter Call-back Routine

Loser uses the file filter call-back routine to select the file names that will be displayed in the dialog box's list box. As *SFPGetFile* reads through the file names in the current folder, it calls the file filter routine for each file. If the routine returns *0*, *SFPGetFile* displays the file name in its list box. If the routine returns *1*, *SFPGetFile* won't display the file. The file filter call-back routine is shown in Figure 9-5.

```
static  pascal uchar
loserGetFileFilterProc (FileParam  *paramBlkPtr)
{
    Boolean         invis;
    pBoolean        result;

    // test the invisible bit
    invis = (paramBlkPtr->ioFlFndrInfo.fdFlags & fInvisible) ?
            true : false;

    if (sLoseMode)       /* in lose mode, show visible files */
        result = invis                     // display visible files;
    else
        result = invis ? false : true;     // display invisible files

    return (result);
}
```

Figure 9-5.
The loserGetFileFilterProc() *routine is Loser's file filter proc function.*

The calling convention for this routine is described by this prototype:

```
pascal unsigned char
fileFilter (FileParam *fileParams);
```

Notice that the return type of the file filter procedure is an *unsigned char*, an 8-bit data type. This means that when the function returns *1*, it must return an 8-bit value, *0x01*—not *0x0001*.

SFPGetFile passes the file filter routine a pointer to a File Manager data structure, a file parameter block, for each file it finds in the current folder. This is where we get the file's invisible attribute-bit, in the *ioFlFndrInfo.fdFlags* field of this structure. The *loserGetFileFilterProc()* routine uses the invisible bit to figure out whether the file is visible and returns an appropriate value based on the current Loser state.

The Loser state depends on the user's selection—either the Lose File button or the Find File button. The static variable *sLoseMode* maintains the value of this state in the program. As we'll see when we look at Loser's button processing, if the user has selected the Lose File button, *sLoseMode* is *true*; otherwise, *sLoseMode* is *false*.

If Loser is in Lose File mode, which means that it is to hide files, it should display the file names that are candidates for invisibility, that is, the visible files. The function *loserGetFileFilterProc()* therefore returns *0x00* if a file is visible, and *0x01* if the file is invisible, when Loser is in the Lose File state. If Loser is in Find File mode, it should display those files that are candidates for visibility, that is, the invisible files. The file filter proc therefore returns *0x00* if a file is invisible, and *0x01* if the file is visible, when Loser is in the Find File state. Figure 9-6 illustrates this logic.

Loser Mode?	***File Visible?***	***Display File Name?***
Lose File	no	no
Lose File	yes	yes
Find File	no	yes
Find File	yes	no

Figure 9-6.
The file filter proc truth table.

Dialog Item Lists

Before we look at the dialog box hook procedure that manages the radio buttons, we need to understand how the Dialog Manager associates items with a dialog box window. The Standard File Package routines use the Dialog Manager to display the Loser dialog box, so we'll need to know something about the dialog box item list in order to understand how Loser manages the dialog box's two radio buttons, Lose File and Find File.

The definition of a dialog box includes two parts: a dialog box template that describes the dialog box's window; and a dependent item list that contains information about the buttons, check boxes, radio buttons, text items, ICONs, PICTs, and user-defined items that will appear in the dialog box. Resource creation programs like ResEdit store the window template information in a DLOG resource and the item list data in a DITL resource. When an application creates a dialog box on the screen, the Dialog Manager creates a window based on the DLOG resource, finds the corresponding DITL information, and loads the items in the item list, allocating space in the heap for the items—controls, ICONs, PICTs, user items.

Each item in the DITL has a reference number, its list index. Indexes begin at 1. In your program, you use an index to specify a particular item in a list. When you create a dialog box and its item list using ResEdit, you have to keep note of an item's item number so that you'll have the correct index in your program to access it. Convention dictates that you define a symbolic constant for each item in your source code, usually in a header file. If you follow the directions in the sidebar "Creating the Loser Dialog Box" at the end of this chapter, your Lose File button will be item

#12, and your Find File button will be item #13. We've defined these constants accordingly in LoserConstants.h and repeat the definitions here for your edification.

```
#define    kLoserLoseButton    12
#define    kLoserFindButton    13
```

Because Loser changes the text string in what would normally be the Open button to Lose or Find, depending on the Loser mode, you'll need the index number for this button as well. The Open button is always item #1.

A note about the item list indexes of Standard File Package items, or those of any other system resource, for that matter: The *SFPGetFile* routine expects the Open button to be item #1, the Cancel button to be item #3, the list box user item to be item #7, and so on. Don't mess with these numbers. The Standard File Package expects these items in their proper sequence. Always add items to the end of an item list, never to the middle.

The Open button index defined by the Standard File Package is 1, so Loser defines a constant for it as

```
#define kSetButtonID     1
```

An item list data structure is designed to be versatile enough to account for a variety of potential item types. The structure contains a pointer, a bounding rectangle, a type declaration byte, and an array of additional data for the item. This structure is not defined in *Inside Macintosh,* but taking a hint from the DITL resource format, we can say that it might look something like this:

```
struct ditlItem
{
    Ptr   ptr;
    Rect  bounds;
    char  type,
          length,
          data [255];
}
```

The *type* field identifies the kind of item an element is—button, check box, static text, and so on—and the content of the *data* field depends on this type. For resource-based controls, ICONs, or PICTs, the *data* field contains the resource ID of the item. For text items, the *data* field contains the text. For buttons, check boxes, and radio buttons like those used in Loser, the *data* field contains the control's title.

Because this data structure is considered internal to the workings of the Dialog Manager, we never access any of its fields directly. When the Dialog Manager creates the dialog box, it uses the resource item to create a control, an ICON, or whatever the template describes, in the heap. You therefore access these heap objects with a Dialog Manager routine, *GetDItem*, which returns the bounding box, item type, and handle to the heap object. We're interested in controls for Loser right now, which are managed by the Control Manager.

Managing Loser's Radio Buttons

The Control Manager allocates heap space for each control and returns the control's handle to the application. You access the control, set its value, show or hide it, or whatever, using this handle. When a control is embedded in a dialog box, the Dialog Manager makes all the Control Manager calls to create the control, but the application must read and set the control's value.

If you know the control's item number, you can get the control handle with the Dialog Manager routine *GetDItem*. *GetDItem* accepts a dialog pointer to the dialog box and item number and returns the control handle, bounding rectangle, and item type. Here's an example, a call to *GetDItem* that gets the Lose File button's control handle:

```
DialogPtr      theDialog;
short          itemType;
ControlHandle  loseButtonHdl;
Rect           box;

GetDItem (theDialog, kLoserLoseButton, &itemType, &loseButtonHdl, &box);
```

The Lose File and Find File buttons are managed in Loser's dialog hook call-back routine, *loserGetFileDlgHook()*, which is shown in Figure 9-7. The Standard File Package makes it easy to manage radio buttons in the SFPGetFile dialog box. Once you've installed *loserGetFileDlgHook()* as the hook proc, the Standard File Package calls the proc with the dialog pointer and the number of the item in which a mouse-down occurred. It's therefore up to the hook proc *loserGetFileDlgHook()* to toggle the radio buttons and set the *sLoseMode* value according to the button selection.

```
static pascal int
loserGetFileDlgHook (DialogPtr dialogPtr, short item)
{
    short           itemType;
    Rect            box;
    ControlHandle   loseButton, findButton, okButton, h;

    /* get the control handles */
    GetDItem (dialogPtr, kLoserLoseButton, &itemType, &loseButton, &box);
    GetDItem (dialogPtr, kLoserFindButton, &itemType, &findButton, &box);
    GetDItem (dialogPtr, 1, &itemType, &okButton, &box);

    switch (item) {

        case getOpen:           // the standard items
        case getCancel:
```

Figure 9-7. *(continued)*
Loser's dialog hook call-back routine, loserGetFileDlgHook().

Figure 9-7. *continued*

```
        case getEject:
        case getDrive:
        case getNmList:
        case getScroll:
            break;

        case -1:                // initialization
            SetCtlValue (loseButton, sLoseMode ? true : false);
            SetCtlValue (findButton, sLoseMode ? false : true);

            /* install graphics items for auto-refresh */
            GetDItem (dialogPtr, kGetFileSepLine, &itemType, &h, &box);
            SetDItem (dialogPtr, kGetFileSepLine, itemType,
                sepLineProc, &box);

            GetDItem (dialogPtr, kGetFileOutline, &itemType, &h, &box);
            SetDItem (dialogPtr, kGetFileOutline, itemType,
                buttonProc, &box);
            break;

        case kLoserLoseButton:          // my items
            if (GetCtlValue (findButton))
            {
                SetCTitle (okButton, "\pLose");
                SetCtlValue (loseButton, 1);
                SetCtlValue (findButton, 0);
                sLoseMode = true;
                item = 101;    // reread the directory
            }
            break;

        case kLoserFindButton:
            if (GetCtlValue (loseButton))
            {
                SetCTitle (okButton, "\pFind");
                SetCtlValue (loseButton, 0);
                SetCtlValue (findButton, 1);
                sLoseMode = false;
                item = 101;    // reread the directory
            }
            break;
    }

    return (item);

} /* loserGetFileDlgHook */
```

Loser needs to process only those events that occur in either of its two radio buttons—those events tagged with the item number of either *kLoserFindButton* or *kLoserLoseButton*. When the user mouses in a file system navigation control, *loserGetFileDlgHook()* simply returns the item number to the Standard File Package so that it can process the event.

When the user clicks the mouse in either of the radio buttons, *loserGetFileDlgHook()* sets that control's value to *1* and sets the value of the other radio button to *0*, using the Control Manager routine *SetCtlValue*. (See the sidebar "Managing Radio Buttons.") *loserGetFileDlgHook()* also changes the Loser state stored in *sLoseMode*, changes the Open button so that its text reflects the state, and returns the magic number *101*, which tells *SFPGetFile* to reread and redisplay the file list. Of course, when *SFPGetFile* rereads the list, the file filter proc will use the new Loser state to display the correct set of files, based on the new Loser file mode.

The Standard File Package also calls *loserGetFileDlgHook()* when the dialog box is initialized, just before it draws the dialog box. This gives Loser a chance to initialize the radio buttons before the dialog box appears.

At initialization, the package sends *−1* for the item number. None of the dialog box items can have a negative number, so *−1* is therefore a safe value that uniquely flags the initialization phase and allows the hook proc to do its initialization stuff.

loserGetFileDlgHook() performs two initialization tasks. As we've already mentioned, it sets the radio button values to reflect the correct Loser state. Its other task is to install proc pointers for user items. Most commercial Macintosh applications use this technique to support automatic refreshing of dialog box items.

You're no doubt familiar with the button outline that indicates the default selection in a dialog box. Figure 9-8 shows a button with the "default" outline.

Figure 9-8.
A 3-point outline around a dialog box button tells the user that pressing Return yields the same result as a mouse click in that button.

Inside Macintosh tells us how to draw this outline. Given the item number and the dialog pointer, here's how you draw the outline for the default button:

```
GetDItem (theDialog, theItem, &itemType, &itemHdl, &itemBounds);
PenSize (3, 3);
InsetRect (&box, -4, -4);
FrameRoundRect (&box, 16, 16);
```

Of greater interest is *when* you draw the outline. *Inside Macintosh* only hints at that, so you're on your own. Your first choice might be to simply draw the button when the program initializes the dialog box. This technique works fine—until a screen

Managing Radio Buttons

Radio buttons were named after the push-buttons usually found on older car radios. The salient feature of car radio buttons is that only one button can be selected at a time, and each new button selection clears the previous selection. It's a one-of-many switch, and your application must perform this button logic. *SetCtlValue* is the Control Manager routine you use to change the appearance of the buttons, and it requires a control handle and a value. The control value *1* selects the button. The control value *0* clears it.

The key to implementing radio button logic is in clearing the value of the other buttons when the user makes a selection. You therefore need to have all the radio button handles in a group so that you can set all the button values. Here's some sample code that manages the radio buttons A, B, and C.

```
selectRadioButtons (DialogPtr theDialog, short theItem)
{
    ControlHandle  buttonA, buttonB, buttonC;
    Rect        box;
    short       itemType;

    /* get all the group handles */
    GetDItem (theDialog, kButtonA, &itemType, &buttonA, &box);
    GetDItem (theDialog, kButtonB, &itemType, &buttonB, &box);
    GetDItem (theDialog, kButtonC, &itemType, &buttonC, &box);

    switch (theItem)
    {
        case kButtonA:
            SetCtlValue (buttonA, 1);
            SetCtlValue (buttonB, 0);
            SetCtlValue (buttonC, 0);
            break;

        case kButtonB:
            SetCtlValue (buttonA, 0);
            SetCtlValue (buttonB, 1);
            SetCtlValue (buttonC, 0);
            break;

        case kButtonC:
            SetCtlValue (buttonA, 0);
            SetCtlValue (buttonB, 0);
            SetCtlValue (buttonC, 1);
            break;

    }
}
```

saver utility like *Pyro* blanks the screen. When the screen is eventually redrawn, the Dialog Manager draws everything in the dialog box except the outline. Figure 9-9 illustrates the problem.

Figure 9-9. *The dialog box looks fine when it's first drawn. After a screen saver utility erases the screen and redraws it, the default button outline and the line between the Cancel and Desktop buttons are missing.*

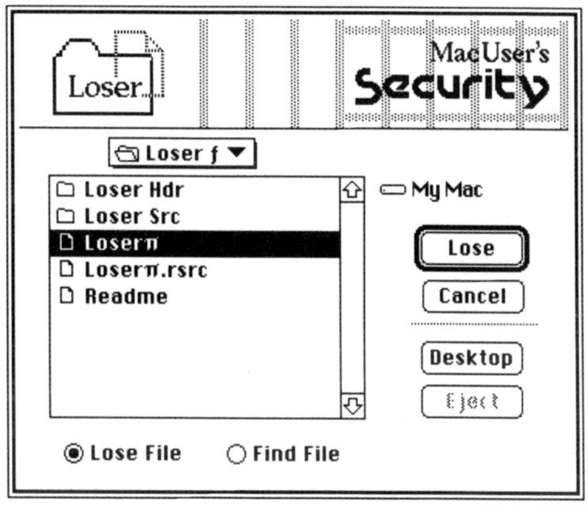

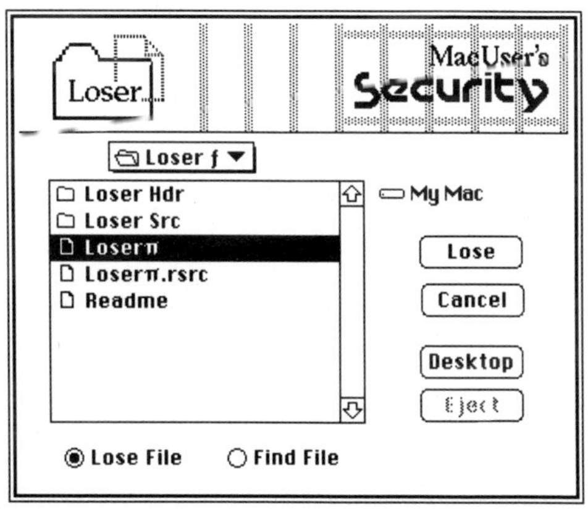

A better solution is to draw the outline whenever there's an update event, and, if you read between the lines in the Dialog Manager chapter of *Inside Macintosh,* you'll figure out that the Dialog Manager supports a method of doing just this. If a dialog box item is a special type of item, called a user item, and if you install a pointer to a function as the item handle, the Dialog Manager will call the function when it receives an update event. If you therefore install a pointer to a function that draws the button outline, *Voila!*The outline will be drawn when the dialog box gets an update event.

There's a trick to using this technique with the button outline. You can't install a function pointer in the button item—you'd lose the Control Manager information for the button, and it would cease to be a button. The trick is in creating the user item on top of the default button.

You use the Dialog Manager routine *SetDItem* to install a function pointer in a dialog box's item handle. This doesn't affect the DITL resource—only the in-RAM representation of the dialog box item. Normally, a user item has a *null* handle. If the handle's value is non-null, the Dialog Manager assumes that the value is a function pointer.

Loser's outline drawing function, which is yet another hook proc and declared with the *pascal* keyword, appears in Figure 9-10. Note that although Loser uses this routine to update the user item, which is the outline, it uses the button's bounding rectangle, not the user item's. That way, we're sure that the outline will be centered on the button.

```
pascal void
buttonProc (DialogPtr theDialog,
            short theItem)    // outline the dialog button
{
    short           type;
    Rect            box;
    Handle          itemHdl;

    GetDItem (theDialog, kSetButtonID, &type, &itemHdl, &box);

    PenSize (3, 3);
    InsetRect (&box, -4, -4);
    FrameRoundRect (&box, 16, 16);
    PenNormal ();

} /* buttonProc */
```

Figure 9-10.
The buttonProc() *routine outlines a dialog box's default button.*

We've included another user item in the Loser dialog box. A dotted line is drawn between the Cancel and the Desktop buttons to separate their button "groups."

You'll find the code for drawing and redrawing the dotted-line user item in the source file DialogUtil.c.

The filter hook proc

The *filterProc* routine is the last of the three *SFGetFile* hook procs and is actually a Dialog Manager hook that responds to dialog box events that occur within the Dialog Manager routine *ModalDialog*. Loser uses this hook proc to detect a press of the

Return key or of the Command-period key combination. Users are accustomed to having the Return or the Enter key select a dialog box's default button, and to having the Command-period combination cancel the dialog box. The filter proc supports these actions.

You'll find the code for the filter proc in *DLOGfilterProc1()* in DialogUtil.c. The routine gets the actual event record from the Dialog Manager and manipulates the *what* and *where* fields of the event record to fool the Dialog Manager into thinking that a button press has occurred in either the Find/Lose button or the Cancel button.

Manipulating the Invisible Bit

We shouldn't become so deeply involved in managing the dialog box that we lose sight of Loser's prime directive: to set or clear a file's invisible bit. In theory, we already know what to do, but let's look in detail at what's required.

Figure 9-11 shows the essence of the program. The *doLoserGetFile()* routine is essentially the Loser user interface. When *doLoserGetFile()* returns with a mode and a selected file, Loser calls the File Manager routine *GetFInfo* to fill the *FInfo* record with current data for the specified file. Hiding or displaying the file is simply a matter of setting or clearing the bit in the *fdFlags* field of this structure, based on the value of the static variable *sLoseMode*. Loser then calls *SetFInfo*, which rewrites the entire record back to the file system.

```
if (doLoserGetFile (&docParams))
{
    fileName = docParams.fileParams.fileName;
    volRefNum = docParams.fileParams.volRefNum;

    if (err = GetFInfo (fileName, volRefNum, &fndrInfo))
        doFileCantAlert (fileName, kRead, err, "\pGetFInfo");
    else
    {
        if (sLoseMode)
            fndrInfo.fdFlags |= fInvisible;
        else
            fndrInfo.fdFlags &= ~fInvisible;

        if (err = SetFInfo (fileName, volRefNum, &fndrInfo))
            doFileCantAlert (fileName, kWrite, err, "\pSetFInfo");
    }
}
```

Figure 9-11.
The heart of a Loser.

Loser is a small application; unlike Generic App, it has no use for window and document management utilities and therefore doesn't need routines for them. The source code for Loser resides in five source files: DialogUtil.c, FileUtil.c, Loser.c, MiscUtil.c, and WindowUtil.c. You'll find that these files contain a very few routines, with the exception of Loser.c, which contains the bulk of the code.

Creating the Loser Dialog Box

The Standard File Package's SFGetFile dialog box contains buttons, a list box, and other controls for file system navigation—and its procedures expect these items to appear in the proper order. You can customize this dialog box by adding new items to the end of the list of dialog box items. Loser's dialog box needs five additional items: a title, the two radio buttons, and two user items.

Although the modified DLOG -4000 resource is included with the complete source code for Loser, available on the disk that accompanies this book, you might be interested in learning how to modify this resource yourself.

Using ResEdit 2.1, open the System file and read the warning.

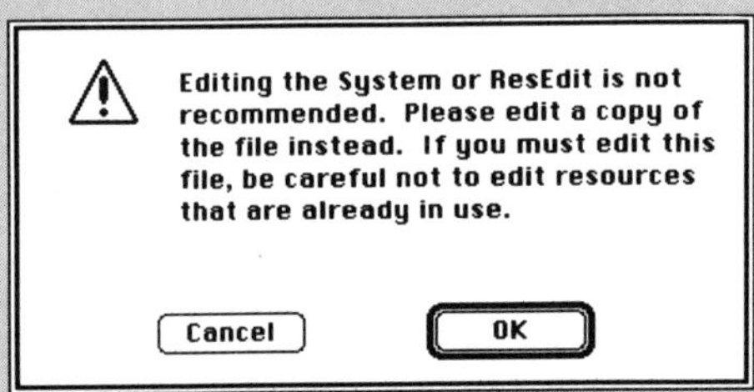

The warning you see when you open the System file in ResEdit.

Tread lightly in here. This is the currently running system, after all, and if you mess up, you mess up permanently.

In the System window, you'll see the resource icons, as shown at the top of the next page.

Find the resource named DLOG, and double-click on it. This reveals all the dialog templates contained in the System file, as shown on the next page.

Find template -4000, select it with a single click, and choose Copy from the Edit menu. This places a copy of the template on the Clipboard.

Now open the Loser resource file by pulling down the Open submenu and navigating to your Loser resource file, Loserπ.rsrc. Select the Loser resource file by clicking in its window, and paste the DLOG -4000 template into it.

Despite its size, Loser is an excellent teaching tool that contains many examples of using the Standard File Package and the Dialog Manager. We'll use this knowledge in Chapter 11's Browser, the final application in this book. But before we can write Browser, we'll need Chapter 10's background information on the File Manager.

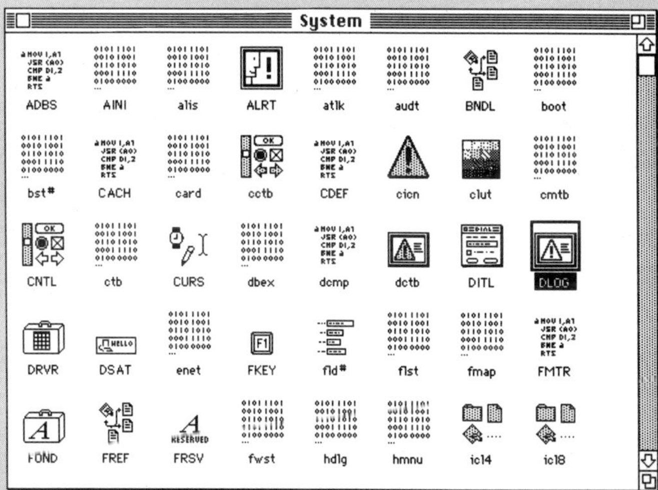

ResEdit Window after System is opened, showing the resource icons.

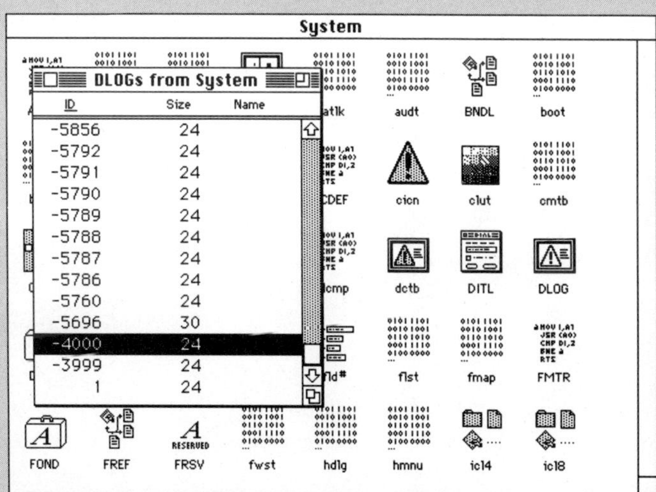

The System DLOG templates. DLOG -4000 is for the SFGetFile dialog box.

You now have a copy of the resource template in the Loser resource file. Next, you need to copy the item list. Repeat this process for DITL -4000, copying the template from the System file and pasting it into the application's resource file.

You now have all the necessary resources in Loser's resource file, so close the System file by using the close box in the upper left corner of the appropriate windows. Don't save any changes in the System file. If you have inadvertently modified the System file, perhaps by choosing Cut instead of Copy, you'll see the *Are you sure that you don't want to save?* message when you close the System window. The purpose of this exercise is *not* to modify the System file, so don't save changes in the System file. You could do some serious damage.

You should be working exclusively with the Loser resource file now. Renumber the new DLOG and DITL resources so that their numbers match their numbers in the Loser source files. Navigate to the new DLOG, and renumber it *65*. You do this by finding it, selecting it (again, with a single click), and using Get Resource Info in the Resource menu. You are then presented with a dialog box that allows you to change the ID number of the resource. If you already have this resource in your file—because you are working on the source disk's Loser resource file—ResEdit won't let you set this number to *65*. Don't worry. Use *66* in that event. Next, renumber the DITL resource the same way, using either *65* or *66*, so that its ID number matches the DLOG's ID number.

Then you'll need to link the DITL to the DLOG. Open the DLOG (*65* or *66* depending on what you just did). In the dialog box, change the value of the field DITL ID to the number you've just assigned to the DITL.

Next, you need to expand the window to make room at the bottom for the controls. You could do this in one of two ways, but you're already looking at the text representation of the DLOG, so it's easiest to enter the numbers into the edit boxes. The values for Loser's window are Top: *32*, Left: *41*, Height: *282*, Width: *342*. While you're in there, select Set 'DLOG' Characteristics from the DLOG menu and make sure that the *procID* field value is *1*. This defines the window type that the Window Manager will draw for the dialog box. The complete contents of the editing window are shown at the top of the next page.

A miniature representation of the dialog window on a Macintosh screen is shown in the DLOG editing window. Double-click on this window, and the DITL contents should zoom into a full-size window for editing. All the items in this particular DITL have to be in the list and in the right order. If they aren't, the Standard File Package won't know what's what. There are even a couple of items that you don't see, off-screen.

Every item in a DITL has an item number, which is how you access it in your application. Try double-clicking the Cancel button. You will see ResEdit's DITL

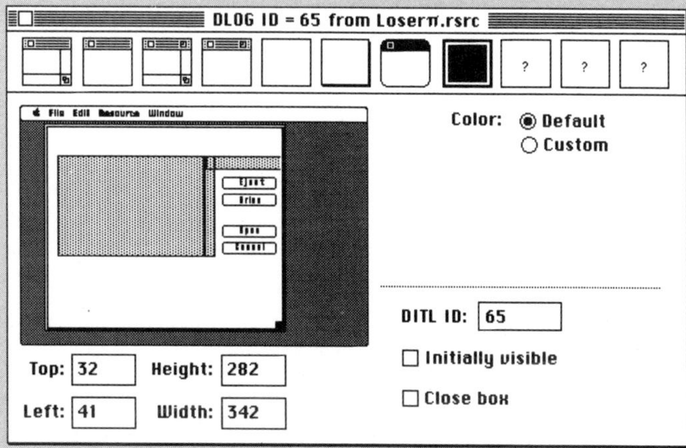

The DLOG editing window.

item editing box, like the one shown below. The title of this window is Edit DITL item #3 from Loserπ.rsrc because the Cancel button is the third item in the DITL list. Don't change the order of the controls. When you've finished looking, close the window with the close box in the upper left corner.

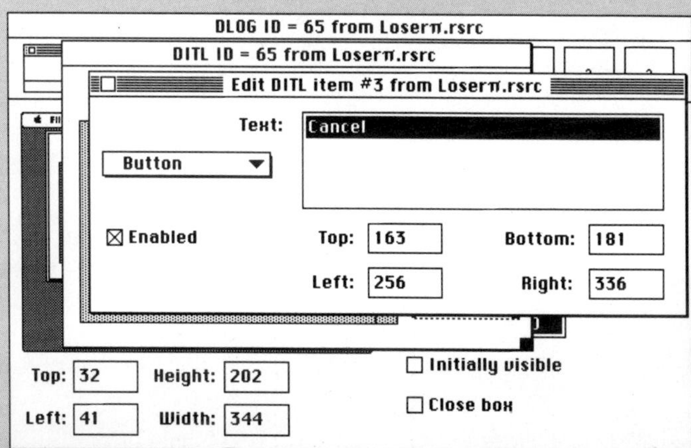

The DITL item editing dialog box, with the third item, which is the Cancel button, selected.

Now comes the painful process of moving all the existing items down in the window to make room for Loser's title. Select each item, one by one (use a single click on the item), and drag it south about 60 pixels or so (three-quarters of an inch). A selected item has a highlighted "handle" at its lower right corner. Don't try to use this handle to drag the item—it resizes the item—but rather, drag the item from its center. Try to move all items to the same locations relative to one another. For finer tuning, you can double-click on an item and enter its new local coordinates in the DITL edit window.

This ResEdit DITL edit window is the interface you use for both creating new items and editing existing items. Items are assigned numbers sequentially. The next free item in the GetFile dialog box is #11, so Loser will use items #11, #12, and #13 for the dialog box title, the Lose File button, and the Find File button and items #14 and #15 for the user items. We've included a PICT resource in our resource file for the Loser title item, but, for the purposes of this example, we'll ask you to create a Static Text item.

After you've moved SFGetFile's existing items out of the way, you'll create the new items. To create a new Static Text title item, drag the Static Text icon from the DITL toolbox to the DITL window.

Double-click the new item to open the DITL edit window. Now type

```
Loser loses found files, and finds lost ones.
```

or any title of your choice in the edit box. This is the text that will go in your title. Click in the close box to close the Edit window. The new title should appear, smack-dab in the middle of the window. Drag the item to the top of the window, and resize the bounding rectangle with the small gray handle in the lower right corner. The text will flow into the allotted space, as shown below.

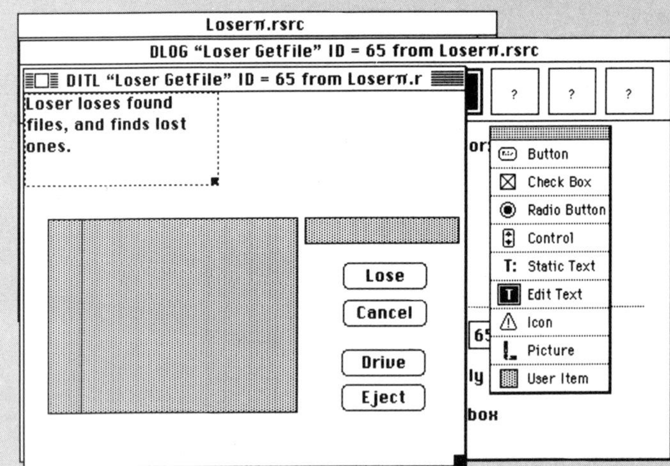

Creating the title.

Next, create the radio buttons, one at a time. Again, drag the new item (radio button) from the DITL toolbox to the DITL window. Double-click the item to open the Edit window, and name it "Lose File" or "Find File." Again, you'll have to size and place the items in the larger dialog window, as shown below.

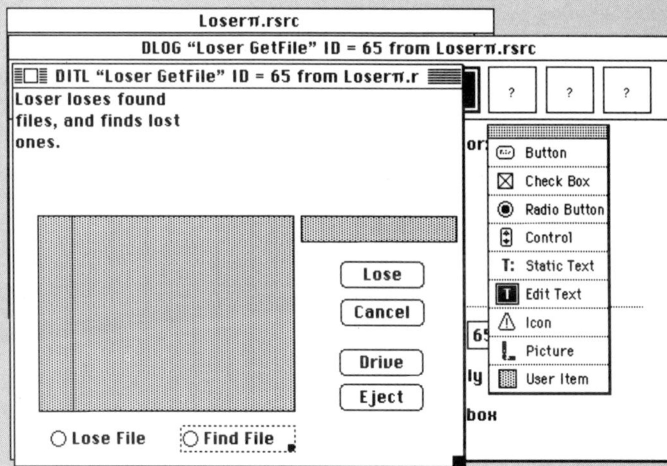

Creating the radio buttons.

Finally, you'll create the user items. Drag the user item from the toolbox to the DITL window. Position the user item so that it overlaps the Lose button.

The last user item will be for the dotted line between the Lose and Cancel buttons and the Drive and Eject buttons. Using the same procedure, drag the user item to the area between the buttons. The item should be approximately 80 pixels wide and 3 or 4 pixels high. Center the rectangle between the two groups of buttons as shown below.

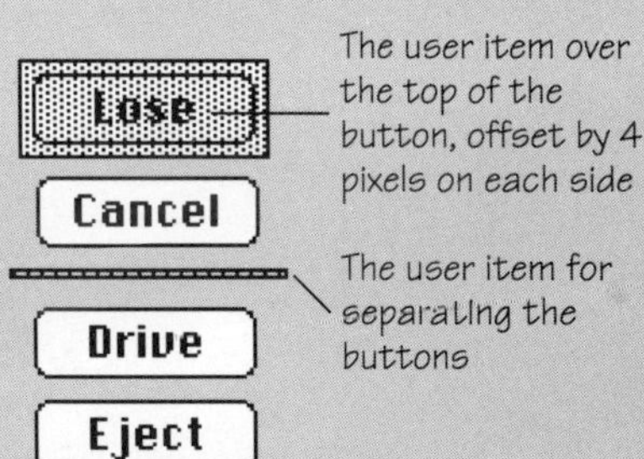

Creating the button outline and button separator user items.

Once you have added all the new items, do your final adjustments to the items in the dialog window so that it all looks nice and neat, and then save your changes and choose Quit.

10

THE MACINTOSH FILE SYSTEM

The Macintosh file system combines disk drives, system software, and data to give you long-term data storage. In this chapter, we'll discuss the major features of the file system and describe how an application uses File Manager routines to access data.

File System Etiquette

The Macintosh file system has a great deal of flexibility. The number of files and folders in the system is limited only by the size of the hard disk. Files can grow and shrink and can be copied, moved from one folder to another, or deleted from the system. If they are in different folders, they can even share common names.

To keep things straight, the File Manager maintains a complex, cross-referenced set of data structures on disk and in memory. These data structures impose some formality on your dealing with files. If your application needs to read from a file, for example, it must first set up the operation by opening the file. Other operations, like deleting a file or moving a file from one folder to another, can be done only when the file is closed.

The first step in getting at a file's data is to open the file. Opening the file sets up an "access path" to the file. An open file can be read, written to, locked, or unlocked. Opening a file yields a file reference number, an integer used by an application for file access during the time the file is open.

Your application can perform three kinds of operations on an open file: reading, writing to, and controlling. Reading a file is retrieving the file's data. Reading transfers a specified number of bytes from the file to a local buffer, which must be large enough to hold the requested data. Writing to is adding to or changing a file's data. Writing transfers data from a local buffer to the file. Locking is a way of arranging exclusive access to a piece of a file in a multiuser environment, and unlocking reverses the process. Locking and unlocking are both file "control" operations.

Closing a file writes all pending data (that might be in an internal file system buffer) to the file—a process called "flushing"—and frees the access path structures. The file reference number is not valid after the file is closed, and further reading or writing using the access path will produce an error.

File System Hardware

Before we go into the details of the File Manager, let's look at the hardware level. The file system is based on a collection of drives and their contents. Drives can be "fixed," the way a Winchester hard disk drive is, or "removable," the way a 3.5-inch microfloppy disk is. (We're limiting our discussion here to traditional magnetic storage media, although we certainly acknowledge the newer optical technologies, such as the magneto-optical and CD-ROM drives.)

In strict hardware hacker terminology, the "disk" contains the recording medium. The "drive" contains the motors, the spindle, and the heads that spin the disk and read or write the data. The "controller" is the electronic device that tells the drive what to read and write. And the "disk drive" is all these things in a package.

Disk Drive Nomenclature

We define basic hard disk terms for our discussion, but different people call parts of the drives by different names. Some find "disk drive" too formal and say "drive," but they call the motors, spindle, and heads the "drive," too. If you don't know what part of the disk drive someone's talking about, ask.

A recording medium, which on floppies and hard disks is a coating of electromagnetically sensitive material, covers the platter surface. On this surface, the File Manager stores the bits and bytes that make up your file. Most fixed drives have more than one platter, increasing the available surface area and therefore increasing the storage capacity of the drive. Both sides of a platter are used to store data. A read/write head services a single side of a platter, so the number of heads indicates the number of platter sides in a disk drive. Figure 10-1 shows the inside of a hard disk drive that has four platters.

A low-level format divides each platter into "tracks," which run in concentric rings around the surface of the disk, and "sectors," which are formed from the intersection of pie-slice shaped divisions of the disk's surface and the track boundaries. A sector contains 512 bytes of data, and a track generally has 16 or more sectors around the circumference of the platter, although these numbers are determined by the software that formats the drive and can differ for each drive and, indeed, even within a drive. On a multiple-platter drive, corresponding tracks make up a cylinder. The number of tracks each cylinder has is another way to express the number of read/write heads that a drive has. Figure 10-2 illustrates this physical organization of disk real estate.

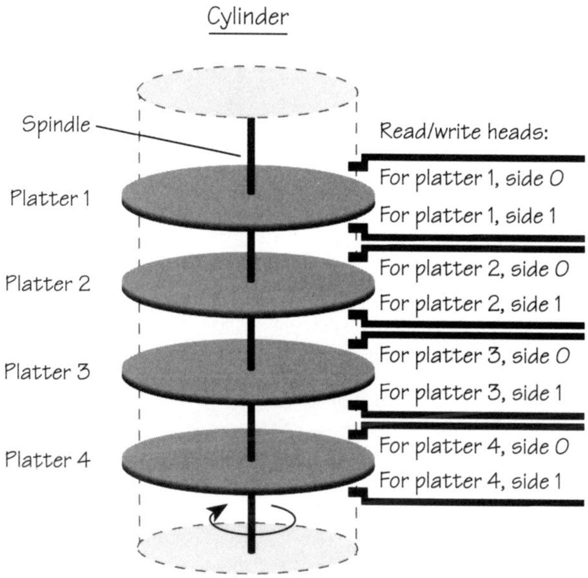

Figure 10-1.
A physical hard disk with four platters and eight heads.

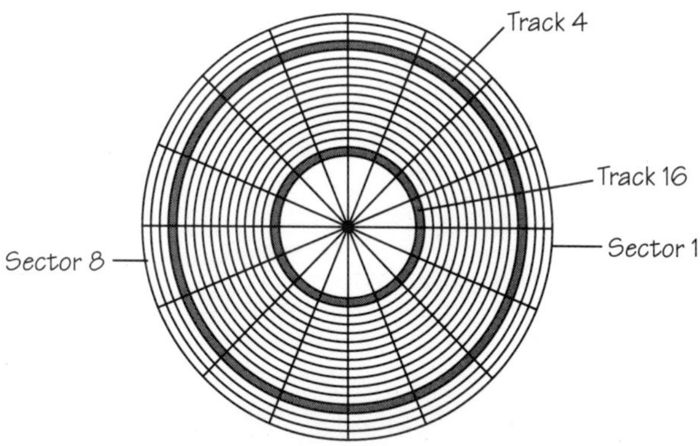

Figure 10-2.
Tracks and sectors.

After the low-level format, the disk is ready for a Macintosh file system, written during a high-level format by the Mac's Disk Initialization Package. The high-level format writes a "volume record" on the disk that describes its size, holds references to files, and organizes the remaining disk sectors in a list of "free blocks." Figure 10-3 on the next page shows the volume information block in relation to other disk blocks and the kinds of information it contains.

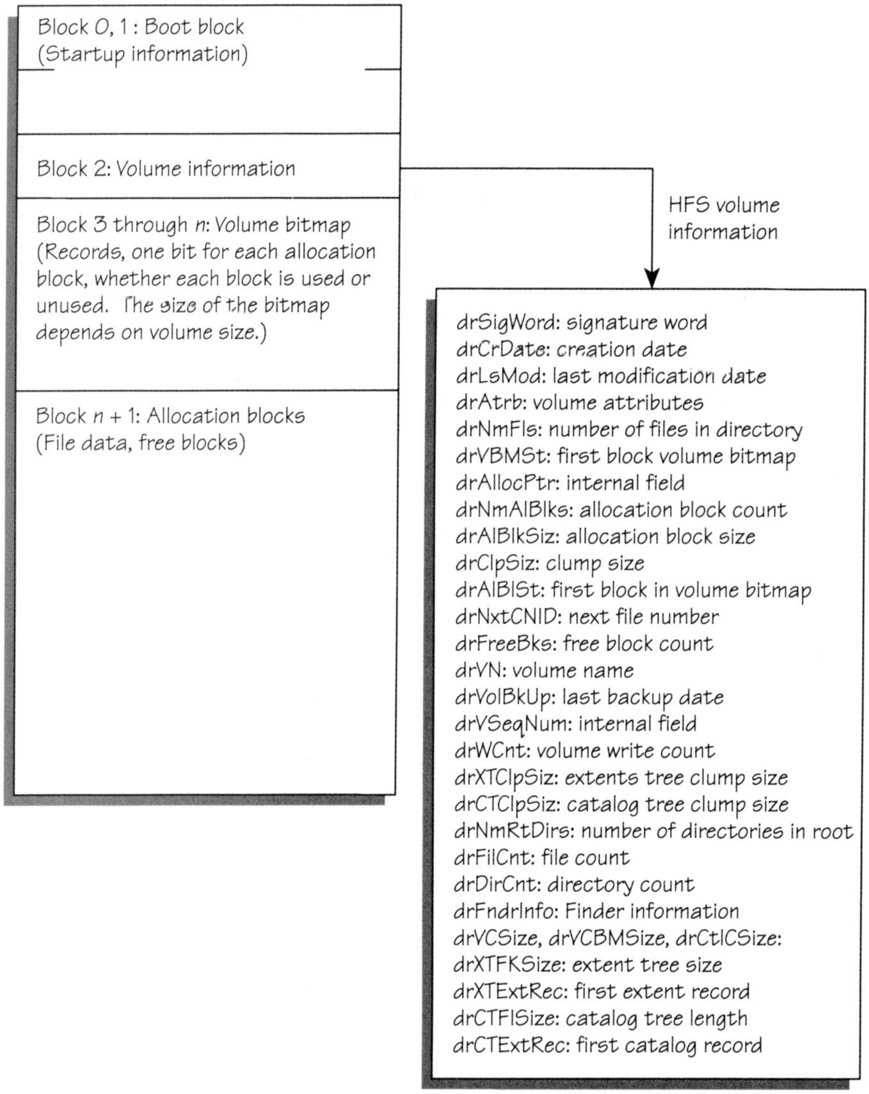

Figure 10-3.
The volume layer.

A block is a logical sector. Although a physical sector is 512 bytes of data, a logical sector can contain 512, 1024, 1536 bytes, and so on—any multiple of the 512-byte sector size. A block is the smallest unit of data available on the drive. The disk's driver always reads an entire block into RAM, even if you have requested only 1 byte of the file, which is why it's always more efficient to do program I/O in a multiple of the block size. Blocks are numbered sequentially from 0 through *n* and cover the entire disk.

The Macintosh file system and the File Manager routines use blocks to hold file and folder data. Finder, the user interface to the Mac OS, uses File Manager routines to support the desktop metaphor. When you drag a file from a hard disk folder onto a microfloppy disk's icon, Finder calls File Manager routines that in turn call the disk drivers to read a list of blocks on the source disk while at the same time allocating blocks on the microdisk for the destination file. The whir of the disk drive and the clicks from the read/write arm stepper motors are the acoustic evidence that all is working on the physical level.

Volumes

The file system considers each drive in the system a volume. In the Macintosh file system, each volume has an icon that the System places in the desktop when the disk is mounted. Each volume in the file system has a volume reference number that you use to access the volume or a file located in the volume. Generally, we're not interested in the volume *per se* except as a container for a file. In fact, a volume reference number and a file name are all you need to specify a file.

A volume must be both mounted and online before you can access any data on it. The File Manager automatically mounts removable volumes, like floppy disks, when they're inserted in the drive and mounts fixed drives at boot time. When the File Manager mounts a drive, it creates a volume-control block data structure and allocates space for volume buffers in the system heap. The File Manager uses the volume-control block in its management of the volume while the volume is online and uses the volume buffers for the transfer of data to and from the volume.

The File Manager has routines to unmount a volume (*UnmountVol*) and to place a volume offline (*PBOffLine*) that you might use to free up system heap space. When a volume is unmounted, no trace of it remains in the heap. Of course, you have to mount the volume again before you can get at any of its files. When a volume is offline, its buffers are free, but the volume-control block stays in the heap.

Bad Blocks

Most platters have a few small defects—areas of the platter where the recording medium isn't regular or thick enough to reliably hold data. Low-level formatting tests the quality of the recording medium by writing a pattern to a sector and reading it back. If what's read doesn't match what was written, the sector is marked "bad." The disk's driver routines keep a list of these "bad blocks" in a table and will spare these sectors from file system use.

Filling Up the System Heap

In Chapter 5, we described the system heap as the area in which the Operating System code as well as the code for any CDEVs or INITs that are loaded is stored, and as the place in which other system-wide data—fonts and resource templates used by active desk accessories, for example—resides. Needless to say, the system heap is a very busy area of memory and tends to fill up when a lot is going on.

If you're a hardware hound like Thom, who has at least five or six assorted volumes of hard drive, Bernoulli drive, and CD-ROM drive mounted on his Mac at all times, you'll find yourself running out of system heap space—apparently without warning. Indiscriminate use of volume partitions results in the same problem because the OS perceives partitions as separate volumes. The symptoms Thom has experienced range from unexpected system crashes to missing characters when he printed documents in certain fonts. (See "The Expert's Edge," *MacUser,* March 1990.)

The Hierarchical File System (HFS)

Directories and subdirectories are the internal structures that correspond to folders in your desktop. The File Manager uses directories and subdirectories to group files. Old-timers whose experience reaches back to the early Macs might remember that only one level of directory was allowed back then—the early Macs used the so-called "flat file system." At the advent of the 128K ROMs in the Mac Plus, folders within folders were supported, for the UNIX-like hierarchical file system (called HFS for short) of today's Mac software. Figure 10-4 illustrates such a system.

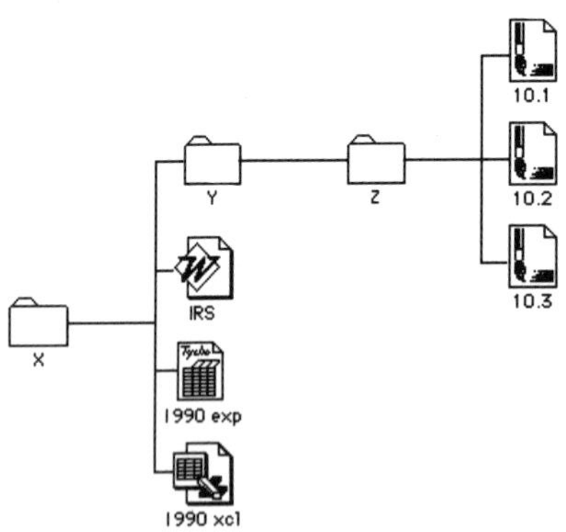

Figure 10-4.
A hierarchical file system of folders and files. Folder X contains three files (IRS, 1990 exp, and 1990 xcl) and a folder, Y. Folder Y contains one folder, Z, and no files. Folder Z contains three files (10.1, 10.2, and 10.3).

This radical change in the structure of the file system occasioned a rewrite of the File Manager documentation, so the File Manager documentation in Volume II of *Inside Macintosh* is superseded by the information in Volume IV.

In order to maintain compatibility of the new hierarchical file system with the old flat file system, Apple borrowed a concept from UNIX: the "working directory." The working directory provides an alternate means of accessing files in a folder. A working directory reference number is associated with each folder in a volume. The working directory's number is that of the current folder when a program is launched from the Finder. In the hierarchical file system, File Manager routines return a working directory reference number instead of a volume reference number, so the two terms have become synonymous.

In the hierarchical file system, a directory is a logical volume. Each subdirectory or folder is considered a subvolume, so File Manager routines that once accepted a volume reference number as an argument under the old Macintosh (flat) file system (MFS) accept a working directory reference number under the hierarchical file system (HFS).

Specifying files

We saw in Chapter 9 how to use the Standard File Package to select a file. Most applications use the *SFGetFile* interface routine to let the user specify the file to open. Two values returned by *SFGetFile* in the *SFReply* structure, *vRefNum* and *fName*, fully specify a file in either the MFS or the HFS. Here's the *SFReply* structure:

```
typedef struct SFReply
{
    char        good;
    char        copy;
    long        fType;     // array[1..4] of char;
    int         vRefNum;
    int         version;
    unsigned char  fName[64];
} SFReply;
```

The *fName* field contains a "partial pathname" for a file. This is a fancy term that simply refers to the file name without its hierarchical information. Consider the file Z in Figure 10-4. Z is the partial pathname (the file name) of this file, whose full pathname is X:Y:Z.

In the MFS, *SFGetFile* returns the file's volume reference number in the *vRefNum* field of the *SFReply* structure. This value and the file name are all that's needed to specify a file. The MFS has no directories: That folders seem to be offshoots of the volume's root directory is sleight of hand, mere trickery perpetrated by the File Manager.

In the HFS, *SFGetFile* returns the file's working directory reference number in the *vRefNum* field. This value is analogous to the volume reference number but refers to the directory that contains the file, not to the entire volume. Figure 10-5 illustrates the working directory concept.

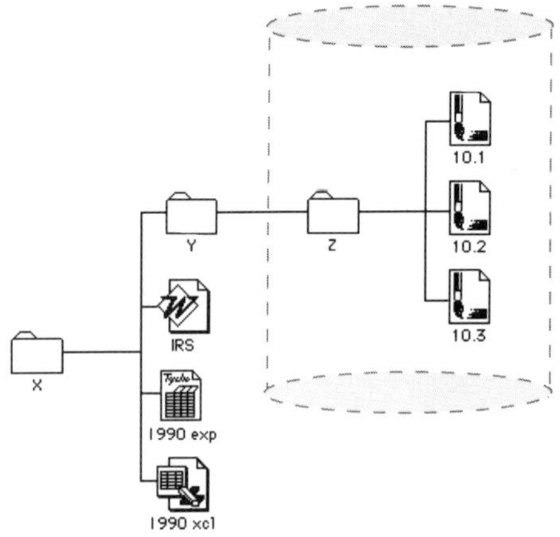

Figure 10-5.
A working directory. Using a working directory is like using a logical volume. In this case, Z is the working directory.

Files

A little icon in the desktop represents the collection of blocks of raw information known as a file. A Macintosh file is really two files in one: It has two "forks," the resource fork and the data fork. The file's resource fork is a collection of resources that are accessed by means of Resource Manager routines. The data fork is generally used to hold application data. Its contents are application specific.

If you've done any programming before, you're probably familiar with the concept of a file's data fork. In environments like UNIX or MS-DOS, the data fork is the file: It holds application-specific data in an application-specific format. Unique to the Macintosh is the resource fork. It contains resources—font bitmap data, dialog box templates, window templates, conversion tables, strings, and, if the file happens to be an application, the application's code segments—in an Apple-specified format.

The Resource Manager is actually a small database manager, so the format of a resource file is designed to facilitate speedy access of a resource. This quick access is what helps the Mac achieve its responsive user interface.

The Resource Manager provides a structured programming interface to a resource fork. Using its routines, the Resource Manager can retrieve an individual resource with its "resource specification": a four-character key, called the "resource type," and a resource number. The resource number is a signed integer that uniquely identifies resources of the same type and also has an intrinsic meaning. A resource number in the range –16384 through 127 indicates that the resource is a system resource; a resource number greater than 127 indicates that the resource is an application resource.

The resource type is defined as a packed array of four characters, and in THINK C is specified as a string between single quotes, as in 'ALRT'. Common Macintosh resource types are shown in Figure 10-6.

Type	*Description*
'ALRT'	Alert box template
'BNDL'	Finder bundle
'CNTL'	Control template
'CODE'	Code segment
'DITL'	Dialog box item list
'DLOG'	Dialog box template
'DRVR'	Desk accessory
'FOND'	Font family
'FONT'	Font data
'ICN#'	Icon list
'ICON'	Icon
'MBAR'	Menu bar
'MENU'	Menu template
'PICT'	Picture
'STR#'	String list
'vers'	Version data
'WIND'	Window template

Figure 10-6.
Common Macintosh resource types.

Data fork and resource fork, a file is an ordered list of bytes with a beginning and an end, and therefore the data contained in the file has a size, in bytes. Each byte in a file is addressable as an offset from the beginning of the file.

Macintosh documentation calls this offset the file's "mark." If the mark is at offset 0, a read operation will begin with the first byte in the file. When the mark is at the last byte in the file, it is the end-of-file (eof) mark. A write operation will append characters to the file and therefore expand the file size. The eof mark follows the last byte of the file. Figure 10-7 on the next page illustrates the concept of a file as an ordered stream of bytes.

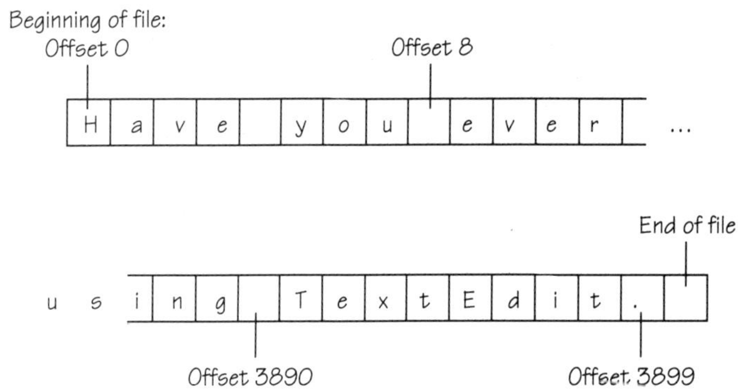

Figure 10-7.
A file as a stream of bytes. Each byte is addressable as an offset from the beginning of the file.

File Formats

The format of a file's data fork is defined by the application's developers. Some file formats are matters of public record, like Excel's Sylk file format, but most file formats are closely guarded secrets. Why are so many file formats kept secret?

Market share. Think of it from the software publisher's point of view. Say that your company sells the leading wazoo processing program with an installed base of one million users, all busy creating files in your proprietary format. What if your main competitor comes up with a better product? What's to prevent those million users from jumping ship to your competitor's product, before you have the chance to sell them your new and improved version?

The answer is those hundreds of files they've already created in your secret format. The competition's product can't read those files, and people can't walk away from their old data any more easily than they can walk away from their computers. How many disks do you have in your possession that can't be read by the computers you now own?

It's probably safe to say that every new application that hits the shelves in your local software store has a unique data format.

Of course, a smart company that's not in a market leading position will discover that it's wise to publish its program's file format. The adoption of that format by others (even if only to read in information) will lead to wider recognition and support for the product.

Although you can think of a file as a stream, its data is really held in "allocation blocks," which on a floppy disk are fixed-sized multiples of 512 bytes. As a file grows, more 512-byte blocks are allocated to it. Depending on the file's length, there can be unused bytes in a file's last block, after the eof mark. If a hypothetical file foo contained exactly 3900 bytes of data, the file would actually take up 4096 bytes, or eight allocation blocks, on disk. The file's size would cause the waste of 196 bytes in the file's last allocation block. If you checked the Get Info dialog box for the file, it would report the file's size along these lines: "3900 bytes used, 4K on disk."

To reconcile this difference, *Inside Macintosh* differentiates between the *logical* end of file, which is at byte 3900 in our example, and the *physical* end of file, which is the number of bytes occupied by the blocks allocated to the file—4096 in our example. Figure 10-8 illustrates such a file's allocation. When we refer to the eof, we mean the logical eof because it tells us the actual size of the file.

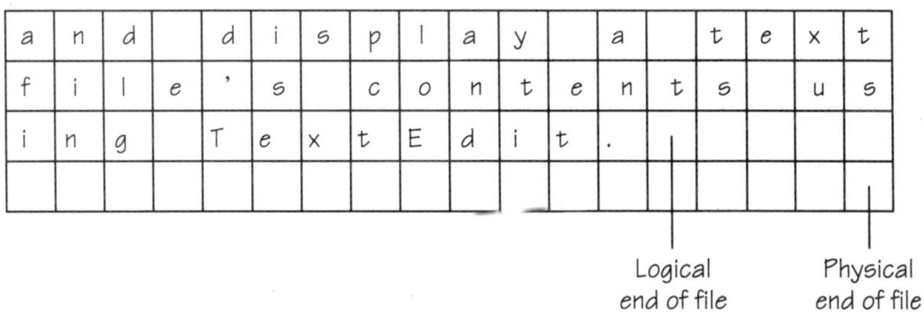

Figure 10-8.
The last block of a file is usually only partially filled.

The File Manager

The File Manager, responsible for this file and folder hocus-pocus, is probably the most powerful of all collections in the Toolbox. But this power comes at a high cost. The File Manager documentation is confusing, contradictory, and voluminous—four ways to specify a file, three variants of the standard I/O parameter block, two levels of using the Manager, and more information than one person would want to know about any file system. A user might find navigating through the file system itself a breeze. A programmer can find working his or her way through the File Manager documentation a real ordeal.

For a novice programmer, the worst choice is the low-level interface to the File Manager. These routines are distinguished from the high-level routines by the prefix *PB*, as in *PBRead*, *PBWrite*, and *PBGetEOF*. The *PB* reminds us that we're using a variant of the Device Manager parameter block to pass data in and out of the routines.

To add to the confusion, when the new hierarchical file system was introduced, each primary routine had its matching hierarchical routine. So, we have a *PBOpen* and a *PBHOpen*; we have a *PBGetFInfo* and a *PBHGetFInfo*. The *H*, of course, stands for "hierarchical."

The interface to these routines is based on the concept of a variant record parameter block, implemented with a union in C. You use one of three variants of the parameter block, your selection depending on which File Manager routine you're calling. The input requirements are different for each routine.

The parameter block contains everything you want to know about a volume, file, or access path, depending on the variant. Each *PB* routine has its own set of input and output parameters of interest, so you can't work with these routines without a copy of *Inside Macintosh* open on your desk. Even then, you're in deep muck.

Figure 10-9 is an excerpt from the documentation for the call *PBHGetFInfo*, which returns file system information about a file in the hierarchical file system. It should give you a feel for the low-level documentation.

```
OSErr PBHGetFInfo ( HParamBlkPtr paramBlock, Boolean asynch );

Parameter Block

-->  12   ioCompletion    pointer
<--  16   ioResult        word
<->  18   ioNamePtr       pointer
-->  22   ioVRefNum       word
<--  24   ioFRefNum       word
-->  28   ioFDirIndex     word
<--  30   ioFlAttrib      byte
<--  32   ioFlFndrInfo    16 bytes
<->  48   ioDirID         long word
<--  52   ioFlStBlk       word
<--  54   ioFlLgLen       long word
<--  58   ioFlPyLen       long word
<--  62   ioFlRStBlk      word
<--  64   ioFlLgLen       long word
<--  68   ioFlRPyLen      long word
<--  72   ioFlCrDat       long word
<--  76   ioFlMdDat       long word
```

Figure 10-9.
PBHGetFInfo *documentation excerpted from* Inside Macintosh.

Note the arrows. The ones that point east (-->) specify inputs to the routine. The ones that point west (<--) specify outputs. The ones that point both ways (<->) specify data that passes in and out of the routine, whatever that means.

Which variant of the parameter block do you use? Notice the *Fl* in the names of the fields *ioFlAttrib*, *ioFlLgLen*, *ioFlCrDat*, and so on. This *Fl*, and the fact that you're getting file information, is the tip-off that you use the *fileParam* variant. The other two variants are *ioParam* to access open files and *volParam* to return volume information.

Look at the numbers column's *12, 16, 18....* These numbers are offsets of the fields from the beginning of the structure, which should tip you off—these calls are for assembly language programmers. If you're going to do your work down here, you'd better know what you're doing.

PBHGetFInfo returns a hodgepodge of data about the file: the open file's number and its directory number, data about the file's Finder Information in the *ioFlFndrInfo* field, the file's data and resource fork sizes and logical and physical end-of-file marks, and the file's creation and modification times.

Our problem with this low-level File Manager interface is that it's really a Device Manager interface, and, as proponents of layered design, we believe that applications should not be mucking around with devices.

Fortunately, there is an alternative: the high-level interface to the File Manager. For most applications, the high-level interface routines are sufficient, and they're easier to use. These are the routines that don't begin with *PB*. Some begin with the prefix *FS*, as in *FSOpen*, *FSRead*, and *FSWrite*. Others are named according to their actions, as in *Create*, *GetEOF*, and *SetVol*.

The high-level interface provides 75 percent of the functionality of the low-level interface, and its procedures are easier to understand. The routines are more specific and therefore more modular—you won't be getting a lot of data that you won't use. For example, *GetFInfo*, which returns the Finder information data in the *FInfo* data structure and whose declaration is shown in Figure 10-10, returns the same data found in the *ioFlFndrInfo* field of the *ioParamBlk*.

```
OSErr GetFInfo (Str255 filename, int volRefNum, FInfo fndrInfo);

typedef struct FInfo
{
    OSType      fdType,
                fdCreator;
    int         fdFlags;
    Point       fdLocation;
```

Figure 10-10.
GetFInfo *declaration*.

Finding the Free Space in a Volume

Sometimes you have to use the low-level File Manager. If your application needs to know the amount of available space on a disk, it has to get at volume information. The volume record, which resides on block 2 of the disk, contains information such as the volume name, the number of files in the volume, the block size of the volume, and the number of blocks in the volume. Access to this data is by means of the *PBHGetVInfo* routine, which is a low-level File Manager routine. *PBHGetVInfo* returns data in a hierarchical volume information parameter block. The fields *ioVFrBlk* and *ioVAlBlkSiz* in the parameter block contain the number of free blocks and the block size. You multiply these values to get the total number of free bytes in a volume. This code fragment shows how to get the available bytes:

```
unsigned long       sizeAvail, blkSize, freeBlks;
HParamBlockRec      blk;
OSErr               err;

/* initialize parameter block */
blk.volumeParam.ioCompletion = 0L;
blk.volumeParam.ioNamePtr = 0L;
blk.volumeParam.ioVRefNum = volRefNum;
blk.volumeParam.ioVolIndex = 0;

err = PBHGetVInfo (&blk, false);  // get the volume information

/* do everything as long arithmetic */
sizeAvail = 0L;
if (err == noErr)
{
    freeBlks = blk.volumeParam.ioVFrBlk;
    blkSize = blk.volumeParam.ioVAlBlkSiz;

    sizeAvail = freeBlks * blkSize;
}
```

The initialization of the parameter block determines where *PBHGetVInfo* searches for the data. If the value of the *ioVolIndex* field is *0*, as it is in the example we show here, *PBHGetVInfo* uses the volume reference number, passed in *ioVRefNum*, to access the volume.

Using the File Manager

Users of most applications will want to create a file, write some data in it, and close the file. Later the user will want to read the data in the file. In Figures 10-12 and 10-13, we'll show code that performs the basic File Manager routines using the high-level interface and the low-level interface.

When the user creates a new file, the application still needs to open it in order to write the data. In Figure 10-11, *createFileFS()* uses the high-level interface to the File Manager to create a file, open it, and return a file reference number. The file creator is 'KWGM', and the file type is 'TEXT'.

Notice that *createFileFS()* always checks the return values of the File Manager routines, which are placed in the local variable *err*. This error checking is important. Many things can go wrong with File Manager calls that create files or that otherwise modify data in a volume: The disk could be locked, the volume could be locked, the directory could be full, the disk could be full, and so on. We'll present a general purpose File Manager error handler in the next chapter.

```
/*
    createFileFS--uses high-level File Manager routines to
                  create a file specified by fileName and volRefNum,
                  open the file, and return a file reference number.
                  Returns -1 if failed.
*/
short
createFileFS (StringPtr fileName, short volRefNum)
{
    short       fileRefNum;
    OSErr       err;

    fileRefNum = -1;
    if (err = Create (fileName, volRefNum, 'KWGM', 'TEXT'))
    {
    /* process error */
    }
    else
    {
        if (err = FSOpen (fileName, volRefNum, &fileRefNum))
        {
        /* process error */
        }
    }

    return (fileRefNum);
}
```

Figure 10-11.
createFileFS *uses the high-level interface to the File Manager routines to create a file.*

In Figure 10-12 on the next page, *createFilePB()* uses the low-level interface to the File Manager, which calls for much more code. The parameter block has to be initialized with the file name and the volume reference number that were passed to the function as parameters. We also have to set the function pointer *ioCompletion* to *null*. If this value were nonzero, the File Manager would treat the value as a function pointer and try to execute at this location.

When we use the low-level interface, we have to explicitly set the file signature data, but, before we can set the information, we must get the existing information with *PBGetFInfo*. This initializes the parameter block so that all values are correct when we write it back with *PBSetFInfo*.

```
/*
    createFilePB--uses low-level File Manager routines to
                  create a file specified by fileName and volRefNum,
                  open the file, and return a file reference number.
                  Returns -1 if failed.
*/
short
createFilePB (StringPtr fileName, short volRefNum)
{
    short       fileRefNum;
    OSErr       err;
    ParamBlockRec  filePB;

    fileRefNum = -1;

    filePB.ioParam.ioCompletion = 0L;
    filePB.ioParam.ioNamePtr = fileName;
    filePB.ioParam.ioVRefNum = volRefNum;
    filePB.ioParam.ioVersNum = 0;

    if (err = PBCreate (&filePB, false))   // create the file
    {
        /* process error */
        return (err);
    }
    else
    {
        filePB.ioParam.ioNamePtr = fileName;
        filePB.ioParam.ioVRefNum = volRefNum;
        filePB.ioParam.ioVersNum = 0;
        filePB.ioParam.ioCompletion = 0L;
        filePB.ioParam.ioPermssn = fsWrPerm;
        filePB.ioParam.ioMisc = 0L;
```

Figure 10-12. *(continued)*
createFilePB *uses the low-level (parameter block) interface to the File Manager routines to create a file.*

Figure 10-12. *continued*

```
        if (err = PBOpen (&filePB, false))
        {
            /* process error */
            return (err);
        }
    }

    /* set up fcb for Finder Info */
    filePB.fileParam.ioFVersNum = 0;
    filePB.fileParam.ioFDirIndex = 0;

    if (err = PBGetFInfo (&filePB, false))
    {
        /* process error */
        return (err);
    }

    /* set file type and creator */
    filePB.fileParam.ioFlFndrInfo.fdType = 'TEXT';
    filePB.fileParam.ioFlFndrInfo.fdCreator = 'KWGM';
    filePB.fileParam.ioFlFndrInfo.fdFlags = 0;

    if (err = PBSetFInfo (&filePB, false))
    {
        /* process error */
        return (err);
    }

    return (fileRefNum);
}
```

Writing the file is simply a matter of calling *FSWrite* or *PBWrite* using the open file's reference number. Figure 10-13 shows how to write the file using the high-level interface.

```
/*
    writeFileFS--uses high-level File Manager routines to
                 write the size in bytes from the buffer to the file
                 referred to by fileRefNum. Returns the number of
                 characters written if OK; error if not OK.
*/
```

Figure 10-13. *(continued)*
Writing data to a file using the high-level interface to the File Manager routines.

Figure 10-13. *continued*

```
short
writeFileFS (short fileRefNum, Ptr buffer, long size)
{
    OSErr       err;
    long        nw;

    nw = size;

    err = FSWrite (fileRefNum, &nw, buffer);
    if (nw != size || err)
    {
        /* process error */
        nw = err;
    }

    return (nw);
}
```

Figure 10-14 shows you how to write the file using the low-level interface.

```
/*
    writeFilePB--uses low-level File Manager routines to
                write the size in bytes from the buffer to the file
                referred to by fileRefNum. Returns the number of
                characters written if OK; error if not OK.
*/
short
writeFilePB (short fileRefNum, Ptr buffer, long size)
{
    OSErr       err;
    long        nw;
    ParamBlockRec  filePB;

    filePB.ioParam.ioCompletion = 0L;
    filePB.ioParam.ioRefNum = fileRefNum;
    filePB.ioParam.ioBuffer = buffer;
    filePB.ioParam.ioReqCount = size;
    filePB.ioParam.ioPosMode = fsFromMark;
    filePB.ioParam.ioPosOffset = 0L;
```

Figure 10-14. *(continued)*
Writing data to a file using the low-level interface to the File Manager routines.

Figure 10-14. *continued*

```
        err = PBWrite (&filePB, false);

        if (filePB.ioParam.ioReqCount != size || err)
        {
            /* process error */
            nw = err;
        }

        return (nw);
    }
```

There is a third, THINK C, alternative to the low-level interface. The THINK C compiler supports the full ANSI C *stdio* library. This library has more functions than the high-level routines and is handy if you want your I/O modules to maintain compatibility with non-Mac systems. These are the routines based on the standard file streams. THINK C provides the same interface routines you'd find in a UNIX or MS-DOS environment, along with source code. Studying the source code is a great way to learn about the low-level File Manager interface.

In the next chapter, we'll look at Browser, a file browser that uses the File Manager routines to read files on disk. You'll see examples of how to read both the data fork and the resource fork.

11

BROWSER: OUR CULMINATING APPLICATION

In the last chapter, we saw how the File Manager interacts with the hardware at one end and with programs at the other to create the illusion of the Macintosh's hierarchical file system. Because of the volume of File Manager information, Chapter 10 had to have a theoretical slant. In this chapter, we'll put theory into practice, using the File Manager to support the foundation of our handy file viewing utility, Browser.

Browser can open any file in the desktop—even those files represented by the generic desktop icon. Browser can open files in two modes: In the text mode, it opens ASCII files and displays them using TextEdit; in the binary mode, it opens any file, either its data fork or its resource fork, and has a debuggerlike interface.

Browser is based on the multiple window generic application multiGeneric of Chapter 7 but also uses the scroll bars of Chapter 8 and the Standard File Package described in Chapter 9. Browser is the "thesis" application of this book—it combines all the skills we've discussed so far into a single application.

In the beginning of this chapter, we'll revisit the Standard File Package to see how to limit *SFGetFile*'s file list to text-only files. Then we'll see how to use the File Manager routines in an application. Finally, we'll look at Browser's implementation of the two display modes, text and binary.

Inside Browser

Browser's main task is to display a file's contents. In order to do that, it needs to

- put up *SFGetFile* for file selection
- open the selected file
- read some of the file data into a document buffer
- set up a document according to viewing mode and display it in response to an update event

In text mode display, the file's data has no format and appears as it would in any editor. Figure 11-1 shows text mode output.

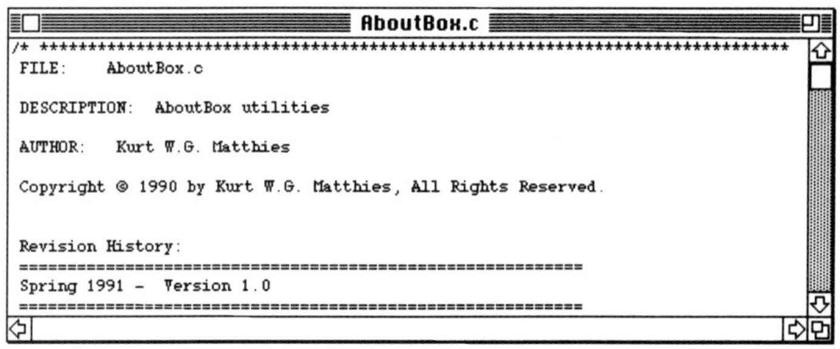

Figure 11-1. *Browser's text mode display.*

Browser's binary mode display is evolved from a long line of file dump utilities: UNIX's od, CP/M's DUMP, and MS-DOS's DEBUG. Browser displays 256 bytes, 16 lines of three columns each, of the file at a time. Figure 11-2 shows an example of Browser's binary mode output.

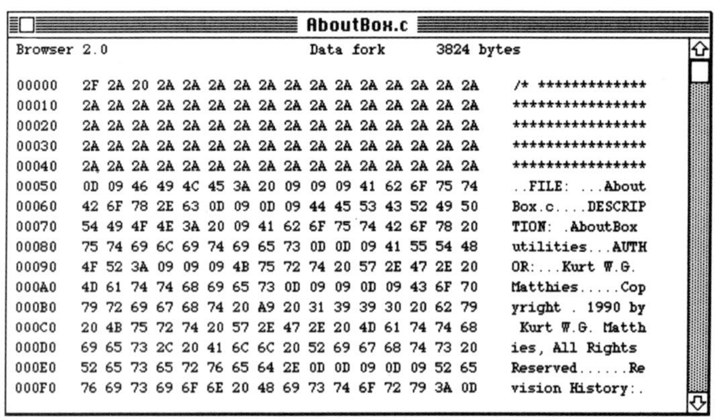

Figure 11-2. *Browser's binary mode display.*

In the far left column in the window, Browser displays the current file offset relative to the beginning of the file. To the right of the offset, the file's data is displayed twice: In the center column, Browser displays the bytes in hexadecimal format, 16 characters to a line; on the far right, Browser repeats the line in ASCII form, displaying nonprintable characters as dots.

The underlying scroll engine differs for the two display modes. In text mode, Browser scrolls a line at a time, so Browser's *curScroll* tracks the line number and *maxScroll* contains the total lines of text. In binary mode, Browser scrolls one page at a time. Browser's *curScroll* value therefore tracks the page number, and *maxScroll* contains the total pages.

Data buffering also differs in the two modes. In text mode, Browser reads all of the file's data into a TextEdit structure and stores the corresponding *TEHandle* in the *contentHdl* field of the *Doc* structure.

Using TextEdit for display has a built-in limitation. According to *Inside Macintosh,* a TextEdit structure has a 32,000-character limit. Browser's text mode simply accepts this limit: It truncates the file to 32,000 bytes, ignoring any file data that's over the limit. Use of Browser's text mode for editing is of course limited to files of the size Browser can view in text mode. We'll leave it to you readers to figure out how to extend the text editing capabilities of Browser. (Hint: Arbitrarily split files into smaller chunks, and make separate TextEdit structures for each chunk. Manage the chunks so that the seams between them are invisible to the user. Alternatively, rewrite Browser's binary mode code so that it uses TextEdit to display a file, a page at a time.)

Browser's binary mode has no such character limit. In binary mode, Browser buffers a screen of characters—256 at a time. When the user scrolls the document forward, Browser reads the next 256 characters according to the scrolled document's position. As the user scrolls the document backward, Browser reads the previous 256 characters. The buffering process is quick, and, because the buffer is small, the binary mode requires only a little space for each open document.

Selecting File Types: File Signatures

In binary mode, Browser can open either fork of any file. In text mode, Browser opens only the data fork of an ASCII file.

The file system maintains file identification data—called the file signature—for each file in a directory. The data consists of the file's creator and the file's type. The file creator value identifies the application that created the file; the file type value identifies the kind of data the file contains. This information binds an icon to the file. Finder keeps the information for every file in the desktop. In System 7.0, the information is kept in the "desktop database."

The signature data is of type *OSType*, which is 4 characters packed into two words, defined in THINK C as a *long*. An *OSType* string of characters does not have a count byte, as do Pascal formed strings, nor is it *null* terminated, as C strings are (called ASCIIZ strings in MS-DOS documentation). You can define an *OSType* token string with the THINK C compiler by using the single quotation mark ('), as in

```
'KWGM'
```

which the compiler translates into the 32-bit hexadecimal long word

```
0x4B57474D
```

You would declare a *null*-terminated C string with double quotation marks, as in

```
"KWGM"
```

This string translates into the 5-byte, *null*-terminated hexadecimal sequence

```
0x4B
0x57
0x47
0x4D
0x00
```

Registering File Signatures

An application developer must register his or her application's file creator and type with Apple, who makes sure that no two applications share the same combination of file creator and type. You can express these values in all uppercase characters or in a combination of uppercase and lowercase characters. File signatures expressed in all lowercase characters are reserved for Apple's use. Examples of some standard file types and signatures are shown in the table below.

Application	**File Creator**	**File Type**
System	MACS	ZSYS
Finder	MACS	FNDR
MacWrite	MACA	APPL
MacPaint	MPNT	APPL
MS Word	MSWD	APPL
PageMaker*	ALD3	APPL
Tycho Table Maker	Tyco	APPL

*Version 3.0 and later

Common file signatures.

You declare a Pascal string with double quotation marks and the \p token, as in

```
"\pKWGM"
```

and this string translates into the 5-byte sequence

```
0x04
0x4B
0x57
0x47
0x4D
```

When it's in text mode, Browser is interested in files of type 'TEXT'—text or ASCII files. Browser doesn't care who the creator of the file is. The file creator value simply identifies the application that created and therefore "owns" the file. The Finder uses the file creator value to launch a file's associated application when you double-click on a data file's icon.

Selecting a File—Revisited

In Chapter 9, we used the Standard File Package to put up the familiar Open dialog box that enables the user to navigate the file system and select a file. Browser also uses the SFGetFile dialog box, which appears as a result of the *SFGetFile* routine.

Chapter 9's Loser required some modifications in the SFGetFile dialog box for its two radio buttons. Browser will use the same modified radio buttons for the user's selection of its text and binary display modes. Browser will use the result of the button mode selection to filter the file names that will appear in the dialog box's list box.

In text mode, Browser is interested only in 'TEXT' files and therefore displays only 'TEXT' files in its list box. This file filtering behavior is typical of all Macintosh applications. Our Tycho Table Maker application is interested only in its native table file type, 'Tabl' files; Microsoft Word can open its native file type (type 'WDBN'), MacWrite files (type 'WORD'), and MacPaint files (type 'PNTG').

The *SFGetFile* routine supports file filtering by type through its *typeList* argument. You tell the *SFGetFile* routine which file types you're interested in, and the Standard File Package displays file names of only that type in the SFGetFile list box. Here's how it's done:

```
SFTypeList      typeList;
short           numTypes;

typeList [0] = 'TEXT'; // TEXT type
numTypes = 1;          // one type only (can be up to 4)

SFGetFile (aPt, promptStr, 0L, numTypes, typeList, ...
```

Browser therefore has no need of the file filter hook proc, as Loser did in Chapter 9.

Opening a File

Once the user has selected a file in the Browser SFGetFile dialog box, Browser's next step is to use the File Manager to get the file's data, or "read" the file. But remember from Chapter 10's discussion of the File Manager that, before you can read a file's data, you must first open the file, which sets up an access path to the file.

When the user selects the Open button in the SFGetFile dialog box, *SFGetFile* fills an *SFReply* record with the name and the volume reference number of the selected file. Browser uses this information to open the file.

Regardless of whether you're using the MFS (unlikely, but it's always a good idea to support the widest user base possible) or the HFS, the values returned in the *SFReply* record are all that the application needs to open the file. We've mentioned this before, in Chapter 10, but it's important enough to repeat: In the MFS, the volume reference number is a true volume reference number; in the HFS, the volume reference number is a working directory reference number. Both kinds of references, when used with the partial pathname returned in the *fName* field of the *SFReply* structure, specify a file in a volume.

Browser uses the function *openFile()* in the source file FileUtil.c to open either file fork—the resource fork or the data fork—for reading. Called from the Open menu command, *openFile()* is passed a pointer to a *FileParams* structure.

Browser uses the *FileParams* structure to pass information into and out of the File Manager utility routines such as *openFile()*. On entry to *openFile()*, *FileParams* contains the partial pathname and volume reference number that were acquired from the *SFReply* structure. On exit, *FileParams* contains the open file reference number and the file length.

openFile() performs three standard file system tasks:

1. First, it opens either the resource fork or the data fork of the file. Browser's user interface routine, *doGetFile()*, sets a bit in the *attributes* field of the *DocParams*, based on the user selection. *openFile()* checks this bit and calls either *FSOpen*, which opens the file's data fork, or *OpenRF*, which opens the file's resource fork.
2. Once the access path is established, *openFile()* gets the file's size with *GetEOF* and stores the size in the *FileParams* structure. *GetEOF* is a File Manager routine that returns the logical end-of-file position.
3. Finally, *openFile()* sets the file mark to the beginning of the file with *FSSetFPos*, the File Manager routine that changes the position of the file mark. Figure 11-3 shows the code for *openFile()*.

```
/*
    openFile--opens a file, gets the file size, seeks to the
              beginning of the file, and returns the file
              reference number 6.20.90kwgm
*/
OSErr
openFile (DocParamsPtr docParams)
{
    OSErr           err;
    long            fSize;
    short           vRefNum;
    Str64           volName;
    FileParams      *fileParams;

    fileParams = &docParams->fileParams;

    /* open the file */
    if (docParams->attributes & kDocDataFork)
    {
        if (err = FSOpen (fileParams->fileName, fileParams->volRefNum,
                &fileParams->openFileRefNum))
        {
            doFileCantAlert (fileParams->fileName, kOpen, err,
                kNulPascalStr);
            return (err);
        }
    }
    else    // resource fork
    {
        if (err = OpenRF (fileParams->fileName, fileParams->volRefNum,
                &fileParams->openFileRefNum))
        {
            doFileCantAlert (fileParams->fileName, kOpen, err,
                kNulPascalStr);
            return (err);
        }
    }

    /* get the file size */
    if (err = GetEOF (fileParams->fileRefNum,
            &fileParams->fileSize))
    {
        doFileCantAlert (fileParams->fileName, kOpen, err,
            kNulPascalStr);
```

Figure 11-3. *(continued)*
openFile() *from FileUtil.c.*

Figure 11-3. *continued*

```
        FSClose (fileParams->fileRefNum);
        return (err);
    }

    /* set the mark to the beginning of the file */
    if (err = SetFPos (fileParams->fileRefNum, fsFromStart, 0L))
    {
        doFileCantAlert (fileParams->fileName, kOpen, err,
            kNulPascalStr);
        FSClose (fileParams->fileRefNum);
        return (err);
    }

    return (noErr);

} /* openFile */
```

Error Handling

We hope that you noticed the calls to *doFileCantAlert()*, which *openFile()* calls whenever it detects a File Manager error—that is, whenever the return value of a File Manager routine is nonzero. Checking the return value of File Manager routines is good, defensive programming—so many things can and do go wrong.

File errors during a file open come in various kinds: damaged medium errors, bad directories, too many files open, errors in name or number, and a host of other problems. If you ignore these errors, you'll create a chain of bugs that will eventually cause your program to crash. If you program defensively by checking the result code of each File Manager routine, your program can notify the user of the error and back out of the problem gracefully.

The functions of the File Manager return an *OSErr* value, which is typed as a *short* integer. This numeric value is a token that represents a file system error. The File Manager returns *noErr*, which is equal to *0*, at the successful completion of a routine, but a host of negative values are possible when things go bad. Symantec ships the *OSErr* tokens as values in the header file Files.h. Figure 11-4 shows some errors an application could encounter during an open operation.

We've developed a set of routines that deal with file system errors. You'll find them in the source file FileErr.c. The function *doFileCantAlert()* is the programming interface to these utility routines. They work in conjunction with a string list resource (STR# 104) in the application's resource file. *getIOErrStr()* in FileErr.c translates a File Manager error number to one of these strings. *doFileCantAlert()* calls *getIOErrStr()* to map the error value returned by a File Manager routine into a string.

Token	Value	Description
dirFulErr	-33	Directory is full
dskFulErr	-34	Disk is full
nsvErr	-35	No such volume
ioErr	-36	Miscellaneous I/O error
tmfoErr	-42	Too many files are open
wPrErr	-44	Disk is write protected
fLckdErr	-45	File is locked
vLckdErr	-46	Volume is locked
volOffLinErr	-53	Volume is offline
permErr	-54	No permission to open

Figure 11-4.
File Manager OSErr *token values and their meanings.*

Using the doFileCantAlert() interface involves calling a single function that accepts four arguments:

1. You pass the name of the file in which the error occurred as the first argument.
2. You pass a token that describes what operation was attempted as the second argument. The tokens, defined in the header file StrRsrcDefs.h, come from the list *kOpen*, *kClose*, *kRead*, *kWrite*, and *kControl*.
3. You pass the error token returned by the File Manager routine as the third argument.
4. You pass a pointer to any additional string that you want to display to the user as the fourth argument. You might put the name of the calling function in this argument as a way of tracing program flow, for example. If you don't want to use this argument, pass the empty *pascal* string pointer, "\p". Be advised: This is not the null pointer, 0L, but a string whose first element is equal to *0*.

The *doFileCantAlert()* routine translates the four arguments into the four *ParamText* values:

^*0* The operation string gets displayed. *doFileCantAlert()* translates its second argument into a string that describes the operation.

^*1* The first argument, *fileName*, gets displayed.

^*2* The error string gets displayed. *doFileCantAlert()* calls *getIOErrStr()*, which digs a string out of the STR# 104 resource that describes the File Manager error value.

^*3* Your discretionary string gets displayed.

Figure 11-5 on page 247 shows the code for *doFileCantAlert()*.

Using *ParamText* in a Dialog Box

The doFileCantAlert() dialog box takes advantage of the Dialog Manager's parameter-text substitution utility. In a process similar to the one UNIX shell programmers know as "parameter substitution," this feature of the Dialog Manager allows your program to change the usually static text strings in a dialog box. You initialize the strings with the routine *ParamText.*

ParamText works this way: If any of a dialog box's text items contains the string ^0, ^1, ^2, or ^3, the Dialog Manager replaces that string with one specified by *ParamText.* The order of the arguments to *ParamText* defines how the strings are substituted: The Dialog Manager substitutes *ParamText*'s first argument in place of the ^0 string, its second argument in place of the ^1 string, its third argument in place of the ^2 string, and its fourth argument in place of the ^3 string. This substitution is shown below.

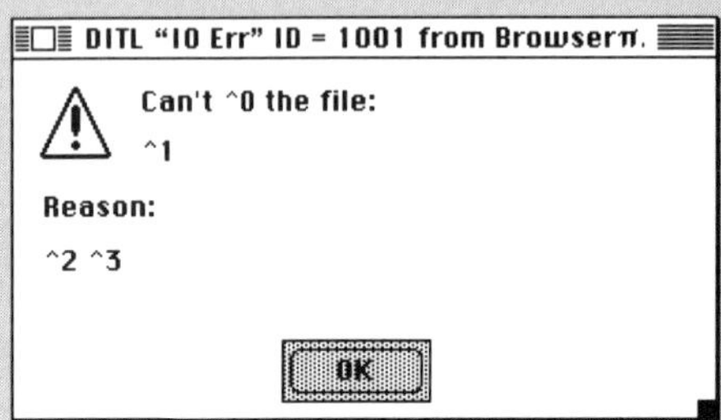

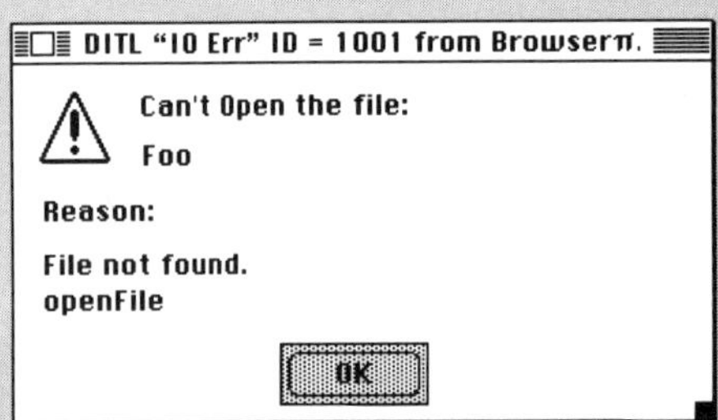

Parameter substitution with ParamText.

The second screen is derived from the first after your program calls

```
ParamText ("\pOpen", "\pFoo", "\pFile not found", "\popenFile");
```

```
/*
    doFileCantAlert--puts up the can't open/close/read advisory; prints
                     other relevant information if supplied; passes null
                     pstrings for fileName; infoStr if not used
    5.28.90kwgm
*/
void
doFileCantAlert (fileName, whatOp, reason, infoStr)
    StringPtr fileName, infoStr;
    short          whatOp, reason;
{
    DialogPtr      theDialog;
    Str255         errStr, whatStr;
    short          theItem, id, itemType;
    GrafPtr        savePort;
    Handle         buttonHdl;
    Rect           box;

    GetPort (&savePort);

    /* get the operation string */
    GetIndString (whatStr, kIOMsgStrID, whatOp);

    if (theDialog = GetNewDialog (kIOErrDLOG, 0L, -1L))
    {
        SysBeep (1);
        GetDItem (theDialog, kOutlineButton, &itemType, &buttonHdl, &box);
        SetDItem (theDialog, kOutlineButton, itemType, buttonProc, &box);

        /* build error string */
        getIOErrStr (errStr, reason);
        ParamText (whatStr, fileName, errStr, infoStr);
        centerWindow (theDialog);
        ShowHide (theDialog, true);

        ModalDialog (0L, &theItem);

        DisposDialog (theDialog);
    }

    SetPort (savePort);

} /* doFileCantAlert */
```

Figure 11-5.
doFileCantAlert() *is called when a File Manager error is detected.*

Mapping the File Manager error to a string

fmErr2AppReason() contains the *switch* statement that performs the mapping of a File Manager error to a string defined in the STR# 104 resource in Browser's resource file. *getIOStr()* calls this routine whenever *doFileCantAlert()* requests a File Manager error value translation and formats the string.

A string list resource of type STR# contains an indexed list of strings. Each string can be as many as 255 characters long. Using a STR# resource is a great way to organize strings in a Macintosh application. Then you don't have to mess with defining a static array of strings in your program; and, because the strings are in a resource, your program is easier to "localize" into another language.

You access each string by its resource ID and index, using the Resource Manager routine *GetIndString*, which returns a *pascal* string from the contents of the resource. Here's an example of how to access the third string in the STR# 104 resource:

```
Str255 buf;
GetIndString (buf, 104, 3);
```

You create the strings in ResEdit, in a window similar to the one in Figure 11-6.

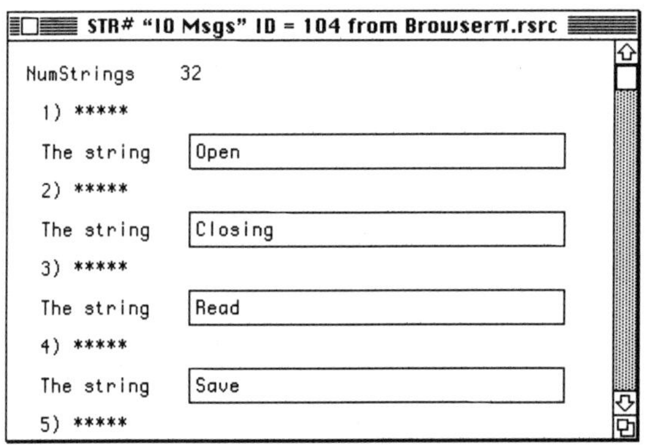

Figure 11-6. *ResEdit's STR# edit window open on Browser's resource file.*

In order to illustrate how the *doFileCantAlert()* set of routines works, we'll modify Browser so that it recognizes a new File Manager error code, *volOffLineErr*. This means that we'll also have to add a new string to the STR# 104 resource in Browser's resource file. Using ResEdit, adding a string to the resource is as simple as scrolling to the bottom of the window, selecting the last ***** marker, and selecting Insert New Field(s) from the Resource menu (or using the keyboard shortcut, Command-K). A new edit box opens in the dialog box so that we can type in the string, as shown in Figure 11-7.

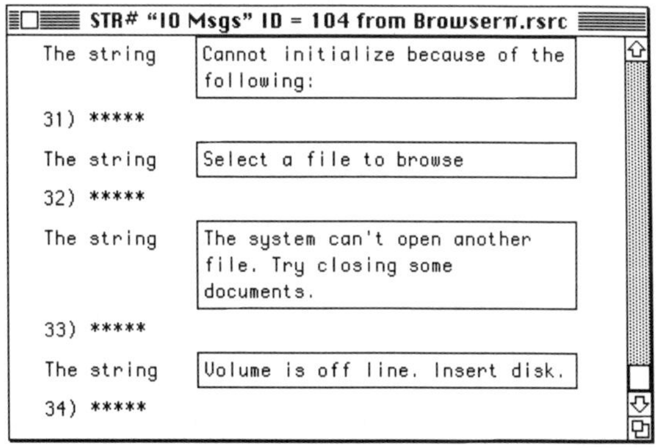

Figure 11-7. *Adding a new string to a STR# resource, using ResEdit.*

After we've added the new string to the resource file, we need to modify the program source code so that it recognizes the new error value. First, we'll need to define a new index constant for the new string. ResEdit tells us, as you can see in Figure 11-7, that the string's index is *33*. Now, in THINK C, we'll open Browser's header file, StrRsrcDefs.h, and define a new constant, *kVolOffline*, with the value *33*. We'll put this definition right after the definition of *kTooManyOpenFiles*, which is index *32*.

The last step is to map the File Manager value *volOffLinErr* to the string index *kVolOffline* in the *switch* statement in *fmErr2AppReason()*. (For the curious: *volOffLinErr* corresponds to *–53*. We don't need to know this—the value is defined in Files.h, a THINK C header file.)

```
...
        case tmfoErr:
            reason = kTooManyOpenFiles;
            break;

/* ### kwgm--added new File Manager error code */
        case volOffLinErr:
            reason = kVolOffline;
            break;
/* ### kwgm */

        default:
        ...
```

Error handling is a vital part of using the File Manager. Whether you use our set of utilities to report errors to your users or simply beep at them when an error occurs, it's always important to have your application check for errors and take appropriate action when it receives notification of one.

Reading the File

Reading the file is a matter of transferring some of the file to a local buffer. Browser uses the high-level File Manager routine *FSRead* to this end. Reading a file minimally requires three items of data:

1. from where—the file reference number
2. how much—a byte count
3. to where—the buffer address

FSRead accepts this data in three arguments—the file reference number, a pointer to a *long* word that contains the number of bytes to read, and a pointer to the buffer in which the read will place those bytes:

```
FSRead (short fileRefNumber, long * byteCount, Ptr buffer);
```

FSRead returns the number of bytes read in the same *long* word that held the requested number of bytes. *FSRead* generally returns the number of bytes you requested, but when your program reaches the end of the file, the number of bytes read will be fewer than the number requested. This is not an error condition but a natural result of reading data into a buffer, so the application has to handle this case gracefully. The *readBuf* function shown in Figure 11-8 illustrates this type of processing. It reads the file and detects an end-of-file mark. If the error is a real File Manager error, *readBuf()* returns the error number. If the "error" detected is reaching the end of the file before the requested number of bytes has been read, *readBuf()* returns *noErr.*

```
/*
    readBuf--reads from file to local buffer
    7.20.90kwgm
*/
readBuf (short fileRef, long *len, char *buf)
{
    long nRead;

    nRead = *len;
    if (err = FSRead (fileRef, len, buffer))    // read the file
    {
        if (err == eofErr)
            err = noErr;         // not an error at eof
    }
    return (result);
}
```

Figure 11-8.
Reading the file and checking the result.

One outstanding issue in Browser remains: how much of the file to read at a time, which dictates the buffer size. We could deal with the answer simplistically, reading the entire file at one time. Of course, if the file the user is interested in is 10 megabytes and only 512K is left in the heap, he or she would be out of luck. The function in Figure 11-9 demonstrates this infinite memory approach.

```
/*
    readFile--reads an entire file into a file buffer; returns handle to
              buffer in data argument; returns true if successful
*/
Boolean
readFile (FileParamsPtr fpp, Handle *data)
{
    Handle      dataHdl;
    long        dataSize;
    Boolean     result;

result = false;
    *data = 0L;

    if ((err = openFile (fpp)) == noErr)
    {
        dataSize = fpp->fileLen;
        /* allocate memory to fit file data */
        if (dataHdl = NewHandle (dataSize))
        {
            HLock (dataHdl);
            if (err = readBuf (fpp->fileRefNum, &dataSize, *dataHdl))
            {
                /* read failed: Notify user, close file,
                dispose of handle */
                doFileCantAlert (fpp->fileName, kRead, err, "\p");
                FSClose (fpp->fileRefNum);
                disposeHdl (dataHdl);
            }
            else
            {
                /* read succeeded; set up for return of data */
                HUnlock (*dataHdl);
                *data = dataHdl;
                result = true;
            }
        }
    }
```

Figure 11-9.
Allocating a buffer for the entire file.

(continued)

Figure 11-9. *continued*

```
    else
        doFileCantAlert (fpp->fileName, kOpen, err, "\p");

    return (result);

}/* readFile */
```

doFileCantAlert() is called if either the open or the read fails. Also note from this example that the buffer is a relocatable object and that because *readBuf()*, which calls *FSRead*, has the potential to move objects around in the heap, we lock the object before passing the master pointer to *readBuf()*. (And don't forget to unlock it after the read.)

Notice the order of operations in Figure 11-9:

1. open file
2. allocate buffer
3. read file

This order flows naturally from the requirements: There's no need to allocate the buffer unless you can first open the file, and you have to allocate the memory before you try to read the file into it.

In text mode, Browser buffers the entire file in the TextEdit structure. In text mode, Browser therefore respects the 32,000-byte limit of the TextEdit structure. In binary mode, Browser reads one screenful of data (256 bytes) at a time.

Text Mode

Browser's text mode uses TextEdit for its display mechanism. We had a brief encounter with TextEdit in Chapter 8: Generic App used TextEdit to display the contents of a TEXT resource. Browser uses a similar technique.

TextEdit revolves around the *TERecord*, the TextEdit data structure that contains all necessary text data. You create an empty *TERecord* structure with the TextEdit routine *TENew*. Browser encapsulates *TENew* in the *makeTERec()* function excerpted here in Figure 11-10. The *makeTERec()* function creates a *TERecord* that encompasses an entire window by calling *makeFrameRect()* and returns a handle to the structure.

```
TEHandle
makeTERec (DocPtr theDoc)
{
    TEHandle  teh;
    Rect viewRect, destRect;

    makeFrameRect (theDoc, &viewRect);
    destRect = viewRect;

    return (teh = TENew (&destRect, &viewRect));
}
```

Figure 11-10.
Creating the TERecord *with* TENew.

Displaying the text in Browser's text mode is identical to what we did in Chapter 8's Generic App. Browser's *drawDocText()* routine offsets the *TERecord* structure's destination rectangle by the current scroll value before calling *TEUpdate.* Look at the discussion in Chapter 8 if you need a refresher on how to manage scrolling using TextEdit.

Binary Mode

Browser's text mode is limited to 32,000-byte files. Its binary mode is memory efficient and can handle any file size because, in this mode, Browser reads only one screenful of data, 256 bytes, of the file at a time and stores this data on the heap in a relocatable object. The handle to the data is in the *contentHdl* field of the document structure.

Buffer management in binary mode is surprisingly simple. Browser keeps track of which 256 bytes of the file it's displaying by managing the file offset, which it stores in the *fileOffset* field of the document structure. When Browser opens a document in binary mode, it reads the first 256 bytes of the file and sets *fileOffset* to *0.* For each screen forward that the user scrolls, Browser bumps *fileOffset* by *256,* seeks to that new file offset, and reads the next 256 characters. If the user scrolls backward, Browser subtracts *256* from *fileOffset* and reads at that new offset. After each scroll, Browser invalidates the current window, which invokes the update mechanism.

Browser's binary mode display routine, *drawByteIF(),* is excerpted here in Figure 11-11. It displays the 256-byte buffer as 16 lines of 16 characters each, constructing each line of the display in the three parts we've shown in Figure 11-2 on page 238: an offset, the data in hexadecimal format, and the data in ASCII format.

```
/*
    drawByteIF--draws a 256-byte screen at the current scroll
            9.20.90kwgm
*/
static void
drawByteIF (theDoc)
    DocPtr          theDoc;
{
    register char *p;
    register short  v, line, i, c;
    short           lineHeight, hOffset, hHex, hAscii;
    Size            fileOffset, fileSize;
    char            offsetbuf [16], hexbuf [64],
                        asciibuf [64], tmpbuf [24];
    FontInfo        fInfo;
    Handle          fileBufHdl;

    fileOffset = theDoc->fileOffset;
    fileSize = theDoc->fileSize;

    if (fileBufHdl = theDoc->contentHdl)
    {
        HLock (fileBufHdl);         // we will move memory here
        p = *fileBufHdl;            // pointer to file data

        printBrowserHdr (theDoc);   // print a file header

        GetFontInfo (&fInfo);
        lineHeight = fInfo.ascent + fInfo.descent + fInfo.leading;

        v = lineHeight * 3;     // leave a space at top of screen

        /* print the file data one line at a time */
        for (line = 1; line <= 16; line++)
        {
            /* build file offset string and increment */
            sprintf (offsetbuf, "%05lX", fileOffset);
            fileOffset += 16;

            /* build hex and ASCII strings, one character at a time */
            hexbuf [0] = 0x00;
            asciibuf [0] = 0x00;
            for (i = 0 ; i < 16 ; i++)
```

Figure 11-11. *(continued)*
Browser's binary mode display routine, drawByteIF().

Figure 11-11. *continued*

```
            {
                if (i + fileOffset < fileSize)
                    c = *p++ & 0x00FF;      // mask upper byte
                else
                    c = 255;                // print box char after eof
                /* hex format */
                sprintf (tmpbuf, "%02X ", c);
                strcat (hexbuf, tmpbuf);  // add to hex string

                /* ASCII format */
                sprintf (tmpbuf, "%c", isprint (c) ? c : '.');
                strcat (asciibuf, tmpbuf);     // add to ASCII string
            }

#define kLeftMargin         10         // left screen margin

            /* draw a line */
            MoveTo (kLeftMargin + theDoc->curScroll.h, v);
            CtoPstr (offsetbuf);
            DrawString (offsetbuf);

            Move (fInfo.widMax << 1, 0);
            CtoPstr (hexbuf);
            DrawString (hexbuf);

            Move (fInfo.widMax << 1, 0);
            CtoPstr (asciibuf);
            DrawString (asciibuf);

            /* double-space for next line */
            v += lineHeight + fInfo.leading * 2;
        }

        HUnlock (fileBufHdl);
    }


} /* drawByteIF */
```

drawByteIF() loops through each line, creating the three parts of the display and drawing them at the bottom of the loop. At the heart of the routine are the three buffers—*offsetbuf, hexbuf,* and *asciibuf*—that hold the corresponding strings derived from the data for each line. *drawByteIF()* uses the C function library utility *sprintf()* to format the three buffers.

The routine creates the contents of *offsetbuf* from a local copy of the file offset. *drawByteIF()* computes the offset value for each displayed line from the initial file offset of the buffer and bumps this offset by 16 for each line.

drawByteIF() creates the hex and ASCII buffers on a character-by-character basis. Within this inner character loop, *drawByteIF()* formats each character as both a hexadecimal string and an ASCII string and concatenates the resulting string to *hexbuf* and *asciibuf* with the C function library routine, *strcat()*. It does some additional processing for the ASCII string: If the character fails the *isprint()* test, which checks that the character falls within the range of printable ASCII characters, *drawByteIF()* substitutes a dot for the character.

drawByteIF() manipulates these line buffers as C strings, so it converts them to *pascal* strings with *CtoPstr* just before displaying them with *DrawString* (which requires a *pascal* string).

The Complete Browser

That's Browser. If you've come this far and aren't completely baffled, congratulations! You're a Macintosh programmer! If you've made it this far and are still stumped, our apologies—perhaps we were unclear about something or you didn't catch some of the points we made in passing. For these folks (not many, we hope), we have a few suggestions:

- Check to be sure that you've used the examples we've presented and that you've compiled them. Try changing pieces of the examples—string names, starting and ending values, and so on—recompile, and see what the new results are.
- Use the debugger to single-step through the programs. Note in particular the initialization that must be done before the actual program actions start, that the program keeps returning to an event processing loop through which all control is passed to subsections of the program, and how ROM Toolbox calls are used.
- Check out the aids available to Macintosh programmers: Read magazines like *MacTutor* and *APDALog*; try out programs that build applications automatically, like Prototyper and AppMaker; study code others have written by downloading examples from CompuServe or Genie.

If you've made it through Browser and want to do more, we have a few suggestions for you:

- Become a certified Apple developer. You'll receive Apple's Developer Notes, CD-ROMs containing example code, HyperCard help stacks, and access to much, much more.

- Get active in the CompuServe MAUG programmer's forum, where you'll meet other Macintosh programmers and have a chance to ask and answer questions interactively. Type

  ```
  go macdev
  ```

  at any ! prompt. Be sure to download code examples and study them carefully. Again, compiling and running new code through the debugger is an excellent way to get a feel for how an application is managing itself.

- Check out your local bookstore. Besides the Apple-sponsored books, you'll find other exceptional books that will expand your knowledge of Macintosh programming, including such classics as Scott Knaster's *How to Write Macintosh Software* (1986).

- Subscribe to *MacTutor*, and consider getting the CD-ROM version of the back issues, which contains all the text and code examples from previous years (five years to date) and makes it easy to search by concepts or by individual routine names.

- Look carefully at how popular Macintosh programs implement the user interface, and try to guess what they have to do to provide the kinds of options they do. Many programs use palettes or option bars, for example, which are, in essence, custom controls. How do you think they were created? Try programming one of your own.

Finally, support programming in general. Let others know what you're up to and let the Macintosh magazines and book publishers know that you're interested in learning more. Buy good programming products, and let the companies that made them know what you did and didn't like about them so that future versions will be better.

Appendix

SYSTEM 7.0 COMPATIBILITY

The release of Apple's System version 7.0 has created a lot of excitement. This new version of the Macintosh OS, touted as a giant leap for Mac-kind, promises to revolutionize the way we compute.

Even if you're not running System 7.0 yet, you're probably aware of its new features from press reports: interapplication communication, virtual memory, outline fonts, and an improved Finder interface. As a reader with a technical bent, you probably also know about the more esoteric details of this release, such as built-in database support, Balloon help, and 1-gigabyte addressing. This is great stuff, but at the same time, we programmers are apprehensive about such a major change in system software. Precedents in the PC world fuel our insecurity.

As a PC application developer, you have to target MS-DOS, Windows, or OS/2 as your host operating system or environment and then adjust your application to accommodate the special characteristics of that environment. Only a handful of high-end developers can afford the overhead of coding and maintaining three separate versions so that programs will run under all systems. As a result, the user can be forced to choose an application on the basis of which operating system or environment it runs under.

We don't want to see Macintosh applications go the way of PC applications. For the next few years, until System 7.0 and its offspring gain widespread acceptance, we envision a user population made up of both version 6.0 and version 7.0 users. If you want your application to be available to all Mac users, running in either environment, you'll have to ensure that the code you write is compatible with both versions.

In your zeal to make your application System 7.0 compatible, don't make it System 7.0 dependent. The dependent program needs System 7.0 to run and crashes under System 6.0. The dependent program is poorly conceived because it assumes too much about the running environment. Compatible programs reflect the best of both worlds: They support features of the new system, but they don't necessarily rely on those features in order to operate.

Sounding for 7.0

Your first step to compatibility is discovering which system version your application is running under. Apple tells us to call the routine *SysEnvirons* to determine the system version. *SysEnvirons* returns assorted pieces of information about the machine as well, such as whether it supports color or has a floating point coprocessor. Figure A-1 demonstrates how to use *SysEnvirons* to get the system version number. System 7.0 supports *SysEnvirons*, so you can use this method to figure out whether an application is running with the new system.

```
short
getSystemVersion ()
{
    SysEnvRec     sysEnv;
    short         version;

    version = 0;
    if (!SysEnvirons (1, &sysEnv))
        version = sysEnv.systemVersion >> 8;

    return (version);
}
```

Figure A-1.
Testing for the system version. The function returns the system version number as a short *integer.*

The Gestalt Manager, a more powerful utility for testing for specific environmental features, shipped in later releases of System 6 (6.0.4 and later) and is available in System 7.0. We anticipate that the *Gestalt* routine will eventually supplant the less informative *SysEnvirons*, but to maintain compatibility with most machines out there now, we recommend that you continue to use *SysEnvirons* to find the system type. In System 7.0, *SysEnvirons* calls the *Gestalt* routine.

You use the *Gestalt* routine to query the system about environment attributes by passing it a selector token that tells the routine what information you're interested in. The *Gestalt* routine returns the requested information in a *long* value, which you pass by reference to the routine. For example, say you have a multimedia application and you're interested in the sound and video capabilities supported by your hardware. Here are the appropriate calls to *Gestalt*:

```
Boolean        gestaltAvail,
               has32bitVideo, hasStereo;
OSErr          err;
long           result;
```

```
gestaltAvail = TrapAvailable ($A1AD);      // check for Gestalt
has32bitVideo = false;
if (gestaltAvail)
{
    if (!(err = Gestalt (gestaltQuickdrawVersion, &result)))
        has32bitVideo = result & gestalt32BitQD;
    else
        ;    // do error stuff

    hasStereo = false;
    if (!(err = Gestalt (gestaltSoundAttr, &result)))
        hasStereo = result & gestaltStereoMixing;
    else
        ;    // do error stuff
}
```

You'll find the documentation for *Gestalt*, its selectors, and its result codes in *Inside Macintosh,* Volume VI.

Paradigm Lost

"32-bit clean" is the watchword for System 7.0 compatibility. (What we say here also applies to getting your Macintosh programs to run with A/UX, Apple's implementation of UNIX.) This "cleanliness" is nothing more than an application's regard for all 32 bits of an address. In earlier versions of the system, only the lower 24 bits of a 32-bit address are significant. In System 7.0, a new 32-bit Memory Manager can take advantage of a full 32-bit address.

Why did the earlier Mac Operating Systems use only 75 percent of the available address bits? After all, 24 out of 32 bits is only a fraction of the total addressable range. To understand this parsimony, we need to look to the 1980s computer engineering paradigm, in which 24 bits were more than enough for any microcomputer address.

At the core of the early Macs is the Motorola 68000. This processor, although possessing a 32-bit program counter register (the register responsible for pointing to the next machine level instruction), is internally limited to a 24-bit address space: It ignores the upper 8 bits of an address. Starting to sound familiar?

In 1980, a 24-bit address space, which maps to a 16-megabyte addressable range of memory, seemed huge, almost infinite, to system designers. This addressable range was as large as an IBM 370 mainframe's.

As technology advanced, the 24-bit limit went away—the 68020 and 68030 have true 32-bit addressing—but the damage was done: The Macintosh team had designed the 68000 addressing limitation smack-dab in the middle of the Mac's Memory Manager.

Even so, restricting an address to 24 bits would have had little effect on our applications today if not for another decision made so long ago. Someone in the Apple system's group got a bright idea about reusing the high bytes of each address.

You have to understand the plight of systems programmers, the engineers who make their living writing operating system software. This miserly group of coders are forever space constrained. Their code has to fit in some small area of ROM, with little or no room for overrun. No wonder they tend to be bit-stingy.

In their never-ending efforts to write "tight" code, systems programmers like to take clever advantage of free bits here and there as flags and placeholders or for temporary data storage. That's what happened in the Memory Manager—someone in the Apple OS group chose to take advantage of the unused high byte in a handle. In the 24-bit Memory Manager, the high byte in every handle contains the corresponding relocatable block's status information. We've illustrated the layout of an old-style 32-bit handle in Figure A-2.

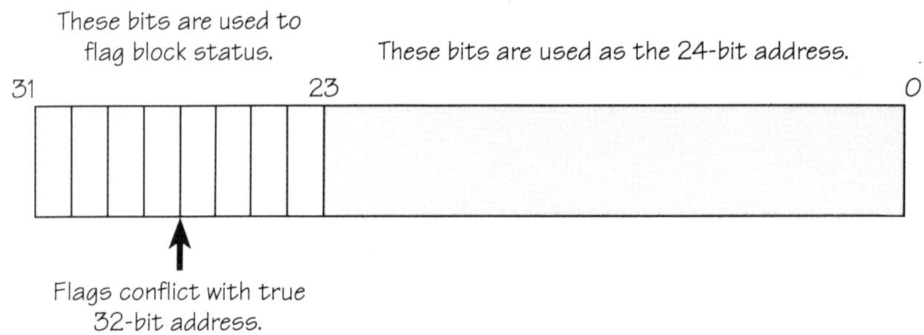

Figure A-2.
The format of a 32-bit handle in the 24-bit Memory Manager. In the old Memory Manager, handles are inherently 32-bit dirty.

In the light of a reasonable speculation that Apple surely had plans at the time to someday support 32-bit addressing, you might call this a gutsy decision. Remember that in a 128K Mac, every byte saved in the System software could be used for an application. The saving grace is that, as a hedge against future enhancement, Apple supplied a set of Memory Manager routines for setting and clearing the high byte's status bits: *HLock*, *HUnlock*, *HPurge*, and *HNoPurge*. And Apple always told developers to use System routines to change values in System data structures if at all possible. To maintain compatibility with future systems, you should always follow this fundamental principle. The two code fragments that follow are an example of what we mean. Both code fragments return the *refCon* field of a *WindowRec* structure. There's a Toolbox routine to return the value of this structure member, so the right way to get its value is to use the routine. The wrong way is to access the member directly.

The right way:

```
Handle     refCon;
WindowPeek     theWindow;
```

```
...
refCon = GetWRefCon (theWindow);
...
```

The wrong way:

```
Handle     refCon;
WindowPeek     theWindow;

...
refCon = theWindow->refCon;
...
```

Most developers got the message and had the good sense to use *HLock* to lock a handle, instead of directly bit-twiddling the upper byte of a handle. But a few developers saw the opportunity to save a few processor cycles by eliminating the overhead of a system call and set or cleared the handle's status bits directly. Their applications are not 32-bit clean and will crash when run under System 7.0.

Here's the bottom line on 32-bit cleanliness: If you already use the Memory Manager routines as Apple recommends, you're home free; if, on the other hand, you've gone out of your way to save a few machine cycles by setting or clearing these bits directly, you've got your work cut out for you.

Don't Forget the *CDEF* and the *WDEF*

Using *HLock* is not the last word in 32-bit Memory Manager compatibility. A similar problem exists in the interface to custom definition procedures. If your application contains either a control definition function (a code resource of type *CDEF*) or a window definition function (a code resource of type *WDEF*), you've got a few more minor modifications to make.

Before System 7.0, there was really no way for a *CDEF* to be 32-bit clean. The Control Manager expects your *CDEF* to clear the high byte of a region handle when the *CDEF* receives the calcCRgns message from the Control Manager. Under 32-bit Memory Manager rules, you can't clear the upper byte of an address without corrupting that address. You're damned if you do, and damned if you don't. Even if you've followed Apple's rules to the letter, your application still isn't 32-bit clean.

The problem with the *WDEF* arises from the fact that the Window Manager uses the high byte of the *WDEF* handle to store the window variant code in the older system software. This situation is remedied in System 7.0.

Making the *WDEF* compatible with System 7.0 is trivial. First, you have a problem only if your *WDEF* supports variations. If it does, remember that the variant isn't stored in the handle anymore. Don't worry about where it's stored—the System routine *GetWVariant* will return the value. By the way, *GetWVariant* has been around since System 5.0.

Fixing the *CDEF* requires a little more from you because you have to support two new messages, calcCntlRgn and calcThumbRgn. Here's where you have to ensure that you're System 7.0 compatible, not dependent. Your *CDEF* still needs to support the old calcCRgns message. System 7.0 won't send this message—only System 6.0 and its predecessors will—so your *CDEF* is still free to clear the upper byte of the handle when it receives calcCRgns. When System 7.0 is running in 32-bit mode, it will send either of the two new messages, calcCntlRgn or calcThumbRgn. You still calculate the appropriate regions for these new messages, but you don't clear the upper byte of the handle when you return it.

StripTease

What if you're running in 24-bit mode and you want to compare the values of two master pointers? In 24-bit mode, the Memory Manager changes flags in the upper byte of a master pointer, so your program should use only the lower 24 bits of the pointers during the comparison. But in 32-bit mode, all of the address bits are significant, so you'll want to compare all 32 bits.

The answer is to call the Memory Manager routine *StripAddress* on the pointers before comparing them. *StripAddress* returns a pointer's significant value, based on the current Memory Manager mode. Passed a pointer when the Mac is in 24-bit mode, for example, *StripAddress* will mask the upper byte in the returned address; but in 32-bit mode, *StripAddress* will return the address unchanged.

You'll rarely find the need to use *StripAddress.* Don't call it every time you use an address—that would choke your application. Use it only when you need to compare two master pointers (a practice of questionable merit) or in the rare event that your application switches the machine from 24-bit mode to 32-bit mode.

Virtual Memory Compatibility

After all you've read about what has to be done to support the new 32-bit Memory Manager, the good news is that you don't have to change a thing in order to support virtual memory. But you might encounter a situation in which you'll need to be wary of the virtual environment. Remember how virtual memory works: Unbeknownst to your application, some of your code or data might be out on the hard disk instead of in RAM. The system brings the code or data back into RAM just before your program needs it. Now, hard disk access is approximately 1000 times slower than RAM access. If your program is executing certain time-critical operations, such as the animation of graphical images, your users can experience a perceptible delay if some of that data first needs to be brought from disk into RAM. To ensure for these time-critical operations that your data is in RAM, you can use the new System 7.0 routines that lock data into physical memory. See the chapter on the Memory Manager in *Inside Macintosh,* Volume VI, for details on these routines.

If you follow the techniques we've talked about so far, you've met System 7.0 halfway. Your application might not support any of the features unique to the new release, but it won't embarrass you by displaying the ubiquitous bomb alert box to your users. You can call your application "System 7.0 friendly."

The final step, bringing your application from friendly to compatible, is to support the features that are the hallmarks of System 7.0. Two of the most important features exclusive to the new system are outline fonts and high-level events.

Outline Fonts

One of the most visible changes in System 7.0—outline fonts—involves the Font Manager. Outline fonts produce an effect similar to Adobe Type Manager's: QuickDraw displays text drawn in an outline font, using the maximum available resolution of the output device. Outline fonts can be displayed at any point size without the jagged appearance typical of a bitmap font.

Bitmap fonts, also called screen fonts, have been around since the Mac's inception. You're probably familiar with the way they're organized: A bitmap font matches the resolution of the screen (72 pixels per inch) because the font designer carefully places each pixel for each character in a bitmap and defines the bitmaps in multiple sizes. This accounts for the fact that when you use a font in a defined size, you get high-quality output. But, when you select a font size that's not defined in the bitmaps, the output appears jagged and distorted.

Font publishers ship a number of point sizes so that their users can do high-quality work. Thom ships his Palo Alto font in point sizes 9, 10, 12, 14, 18, 24, 36, 48, and 72, for example.

Of course, the more point sizes a bitmap font contains, the more disk space it consumes. In Thom's Palo Alto font, bitmap information for each character is repeated nine times, once for each point size set in the font. The larger point sizes take up the most space: Palo Alto 10-point is described in 2420 bytes; Palo Alto 72 uses up 30,516 bytes.

Outline fonts take advantage of a classic trade-off in computer science: trading storage space for computational time. If you're willing to put in some computational effort, you can generally reduce the storage space requirements of a program.

With outline fonts, the information kept for each character is not a bitmap but a description the Font Manager uses to calculate each character's image. The font designer creates a description (an "outline") for each character, at a 1-point size, which the Font Manager can scale to any size. Because the images can be created "on the fly," at any point size, from the 1-point outline, only that one representation per character is needed in an outline font. This saves space: A typical outline font uses up 40K. And you get a high-quality rendering of each character, no matter what the point size. The font size restriction of 127 points is lifted with outline fonts.

Supporting Outline Fonts

Because System 7.0 implements outline font support on the Font Manager layer, your application can take advantage of outline fonts without modification. But bitmap fonts have not gone away. System 7.0 supports both outline fonts and bitmap fonts, and there will be cases in which a system will contain both an outline font and a bitmap font for a particular family. The system default will be the bitmap font. In these cases, you must explicitly tell the system to use the outline font by calling *SetOutlinePreferred*, the new Font Manager routine that changes the default mode from bitmap to outline.

> **WARNING:** *If you use the* SetOutlinePreferred *routine, your application had better be running under System 7.0. System 6.0 doesn't have a* SetOutlinePreferred *call, and calling* SetOutlinePreferred *under System 6.0 treats your user to the bomb alert box—something your user would gladly forgo. Always check the system version (with* SysEnvirons *or* Gestalt*) before issuing a call to system-dependent code.*

Because the Font Manager produces outline font images in any size, you need an Other item on your font menu. The Other command should produce a dialog box that provides your user with an opportunity to enter any positive font size value.

An Event-full Software Release

Although the outline fonts are probably the most visible evidence of software changes in System 7.0, the most extensive changes in the new system involve event processing. The Event Manager has been revamped in System 7.0 to accommodate interapplication communication (IAC).

Rest assured: Your application will still receive an event when the user paws the keyboard or twiddles the mouse button—System 7.0 won't affect those parts of your existing application's source code. But IAC brings a new kind of event—the high-level event—to the system's repertoire.

High-level events enable communication among multiple applications.

If you've had any experience with a message-based operating system (MBOS) like RSX-11 or CTOS, you should be familiar with the theory behind interapplication communication on the Mac. In MBOS lingo, a communication between two applications is a "message," and, on the Mac, an application sends a message by posting a high-level event destined for another application running concurrently on the same system.

Four terms—"client," "server," "request," and "response"—make up the MBOS vocabulary. The application initiating a communication is called the client; the one targeted to receive the communication is called the server. Messages are classified into requests, which are initiated by the client, and responses, which the server posts in response to requests.

Receiving High-Level Events

Your application will receive high-level events just as it receives mouse-down or key-down events: by means of the main event loop. Recall that a Macintosh application receives events by calling *WaitNextEvent* in its main event loop. When *WaitNextEvent* returns a valid *EventRecord*, the event code in the *EventRecord*'s *what* field identifies the event type. In System 7.0, the *what* field value is *23* when the application receives a high-level event.

The Event Manager encodes information that identifies the message in the *EventRecord*. The *message* field of the *EventRecord* specifies the message class, and the *where* field contains the message ID. Both of these *EventRecord* fields are long integers, which the Event Manager uses to pass an *OSType* value, so message class and ID values are similar to application file signatures.

The message class in the *EventRecord*'s *message* field defines the message origin, uniquely identifying the sender of the message in the *message* field. If your application is going to send messages, it's probably a good idea to use the application file signature for this value. The message ID in the *where* field defines the type of message within its message class.

Because of *EventRecord* size limits, all the data associated with a high-level event might not be completely contained in the *EventRecord*. If your application intends to process the high-level event, it should call the new Event Manager routine, *AcceptHighLevelEvent*, which retrieves the extra data associated with the event.

How do you know what extra data, if any, will be sent along with the high-level event? If interapplication communication is to live up to its potential, applications—and application developers—must cooperate. After all, if an application doesn't understand a message format, it can't take advantage of the data the message contains. As IAC evolves, more and more message classes with their associated message formats will be defined.

But don't look for a world in which message formats are shared freely among applications—at least not immediately. We expect that the major software vendors will keep their message formats to themselves. In its early stages, IAC will probably consist of private transactions among a vendor's applications. Currently, the only IAC message format standards come from Apple, and the specification is for what's called an AppleEvent.

AppleEvents

AppleEvents and their format are described in detail in *Inside Macintosh,* Volume VI, and eventually will provide the framework for a scripting interface to both applications and the Finder. The minimal set of AppleEvents an application should support if it is to be "System 7.0 savvy" is shown in Figure A-3 on the next page.

Event	***Action***
Open Application	Open an application
Open Document	Open each specified document
Print	Print each specified document
Quit	Quit the application
Setup	Update the menu items
Get	Return a specific property

Figure A-3.
Essential AppleEvents if an application is to be "System 7.0 savvy."

Although the details of supporting AppleEvents are beyond the scope of this book, you can do something now that will aid your effort to support AppleEvents. Apple calls it "factoring your code."

Isolating User Interface Code

The need to factor your code, that is, to isolate those lines of code that manage the user interface from those lines that perform the actions, arises from the way AppleEvents and the eventual command-line interface to Finder will work.

An example will illustrate what we mean. When the system sends your application an *Open Document* AppleEvent, it will also send the list of documents to be opened. (Your application gets the list by calling *AcceptHighLevelEvent.*) Your application doesn't need to put up the SFGetFile dialog box to get file information from the user—the system sends the information that your application needs to open the documents. You therefore don't want to have the call to *SFGetFile* (which puts up the Open dialog box) in your application's document-opening routine.

If your application is to support an AppleEvent interface, you'll need to isolate the user interface code from the action routines. An action routine is the code that actually performs an operation. In this example, the action routine is the code that opens a document.

If you've been writing modular code all along, you're probably already isolating user interface code from action routines. But, if you've been calling user interface code in the middle of your action routines, you've got some work to do.

The document-opening action routine is particularly instructive because our Generic App already supports the factoring concept. Most existing applications can open a document in response to either a File menu Open command or the user's double-clicking on a document's icon in Finder. If you've written your document-opening action routine to be called from either of these places in your code, you've already factored out the user interface code.

You can begin factoring your code right now, without the AppleEvent specification. Factor out the Open, Print, and Save action routines. When you have the specification, just plug in the code that parses the message data and you'll be off and running in System 7.0.

Note that we recommend that you factor out your Save action procedure, even though that isn't required in System 7.0. Just because Apple hasn't told us to do that now doesn't mean that Apple won't demand just that in the future. You might as well get in the habit of writing factored code now. Try to figure out which other operations in your code can be factored out from the user interface code.

Factoring is the logical result of modular programming and leads to the best way to implement Undo/Redo in your application. All the action routines in our commercial application, Tycho Table Maker, are factored. The input to Tycho's action routines is a parameter block that can be built from either the user interface subsection or the Redo subsection. But that's a topic for another book....

INDEX

References to figures and illustrations are in italics.

Special Characters

A

B

G

H

V

W

Z

About the Authors

Kurt W. G. Matthies and Thom Hogan are microcomputer veterans. Kurt is an internationally known writer, lecturer, and software developer. He is a former contributing editor to *MacUser* magazine, for whom he and Thom cowrote the popular *Power Programming* column. As a software developer, Kurt has collaborated on many Macintosh, MS-DOS, and UNIX programs. He has lectured internationally on C programming and on operating systems and holds a degree in engineering from San Francisco State University. Kurt lives in Boulder, Colorado, where he runs his own software consulting company. This is his first book for Microsoft Press.

Thom Hogan is a software developer, programmer, technical writer, and lecturer. He is the author of several books, including *The Programmer's PC Sourcebook* (now in its second edition) and *The Programmer's Apple Mac Sourcebook* (both from Microsoft Press) and the bestselling *CP/M User's Guide.* Thom has been a regular columnist for *MacWorld* and *MacUser* magazines and a frequent contributor to other computer magazines. He is currently an evangelist for GO Corporation.

The manuscript for this book was prepared and submitted to Microsoft Press in electronic form. Text files were processed and formatted using Microsoft Word.

Principal editorial compositor: Debbie Kem

Principal proofreader: Deborah Long

Principal typographer: Carolyn Magruder

Interior text designer: Darcie Furlan

Principal illustrator: Lisa Sandburg

Cover designer: Studio MD

Cover color separator: Color Services, Inc.

Text composition by Microsoft Press in Garamond Light with display type in Futura Extra Bold, using the Magna composition system and a Linotronic 300 laser imagesetter.

Printed on recycled paper stock.